COACH OF CHAMPIONS

Great Lakes Books

A complete listing of the books in this series can
be found online at wsupress.wayne.edu.

Editor

Thomas Klug
Sterling Heights, Michigan

COACH OF CHAMPIONS

D.L.
HOLMES
AND THE
MAKING
OF
DETROIT'S
TRACK STARS

Keith D. Wunderlich and David L. Holmes Jr.

WAYNE STATE UNIVERSITY PRESS
DETROIT

ISBN 9780814352137 (paperback)
ISBN 9780814352144 (ebook)

Library of Congress Control Number: 2024939544

On cover: D.L. setting up his Holmes Folding Hurdles at an unknown location in 1958. Photo courtesy of the Jean Holmes Wunderlich Estate. Cover design by Brad Norr Design.

Grateful acknowledgment is made to the Friends of the Great Lakes Books Series Fund and the Regional Books Fund for the generous support of the publication of this volume.

Wayne State University Press rests on Waawiyaataanong, also referred to as Detroit, the ancestral and contemporary homeland of the Three Fires Confederacy. These sovereign lands were granted by the Ojibwe, Odawa, Potawatomi, and Wyandot Nations, in 1807, through the Treaty of Detroit. Wayne State University Press affirms Indigenous sovereignty and honors all tribes with a connection to Detroit. With our Native neighbors, the press works to advance educational equity and promote a better future for the earth and all people.

Wayne State University Press
Leonard N. Simons Building
4809 Woodward Avenue
Detroit, Michigan 48201-1309

Visit us online at wsupress.wayne.edu.

This book is dedicated to
Coach David L. Holmes,
Hazel J. Holmes, his wife,
Jean Holmes Wunderlich, his daughter, and
David L. Holmes Jr., his son.

You ran your race at an amazing pace.
Although your leg has ended,
know your baton pass was flawless,
your lead was appreciated, and
the race continues.

CONTENTS

PREFACE

We all heard stories when we were growing up about ancestors we never met. Maybe it was the chain-smoking aunt or the great-great-grandmother chasing a chicken across the yard because it was that evening's dinner. I had a relative who always smoked a cigar—even when swimming. When he dove into the water he would reverse the cigar—with his tongue—so the lighted end and the entire cigar was inside his mouth! His head would pop out of the water and he would reverse the process and produce the lighted cigar—still smoking—without ever using his hands. I heard that story hundreds of times over the years and, to this day, wish I'd been there just once to see it. That "talent" is part of the story of a relative I never met.

Other times, the stories we hear aren't about a relative with one special ability. They aren't about a singular major incident that defined their character. Instead, we hear smaller stories that, over time, build into the foundation of how we know this ancestor we never met.

Such was the case with my grandfather, Coach David L. (D.L.) Holmes. He was my mother's father. Coach Holmes passed away when I was three years old, too early for me to remember anything about him. My memories of him are from stories my mother and uncle told me as I grew older. I also attended Wayne State University Sports Hall of Fame events over the years and talked to many of his track men. I look back on those encounters and wish I'd paid more attention to the stories I heard. I don't remember any of the details, but I know they painted a picture of my grandfather in my mind: kind, gentle, smart, proper, athletic, knowledgeable but humble, inventive, ambitious, loving, with a unique ability to see talent where others could not. He was also light-years ahead of his time in the acceptance of athletes of color and non-Christian religions.

I don't think I ever had an idea of the life challenges he faced before researching this book. He experienced profound disappointments throughout his life. Without spoiling any of the chapters here, Coach Holmes' personal experience with defeat and loss instilled an empathy for his athletes experiencing the same thing. The arm on the shoulder and consoling words Holmes said to an athlete after that athlete lost a race came from the heart. And his athletes knew it.

Coach D.L. Holmes was the athletic director and track and cross-country coach at Wayne State University in Detroit, Michigan from 1917 to 1958. With forty-one years of indoor track teams, outdoor track teams, and cross-country teams, as well as teams in other sports he coached when he was starting out, there were hundreds, if not thousands, of young men whom my grandfather coached. It's a legacy with scores of stories yet untold even within these pages.

This book began decades ago under the authorship of my uncle, Professor David L. Holmes Jr. He was Coach Holmes' son and my mother's brother. His work as a professor at the College of William and Mary, which included writing many other scholarly books, prevented him from ever finishing the book based on his father and my grandfather, Coach David L. Holmes. I desperately wanted him to finish the book because I knew it was an incredible story that had to be told. He was in his late eighties and residing in an assisted living facility when I asked my uncle if I could complete the project, and he agreed. My aunt Carolyn Holmes sent me all the research, newspaper clippings, and interview transcripts from my uncle's work. I dug in and found that I had to include some of the interviews my uncle completed. My uncle was surprised when he found out I had changed directions a bit and he was now *in* the book and not just the coauthor of it!

It was impossible for me not to include my uncle. He did scores of interviews with track men from my grandfather's teams at Wayne State University in Detroit. All but one had passed away by the time I inherited this project. All those conversations would have been lost had my uncle not conducted those interviews decades earlier. The information he gathered was a time capsule of stories that could be told only by the athletes that lived them. The book was nearing completion when, in April of 2023, my uncle passed away at the age of ninety. The responsibility to share his great love and depth of knowledge about Coach D.L. Holmes was now solely on my shoulders.

This book is both nonfiction and speculative nonfiction. The interviews are mostly word-for-word transcripts of conversations my uncle had with Wayne athletes. The interviews have been adjusted slightly to take out "ahhs" and "umms" and off-topic tangents, and to create whole sentences. Each interview is followed by a chapter that will take you back in time to when a particular story occurred. The people in those stories are real. The majority of the facts in those stories are true. The dialogue and some of the situations have been speculatively created to fill in the blanks where the facts aren't known. You may refer to the appendix for references and more information on what is fact and where I exercised some creativity.

Coach D.L. Holmes began at Wayne in 1917 when it was called Detroit Junior College. In 1924, the junior college merged with Detroit College of Pharmacy and Detroit Teacher's College and the name was changed to the College of the City of Detroit. In 1934, the name changed again to Wayne

University. Finally, in 1956, the current name of Wayne State University was adopted.

The term "Old Main" wasn't officially used until the 1950s. Prior to that, it was simply called the Main Building. When D.L. first arrived, it was the *only* building. However, to keep the confusion to a minimum with readers already keeping track of a college that was renamed four times while D.L. was there, I refer to the building as Old Main for the entire book.

Coach Holmes was there for each of those name changes and before Old Main was old. He was there a long time, yet he was a man ahead of his time. He saw talent where other coaches did not. He analyzed the exact movements of athletes to produce the most efficient and effective use of energy possible. He was an inventor of track equipment and innovative training techniques. And he was integrating his track team racially, ethnically, and religiously as early as 1920.

I am still amazed when I read about the times when my grandfather was running in 1908 as a college track man at Oklahoma A&M on a dirt track with primitive track shoes. The times are considerably better than mine in the mid-1970s on a synthetic track with awesome shoes—and I was the fastest 100-yard dash man at my high school and the fourth fastest in my county. I often wish he had been there to coach me. He had a way of taking average talent and turning those athletes into champions.

This book is also about those champions. State champions, national champions, world record holders, and even a few Olympians were produced by Coach Holmes. He took athletes who never even considered going to college and turned them into NCAA champions. In many ways, his athletes achieved more than he ever did on the track. That may have been his unspoken motivation. He was a surrogate father to his athletes and he wanted more for them than he had personally accomplished. And he was more than a surrogate father to many of them.

This book was written for all those who were touched by the life of Coach Holmes. While most who knew him personally are no longer with us, many more have been touched by his legacy. Still more, who never knew him until now, can be moved by a man who taught others that they could be more than they thought they could be.

Keith Wunderlich

ACKNOWLEDGMENTS

In addition to my coauthor and uncle, David L. Holmes Jr., without whom this book would never have been written, I would like to thank and acknowledge the following people:

- Duncan Murrell, Tom Klug, Sandra Judd, and my wife, Mary Wunderlich, for their questions, guidance, foresight, and editing of this book.
- Keith McClellan, author of *The Hero within Us.*
- John Telford, Coach Holmes' last All-American runner and author of *The Longest Dash.*
- Jeffrey Weiss, senior associate athletic director for media relations, Wayne State University.
- Andra Dues Lesley, daughter of Leroy Dues.
- Michelle Preyer, granddaughter of Leroy Dues.
- Crystal Mannino, director of Junior Olympics and Outdoor Sports, AAU Track & Field, Lake Buena Vista, FL.
- Shae Rafferty, Sarah Lebovitz, and many helpful archivists and staff members at the Walter P. Reuther Library, Wayne State University, Detroit, MI.
- David Haberstich, Archives Center, National Museum of American History, Smithsonian Institution, Washington, D.C.
- Greg Bond, curator of the Joyce Sports Research Collection, University of Notre Dame, Hesburgh Libraries, South Bend, IN.
- Jean Holmes Wunderlich, my mother (deceased), whom I wish I had listened to more closely, but who fortunately kept a ton of family history.
- Robert "Bob" Holmes, nephew of Coach Holmes.
- Carolyn Holmes, my aunt and the wife of Professor David L. Holmes Jr., who found all my uncle's notes, sent them to me, and always supported this project moving forward.
- Sandra Korn, acquisitions editor at Wayne State University Press, for her guidance and support throughout the publishing process.

1

WE COULD BE CHAMPIONS

Interview with Tom Adams, Class of 1941
Interviewed by Professor David L. Holmes Jr.

June 6, 1997

Professor Holmes hunched over the top of a small cassette recorder and spoke loudly into the microphone embedded in the unit to verbally note several key identifying characteristics about the interview. He had been interviewing athletes from Wayne State University in Detroit for a few days now as research for a book he was writing about his father, Coach David L. Holmes. Coach Holmes was often noted as the "coach of everything" due to his early years coaching football, basketball, tennis, golf, track, and cross country. His coaching career at Wayne State University in Detroit began in 1917 and ran until he retired in 1958. That he was a coach for so long at the same university is remarkable on its own, especially by today's standards. However, that had nothing to do with the theme of the yet-unwritten book.

"This is David Holmes Jr., son of Coach David L. Holmes, interviewing Tom Adams on June 6. This is the sixth right? Yes, June 6, 1997. Now let me just play that back and make sure this thing is working. One of my interviews was completely lost. I didn't check it and the cassette malfunctioned and I opened it up and it popped out like spaghetti."

Adams chuckled. He was in his late seventies. He had been a "big man on campus" when he attended Wayne, and the years had been kind to him. He was still quite handsome and maintained the physique of a football player. His broad shoulders made you think he could pick up the pigskin right then and perform well. Only his hands betrayed his years on earth. His fingers were thin and the skin on them was just a little too white. And he had a landscape of wrinkles and brown age spots on the back of his hands that resembled the topography of a mountain range. Yet his voice was as strong and deep as it had been when he walked the halls of Old Main decades previously.

When other athletes reminisced about teammates at Wayne, Adams often came up in the conversation. He was not your typical Wayne student. His family had money. He was a rarity in that he didn't have to work his way through school. Yet, he chose Wayne University as the college he wanted to attend. He had choices where other athletes did not. He could have gone anywhere and was recruited by other colleges for his football skill. Adams even had scholarship offers, yet he chose Wayne. Looking back on those years from a 1997 perspective proved it was a good choice for him and ultimately a great one for the university.

Professor David L. Holmes Jr.: [*repositioning the tape recorder*] You were in football and track?

Tom Adams: Yeah, football and track.

Professor: I was surprised to learn the football team wasn't scrimping for funds like track. I always had a sense that the entire school was scrimping.

Adams: They weren't what you would call opulent. The scholarships were narrow, but enough to give them a sort of representative team in the division—they didn't have the divisions then that we do now—but we were obviously not among the top football teams [*laughs*]. But we did reasonably well if we stayed in our own class. Our schedule would include the likes of Michigan Normal [Eastern Michigan], Western Michigan, and Central Michigan. There were all these annual affairs with Ohio teams like Akron, Ohio University, Cincinnati. We played against Michigan State. That was always a real eye-opener. It was a good chance to analyze how incompetent we were or thereabouts! But we would—ah, is your tape recorder all right?

Professor: [*fiddles with his recorder that had been making a rattling sound*] Seems to be fine now.

Adams: Anyhow, we played Temple one year and Carnegie Tech when they had a team. And, oh, Bowling Green.

Professor: I remember going down there to a game. I remember going to Ohio Wesleyan to a game.

Adams: Yes, Wesleyan. Anyway, that was generally the mix.

Professor: I'd be interested in hearing about the Michigan State games. The contrast between the teams.

Adams: Michigan State had not joined the Big Ten as of then, but they were on the verge of it. They were the class of university football that was a

1A kind of school, so it was a tough game for us. But, it was our opening game, too. So, they were not as good as they were going to be later in the season. And we were able to—because of the incentive of playing at Macklin Field up there—we played fairly good football. They had years when we played them when John Pingell was their star All-American and so-called triple flip man. And after that, in my working years, John went into the advertising business and we were competitors there! He was with, let's see, they changed their name, but, ahh, Ross Roy. Ross Roy for a good number of years. He was the first running back I ever tackled! And I would remind him of that! [*laughter*] But, we had a very pleasant friendship and relationship in the following years. And it was a big game. In 1938 we lost 6–34 in front of twenty-two thousand. We played them in 1939. We played them fifty-one minutes of scoreless football. Then, they scored twice in the last nine minutes and we lost 0–16.

Professor: I wouldn't expect to see that, you know. I would expect to see . . .

Adams: Well, you did those other years. That was a decent year, we won four and lost five. That might not sound great. But, our losses were Michigan State, Bowling Green, Cincinnati, Michigan State Normal [Eastern Michigan], and Central Michigan. Those were big schools for crying out loud! We were little Wayne State!

Professor: David against Goliath!

Adams: Exactly!

Professor: My dad was not your football coach. He coached everything for quite a while, but in 1929—strange timing with the Depression—they brought on more coaches.

Adams: Right, but he was my track coach. I was a sprinter. A lot of my football success was due to Coach Holmes. He made me a faster runner. I gained a lot of yards because no one could catch me! [*laughter*]

Professor: I was told about a game against Buffalo.

Adams: [*laughs*] My favorite football story! The Buffalo game was 1940. It had been snowing for days and it kept snowing during the game so it was almost impossible to see the lines. The snow was three to four inches deep on the field. Oh, and cold, too. Really cold. The end zone lines were hidden. We had a drive where I got the ball and I scored. But, the officials never raised their arms. They couldn't tell where I was on the field. No touchdown. We had to run another play. We repeated the same play and I got the ball and scored. The refs were just standing there! I'm in the end zone, but they can't see it so no touchdown. I'm getting frustrated. Finally, on my third try, I went through the end zone and up to the wall of the grandstand. Touchdown! Are you raising your arms this time, ref? Maybe a little overdramatic, but hey, I scored three times on that drive!

Professor: [*laughs*] That's a great story! And that was well before turf, so the ground was probably frozen, too!

Adams: Right! The worst, horrible, just horrible conditions to play.

Professor: You did well in track, too.

Adams: Yes, much better weather in track season! My two biggest accomplishments were winning the 1939 Canadian Indoor Sprint Championships and my 880-relay team winning at the Notre Dame Relays in . . . 1938. Yes, 1938. Even though we were a smaller school, we did very well at relay events. It didn't matter if you only brought a couple relay teams. We would win several relays and place quite well in the standings.

Professor: Was your time at Wayne interrupted by World War II?

Adams: No, it wasn't. I got my degree at Wayne in May of 1941 and the next week I went to the Naval Air Station for training. From there, I went to Corpus Christi, Texas. I was in the first class at Corpus Christi, and a lot of months later I emerged from there thanks to the Japanese. If the Japanese hadn't bombed Pearl Harbor, I don't think I'd have gotten through that whole program. Anyway, I got through it. So, Wayne was not interrupted except for some of my own aberrations. [*laughs*]

Adams failed to include that he was a decorated World War II hero. He received the Navy Cross for heroism during battle in World War II. His citation reads:

> The President of the United States of America takes pleasure in presenting the Navy Cross to Lieutenant Thomas Brooks Adams (NSN: 0–116874), United States Naval Reserve, for extraordinary heroism in operations against the enemy while serving as Pilot of a carrier-based Navy Torpedo Plane in Torpedo Squadron ELEVEN (VT-11), attached to the U.S.S. HORNET (CV-12), during the Battle for Leyte Gulf in the Philippine Islands, on 25 October 1944. Assigned to attack enemy surface forces in the vicinity of the Philippine Islands, in the face of intense, accurate anti-aircraft fire, Lieutenant Adams pressed home his attack and scored two direct bomb hits upon an enemy light cruiser. Lieutenant Adams' outstanding courage, daring airmanship and devotion to duty were at all times inspiring, and were in keeping with the highest traditions of the United States Naval Service.
>
> —Commander 2d Carrier Task Force Pacific:
> Serial 0576 (February 27, 1944)

In a newspaper account asking Adams about his Navy Cross, he downplayed it by saying he received it for "my shenanigans in the Southwest Pacific." In fact, he was hit by anti-aircraft fire and shot down by the Japanese. He managed to return close to his destroyer before crashing into the water and was rescued. In addition to a Navy Cross, Adams also received a distinguished Flying Cross and Air Medal.

While at Wayne, Adams was a football star, track star, singer, and male lead of the university musicals. It was 1938 and he had it all, from good looks to athletic skill to a good voice to money. That final attribute, money, was especially impressive considering America was just getting over the Great Depression.

David L. Holmes Jr., son of Coach Holmes, was not an athlete, or a singer, or the lead in any musicals. He was a professor of religious studies at the College of William and Mary. And every ounce of him said "professor." Before he ever opened his mouth, you knew. Now, not in a bad way. Some professors are equal parts erudite and narcissistic. Their required reading list is all books they wrote, and they ensconce themselves in their offices while a graduate assistant teaches their classes. Not Professor Holmes. He looked the part of "professor," always wearing a sport coat and tie that might or might not have gone with each other, much less the rest of the outfit, and you knew it the minute he started talking; he was brilliant. He had a wry smile and infectious laugh that made you laugh along with him even though you were too far removed from his intelligence quotient to understand the humor.

Professor Holmes' passion was the university classroom. It would never even occur to him to have a graduate assistant teach his class. He loved teaching it himself too much. His love for William and Mary was based on its deeply historical roots and also its smaller size. He felt it was very important for professors to deliver the content of each and every class personally. As a result, he knew his students well. In turn, they cared about him. When he retired, former students established the David L. Holmes Reformation Studies and American Religious History Endowment in honor of his great accomplishments over four decades at William & Mary. A social media post about him summed up the comments of many: "The best teacher I had in four years there. He is a treasure who will be missed."

When talking about his father, however, Professor Holmes often saw the glass as half empty, or even slightly less than half empty. He was not the athlete he thought his father wanted him to be. He never even attended an Olympic Trial, much less qualified for one, like his father did. He was not a lyric tenor like his father. Professor Holmes was not a carbon copy of Coach Holmes. Yet, Coach Holmes gave forty-one years to Wayne State University and Professor

Holmes gave forty-six years to William and Mary. Both impacted the lives of hundreds, possibly thousands, of students. Both left legacies that are different from each other, yet strikingly similar in how they are remembered and cherished. Professor Holmes was not an athlete, but he most assuredly had a stride that matched many of the footsteps of his father.

> **Professor:** What do you remember about my dad as your coach?
>
> **Adams:** There are so many things. But the one thing that comes to mind the most often is that he treated everyone like they were special. Every single practice he would have an individual workout prepared for every team member. He didn't just lump all the sprinters together and say "You all do this. . . ." I had my own set of instructions on what I was to practice that day, every day. But the guy who never scored a point in a meet also had his own individual workout prepared by Coach Holmes. He wanted everyone to be better, even if better was coming in fifth instead of sixth—in the third heat.

Adams paused. He put his head down as if thinking. His hands clasped, elbows on his knees, he rested his chin on his hands as he looked at the floor, almost as if he was praying. Professor Holmes did not interrupt. When he looked up there were tears in his eyes. It was as if he was back at Wayne sixty years before. He took a moment to compose himself.

> **Adams:** He made us believe in ourselves and think that we could be champions. He made us believe that we could accomplish anything. Would I have been successful in my career without his coaching? Maybe. But I guarantee you I was *more* successful in my career because of him. The only thing limiting you is you.
>
> **Professor:** That is truly beautiful and a wonderful tribute to him.

The professor thought for a minute. He knew the question he wanted to ask but didn't want to offend anyone by asking it. However, this was a question with generations of discrimination behind it, and it would be more offensive not to ask.

> **Professor:** But you were also a white kid from a family with money. What about the Black kids and Jewish kids and Eastern European kids?
>
> **Adams:** Well, that's just it. We were all the same. It didn't matter if you were white or Black or anything else. Coach Holmes couldn't have cared less what your skin color was or who you worshipped. All he wanted you

to do was run faster, jump higher, launch a shot further, and believe in yourself. I had a different background than most of the kids at Wayne at that time. They were working-class kids. They didn't have much money. Coach Holmes had no scholarship money. Zero. He would get kids jobs at the college. He made deals with certain department heads, and jobs were reserved for his team members. They all worked their way through Wayne. Paid for it themselves. Talk about believing in yourself! Most of these kids would never have gone to college. Coach Holmes would see them in a Detroit high school track meet and go visit their parents. In the poor white neighborhoods he was the only white man they ever saw wearing a sport coat, tie, and hat. In the Black neighborhoods, he was the only white man not looking for prostitutes. In both neighborhoods he was the only white man in a tie not collecting on a bill. He'd go talk to their parents and say he could make their son a champion. And they came to Wayne. And they became champions.

Professor: He had some success, that's for sure: three Olympians, including one gold medalist, eleven All-Americans, nine national champions, and four world record holders. And that doesn't take into account all the athletes that are now doctors, lawyers, teachers, coaches, administrators, and . . .

Adams: And advertising company executives.

Professor: Yes, and CEOs of major companies like Campbell Ewald.

In business, Adams was also a standout. He was named "Outstanding Young Advertising Man of the Year" in 1955 and was appointed president of Campbell Ewald in 1958. Later, Adams earned the positions of chairman of the board and chief executive officer of the Campbell-Ewald Company. *Sports Illustrated Magazine* named Adams to the 25 Year All-American team in 1965. He was also a member of the Wayne State Board of Governors and the Board of Trustees of Children's Hospital and served as a director of the Economic Club of Detroit.

Adams: One of the qualities I admired most about [Coach Holmes] . . . was how he always deflected any accolades that came his way. He minimized what he did to emphasize what we all did. He gave the athlete all the credit. He never talked about his own success. There was always a story that ran through the team about Coach Holmes and the Olympics. But he never talked about it. He was an Olympian, right?

Professor: Well, that's an interesting story.

2

HOLMES ON DECK

Stockholm 1912 Olympic Trials, Central Division, Evanston, Illinois

June 8, 1912

The fact that he was not alone gave him no comfort. Many of the track athletes at the Chicago Olympic Trials had been overcome by a virus that was fearsome. D.L. was sick, sicker than he'd ever been. Flu-like symptoms of headaches, abdominal pain, and vomiting ran through the dormitory facility like wildfire. The actual qualifying events were still a few days away, but D.L. thought he would not be able to get out of bed for weeks.

He had always had an internal stamina that allowed him to overcome most adverse situations. This virus, however, had knocked him over. There was little anyone could do except allow it to run its course. The small medical facility at the trials was overrun with a tide of very sick young men. In an effort to prevent the virus from spreading further, all of the sick athletes were housed together in a separate tent-like facility and away from other athletes in the dorms. D.L. felt as though he became sicker as a result of the close contact with other sick athletes. He longed to get out of there and have some time to recover on his own. But he knew no one in Illinois, so thoughts of a "break-out" were quickly quashed. His brother, Oliver Wendell (O.W.), was coming to watch his events. But that was three days out, and he was of the mind he should send O.W. a telegram and tell him to stay home.

His hometown of Stillwater, Oklahoma, was gearing up for a fundraiser to send him to Stockholm, should he win the trials. A win was expected. In 1910 and 1911, D.L. was considered one of the nation's top athletes in the running broad jump. He trained in Chautauqua, New York, and beat the country's best at championship meets held there each summer. His best running broad jump (renamed long jump) was 24′6″ and his best hop-step-jump (renamed triple jump) was 47′6″.

D.L. had athletic genes that were evident well before college. As a fifteen-year-old freshman at Oklahoma State Agriculture and Mechanical College Prep High School, D.L. earned a varsity letter in track by accumulating more than the required number of points in sprints, discus, and running broad jump. Normally, varsity letters could not be conferred until an athlete's sophomore year, but his extraordinary achievements gained him the early status. He also excelled at football in high school. His parents, however, were against his participation in the sport and forbade him to play. With incredible quarterback skills, he desperately wanted to perform on the gridiron. The roster showed him as a student manager and water boy for the football team. On the field, a quarterback who looked and played much like D.L. Holmes performed under a different name. It seems his parents never learned of the deception while he was in high school.

In 1904, D.L. enrolled at the Oklahoma Agricultural and Mechanical College located in Stillwater, a natural step forward from the prep school of the same name. It was there that his moniker "D.L." came to be. He was a locally known orator, and his speeches were often published in the *Brown and Blue* college magazine. When he competed in oratorical contests he did so under the name D. Lynn Holmes. Simultaneously attending Oklahoma A&M was his brother, Oliver Wendell Holmes. This was not the same Oliver Wendell Holmes who was a United States Supreme Court justice, although family stories often left out that distinction. Salutations were always formal, using a Mr. or Miss or Mrs. This led to an issue with the Holmes brothers. They were both Mr. Holmes. "D.L." and "O.W." became an easy solution to the mystery of which Mr. Holmes you were addressing. This identification was especially helpful when it came to singing. In the A&M Male Quartet of 1908, D.L. Holmes was second tenor and O.W. Holmes was first bass. Fifty percent of the group was Mr. Holmes.

D.L. was a great vocalist. Professor T. F. Lawrence, of Oklahoma A&M, was incensed that D.L. was not going into music as a career. He was in the male quartet and was a featured vocalist in school plays. Lawrence felt he had a real future in either teaching music or becoming a professional musician. While D.L. loved music, his true passion was athletics. He excelled at just about everything. So, rather than make a decision based on talent, he made one based on desire. And that desire was athletics.

While in college his involvement in football became known even to his parents. He was a football star due to his quickness. He also played basketball and baseball and, of course, ran track and field. He set a college running broad jump record. At one track meet against a Kansas university, D.L. jumped so far on his first jump the Kansas participants in the event dropped out. And, although he was known more as a jumper and sprinter, he participated in a long-distance competition, racing to the top of Pike's Peak. He won and waited ten minutes for the second-place finisher to arrive.

D.L. was involved in track and field not only as an athlete but also as an editorialist. The *Orange and Black*, an Oklahoma A&M publication, called for the addition of a cinder track in 1909. This was a year after D.L. had graduated from A&M, but the effort had D.L.'s influence written all over it. His name was not attached to the editorial, but it was surely his insistence, and possibly his pen, that brought it to print. He was tired of the primitive conditions of the college's track. Modern tracks were made of cinders, not dirt or clay or whatever type of soil happened to be under the spot where the track was made. The composition of fine ash, carbon, and very small pebbles make a cinder track comfortable to run on and easy to drain. The editorial noted, "We need a track that may be used right after and during a rain, if necessary. A good cinder track will give us this, and so why not have one?" The A&M track was dirt. The running approaches to the jumps were dirt. Dirt tracks were sometimes too soft to dig your toes into for a good start, or so hard you couldn't get your toe holes dug at all. And sometimes they were too muddy for the athletes to do anything.

High jumpers and pole-vaulters, of course, landed on their feet. If the dirt wasn't soft enough, serious injury was common. The dirt often became too compacted for a soft landing. Newspaper accounts tell of Olympic athletes who earned a spot on the team with their pole vault but were too injured to go to the Olympics due to a rough return to the ground. Many colleges had already modernized their pole-vault area. Most now had a hole in which to insert the end of the pole for an athlete's vault, rather than a six-inch spike on the end of the hickory pole. Most colleges also now had a two-foot bed of small wood chips to aide in a softer landing, which was certainly needed for a jump of ten to eleven feet in height. A&M was not quite there.

To say D.L. was an overachiever in college would be an understatement. He took part in athletics, music, plays, oratoricals, art, and the Omega Literary Society—with top performance in each. By college graduation he had selected athletics and coaching as his life's work. But his words from a 1908 oratory show he could have just as easily entered politics:

> We are now entered upon the brightest era of the history of our nation. Today, the potentialities for good and bad are grand beyond precedent, and it rests with the living to say what the future shall be. There is

enough that is alarming to excite us to the most vigorous action; there
is enough that is promising to encourage our best efforts with the brightest hopes. The day is not far distant when every man shall be his brother's
keeper—when our swords shall be beaten into plowshares, and the "Dove
of Peace" shall fold its wings over a world of common love and common
interests, and who shall doubt but that our own beloved country shall be,
as ever, the leader in this onward movement of nations.

—D. Lynn Holmes, A&M Oratorical Contest of 1908, excerpt

D.L. was a senior when he wrote that. Seniors at Oklahoma A&M were also
asked to leave free advice to juniors. D.L. offered: "Don't bother with second
thoughts—first ones are good enough."

He took his own advice to heart, as he had no second thoughts when, fresh
out of college in 1908, he accepted a position as the professor of history and
director of athletics at Bethel College in Russellville, Kentucky. The athletic
job title was not nearly as administrative as it sounded. D.L. found himself
personally directing all athletics. Meaning, he was the coach of football, basketball, baseball, track, and cross-country.

Football at Bethel, and at most colleges in the south, was light on rules.
Teams were usually shorthanded, and the football coach was often also a
football player. Such was the case for D.L., and he loved it! He could keep
playing football. Lax rules extended way beyond the player roster. Gambling
and fights were also the norm at college football games. Spectators would
swarm the field—during the game—and players had to dodge them and the
opposing team to gain yardage. Spectators would try to personally change
the outcome of the game to favor their betting position.

Win or lose, players had to be careful. Winning players might find themselves hit by a fence post thrown by a losing bettor. The victorious team often
had to fight its way off the field while threats of bodily harm were hurled at
them. And that's how losing bettors felt about the winning team. Pity the
team that lost them their money. Under Coach D.L. Holmes, Bethel was
nearly always the winner.

In his final year at Bethel, D.L. coached an undefeated football team and
the top basketball team in the south, and his track team broke multiple state
and southern records. Quite an accomplishment for four years at the college.
All the while, he was working on his personal goal of making the Olympic
team for the 1912 Stockholm Olympics.

In the spring of 1912, D.L. mailed in his registration packet for the Olympic Trials. He registered as an "Unaffiliated Amateur," which meant that he
did not belong to one of the athletic clubs that sponsored athletes for the

Olympics and that, until 1912, had controlled almost all American participation in the Olympics.

Things had changed since 1896, when the more formal and more complete Olympics were revived. Up until the 1912 Olympics, track men were selected for the American team in one of two ways. The first method was to prove themselves of Olympic caliber at an Amateur Athletic Union (AAU) regional meet held prior to the Olympics. At that point an athletic club, such as the New York Athletic Club or the Chicago Athletic Association, would incorporate them as members, sponsor them for the Olympics, and pay their expenses to the games. Athletic clubs were upper middle class and upper class in membership. These clubs were both athletic and social centers for the male community leaders.

D.L. was not upper middle class. He was from a poor farming community in Oklahoma, not an urban center. He was not in a position to be helped by an athletic club.

Athletes were also almost automatically included on the Olympic team if they had achieved well at universities known for their track programs. The universities would sponsor, raise money for, and send their best athletes overseas to compete for the United States in the Olympics. In 1900, Princeton, the University of Michigan, the University of Chicago, and some others raised money and sent their best track men to Paris, France. The American Olympic Committee then rubber-stamped their choices without tryouts.

Oklahoma A&M was not one of those prestigious universities. The "A&M" was an abbreviation for Agricultural and Mechanical. It was a state-sponsored school with free tuition. Enrolled students had to pay only for room, board, and books. D.L.'s father had moved to Stillwater so all of his children could attend Oklahoma A&M tuition free and live at home. While this was an astute financial move, A&M was not an upper-class school that had the clout to make an impression on the Olympic Committee.

D.L. had two strikes against him. He was personally not upper middle class and, although he had graduated, his university had no ability to help him. Athletes who attended little-known colleges or who did not belong to prestigious athletic clubs could be left out in the cold.

D.L. was not going to go unnoticed again just because he lacked the right "class" and connections. In 1908, the year of his college graduation, D.L. lacked the money to go to Chicago—the nearest AAU regional meet—and compete. And Oklahoma A&M had no influence in the American athletic world. Without influence or money to fund a trip to the trials or to the Olympics, D.L. was out of luck. He did not go to the Olympic Trials. He might have raised funds to go to Chicago from Stillwater merchants, but fundraising was not an area of expertise for D.L.

In 1912, however, the year Stockholm hosted the games, D.L.'s luck changed.

The process of Olympic selection was broadened in the United States. In that year, the United States attempted to field a team chosen, in part, on merit rather than purely on influence and money. Many of the track athletes, all of whom were male, qualified for the team by performing well at tryouts. The previous methods of obtaining an Olympic position were not totally gone. Some members of the American team that went to Stockholm owed their place largely to the influence of an athletic club. But for the first time, the team had a large number of athletes who had earned a spot by winning or placing well at AAU meets, regardless of their athletic club association. The 1912 team contained a number of minister's sons, and few would have had the private funds to make the trip otherwise.

The 1912 Olympic Trials were taking place on the track at Northwestern University in the Chicago suburb of Evanston. D.L. had money from his job at Bethel College and sponsored himself. Like other nonaffiliated competitors who had no athletic club, no outside sponsor, and no hotel, D.L. was assigned to one of the dormitory rooms. Now, with his sickness, that room assignment had changed to something even less desirable.

D.L. was curled up in a fetal position in a bed in the Olympic Trials sick tent. His dreams had been replaced by intense pain, hot and cold sweats, an inability to keep any food down, and a head that weighed so much he couldn't pick it up off the pillow. Now two days away, his participation in the trials seemed unlikely. The incredible amount of sacrifice, time, and preparation he had put in seemed to have been a waste.

The disappointment was overwhelming. He always worked hard and was rewarded with success. If he had a motto, that would have been it: "Believe in yourself, work hard, succeed." Success was your motivation. Hard work made the success worthwhile. D.L. didn't need, want, or ask for any outside accolades. His motivation was all internal.

D.L.'s brother, Oliver Wendell (O.W.), arrived at the Olympic Trial facility at Northwestern.

"How are you feeling?" asked O.W.

"I've been better," said D.L. in a voice that didn't sound like him at all. "I'd say I'm a 6 out of 10."

"That's not good. You need to be feeling like a 10 if you want to perform well at the trials tomorrow afternoon," said O.W.

"Well, this morning I felt like a 1. So, a 6 is a lot better," said an obviously not well D.L.

O.W. knew he had to get D.L. to drink some liquids and eat some food. D.L. needed more energy. If he could gain some additional strength and get another 20 percent better by tomorrow, he could possibly participate after all.

D.L. could make eye contact for only a few seconds before having to lower his head. His head was still heavy, and the virus was still active within him. O.W. became D.L.'s nursemaid and was able to get some food to stay in him. He cooled his flashes of heat with a cold, wet cloth. A slight bit of color returned to D.L.'s face. Maybe a good night's sleep would help.

The next morning D.L. did feel better, though not nearly 100 percent. He and O.W. went to the track and practiced the running broad jump. O.W. was both foul judge and measurement referee for the practice. It wasn't good. After several attempts the longest jump was 22'3", likely well short of making the cut for the team. D.L. wanted one more practice jump before the trials began. He took some time in mental preparation. He needed to muster all of his strength and ability for this last practice jump. He walked back his pace from the jump box. He turned and stared at his goal. He dug the toes of his shoes into the dirt approach and blasted out of his starting position. O.W. could feel the determination as he came closer and closer to the wooden take-off block that indicated where the measurement began. O.W. watched intently. No foul. D.L. flew into the air and through the air with perfect form and incredible strength. He landed well with his momentum propelling him forward face-first into the sand jump pit. He lay there for a few seconds, half exhausted, but also knowing it had been an excellent jump. O.W. measured and loudly exclaimed "25'1"!" The Holmes brothers looked at each other and the realization became clear. No other American had broken the 25' mark. Had this been during regulation competition it would be an American record! It was Olympic medal material for sure, and quite possibly good enough for the gold medal. O.W. and D.L. clasped hands, then arms, and then exchanged a full-out hug. O.W. raised D.L. into the air with excitement.

Now he needed to repeat that jump when it counted in the afternoon. D.L. could feel the virus surging again in his head and lungs. He wanted to rest a little before his part of the trials began.

Later that day, D.L. was back at the track and stayed loose by stretching and light jogging, but also kept his eye on the competition. There were some good jumps, but nothing spectacular. He had competed against James Wasson, from Notre Dame, before and knew he was a good jumper. He was one to watch closely. Wasson's best so far was a 22'3½" on his second of three jumps. Good, but beatable.

The name Holmes was called. It was time for D.L.'s first jump. D.L. tried to put the lingering effects of the virus out of his mind and concentrate fully on the task ahead. Another 25' jump would be grand, but a 23'6" would do the trick. Toes in the dirt runway, a quick start, arms driving hard, wind in his face, take-off board nearing, adrenalin flowing, he heard the bang of his shoe on the wood, launched off the board in beautiful form, and heard "foul" well before he landed. The referee said the toe of his shoe had been over the edge of the foul line on the take-off board. Jump One, foul.

O.W. came up to D.L. as he waited for his name to be called again. He said the jump was long, almost as long as the 25-footer. The adrenalin of the moment probably threw off his stride. He also told D.L. that Wasson's third jump was under 22'. It looked like 22'3½" was the distance to beat.

"Irons. Frank Irons," said the referee. That name caught D.L.'s attention. He looked up. Irons was from the Chicago Athletic Association and was the gold medalist from the 1908 Olympics in London. Although a small man, standing just 5'3" tall, he was quick and he was a formidable foe. With that gold-medal jump in 1908, Irons held the third spot for all-time longest running broad jump in the world. Irons and D.L. made eye contact for a split second. There was a bit of a nod from each; a mutual respect that can be earned only through competing against each other.

Irons' winning jump in 1908 was 24'6½". He had not jumped that distance since. In 1909, his AAU winning jump was 22'5". He bettered that at the 1910 AAU national meet with a jump of 23'5¼" and also took first place. Yet, neither AAU jump was close to his Olympic jump. D.L. knew he had a chance.

"Holmes on deck."

D.L. was next after Irons. Small but muscular, Irons drove down the approach with determination, hit his penultimate stride perfectly, and soared into the air. His jump looked good. Very good. The ref said, "22 feet, 9½ inches." Better than Wasson, but not nearly what D.L. could jump. "Holmes. David Holmes." D.L. was next.

D.L. walked the running approach and did a couple final stretches near his check mark. He visualized himself running the approach, launching off the jump block, and having perfect form through the air. Now he just had to do it in reality. "Don't foul, don't foul, don't foul," kept running through his head. Toes dug in the dirt, he could see his brother O.W. pacing on the grass nearby. He was ready. Thrusting his right arm behind him, he took off from his starting stance. As he raced down the approach, D.L. thought about hitting the wooden block perfectly this time. "Don't foul, don't foul, don't foul," he said to himself. He could not afford a second foul. This jump, however, was just the opposite. So concerned about having part of his shoe over the foul line, D.L. just barely got a toe on the block before launching into the air. His misplaced shoe on the jump block impacted his form. The jump counted, but he lost 18" or more by hitting the block wrong. 21'3". D.L. knew that wasn't good enough, as Carl Cook from the Cleveland Athletic Club already had a 21'5½". Only the top three got to go to the Olympics.

D.L. had one jump left, and everything was riding on it.

The top three jumpers were Irons, at 22'9½"; Wasson, at 22'3½"; and Cook, at 21'5½". On any other day, D.L. could beat all of those distances easily. Jump one, fault. Jump two, too short. He had to do it on jump three.

D.L. was lost in his own thoughts when O.W. came to say he was next. D.L. hadn't heard his name called. This was it. The Stockholm Olympics was riding on this one jump. He concentrated so fully he was impervious to anything around him. He could see no spectators or officials. His competitors disappeared from his thoughts. The world became silent, and he readied himself for the most important jump of his life. He dug the toes of his shoes into the dirt. He created the perfect sprinter's stance and conjured the sound of a starter's pistol in his head as he took off down the approach. His stride perfect, his mind and body fully engaged, any remnants of the virus seemed to have been left on the track. He hit the board perfectly and flew through the air. Before he even landed he could hear his brother shouting and cheering. It had been a long, long jump. D.L. was ecstatic. He leapt out of the sand and drove his fist into the air in exhilaration and excitement. He looked over at O.W., who was no longer cheering. He looked back. The ref and foul judge were talking, almost arguing, with each other at the jump block. D.L. walked back their way, wondering what they were talking about. The foul judge looked at him and said, "Sorry, kid, foul."

D.L. fell to his knees in disbelief. The pain of the moment was overwhelming. The realization of what had just happened sent shock waves through his entire body. He hung his head and forced back the tears that so desperately wanted to escape.

D.L. Holmes was not going to the Olympics.

The virus that he had pushed out that morning came roaring back. Whether it was due to emotions or sickness or both, his head was heavy and he held it low and slowly walked away from the jump area. O.W. caught up to him and put his arm around him. "Sorry, D.L.," he said. "That had to be really close. I couldn't see a foul. It looked like you hit it right to me." O.W. paused for a minute, trying to think of something helpful to say. "The 1916 Olympics aren't that far away. I know you'll try again." D.L. could only pick his head up slightly and look at O.W. with eyes that showed the depth of his disappointment. He wanted to go to Stockholm badly. But it wasn't going to happen.

The Holmes brothers went back to the sick tent where D.L. had his temporary home.

"You know, I think I just need a little time to myself," said D.L.

O.W. understood and said he'd come back later to check on him.

D.L. stretched out on his cot, buried his head in his pillow, and sobbed.

Exactly three weeks later, on June 29, 1912, D.L. participated in the AAU Central Association Championship Track Meet. Included in the field of competitors in the running broad jump was James Wasson. In that competition, Wasson came in second place with a jump of 22'4½", better than he had jumped in his second-place finish at the Olympic Trials. First place, at 23'9½", went to D.L. Holmes. That distance would have put D.L. in the Olympics.

Although he didn't qualify, D.L. followed the results of the Stockholm Olympics closely, especially the running broad jump. The first-place jump was 24'11¼", a fabulous jump. Second place was 23'7¾". D.L. shook his head and looked away from his newspaper. He regularly jumped further than 23'7¾". And once, just that once, practicing at the Olympic Trials, he had jumped farther than 25'. If he had only been 100 percent healthy at the Olympic Trials, that could have been his name in the newspaper.

D.L. pulled a handkerchief from his pocket to dry his eyes. So much work. So many dreams. So much pain thinking about what could have been. It was the worst timing for a virus to run through Chicago. He had visualized himself on the Olympic podium having a medal placed around his neck. Maybe not the gold medal, but perhaps, just perhaps, he could have brought home a silver medal from Stockholm. He had recurring dreams about the welcome he would have had in Stillwater.

In reality, D.L. had nothing. He had nothing but those dreams. He had no voyage to Stockholm, no competition in the Olympics, no Olympic medal presentation, no ticker-tape parade, no hero's welcome. All he had was a newspaper with the stories of others who did what he wanted to do.

It was one of the greatest disappointments of his life. His only consolation was the thought of the 1916 Olympics. It would be four more years until he could turn his dreams into reality in Berlin. He would be twenty-nine years old in 1916, older than most other athletes, but not the oldest athlete competing. By the 1920 Olympics he would be past his prime.

D.L. set his mind on 1916.

His preparation was especially difficult, not because of the training but because he needed to keep his amateur status. D.L. thought about Jim Thorpe who won both the gold medal in the pentathlon and the gold medal in the decathlon only to have them stripped from him because he had been paid to play minor league baseball. If D.L. was paid as a coach, he would be considered a professional and be ineligible for the Olympics. Bethel College had agreed to pay D.L. for his work as a history professor while he "volunteered" as the athletic director and coach of all sports. He was now moving on to a new job and hoped he could work out the same arrangement with his new employer.

As he did for the Stockholm Olympics, D.L. put together a training and competition schedule to prepare him for the games in Berlin. He did well, winning the running broad jump in almost every competition he entered. Balancing personal preparation with the work of a college professor and coach wasn't easy, but D.L. managed to pull it off. The allure of a chance at another Olympics kept his motivation strong.

While D.L. was preparing for Olympic competition, something entirely different was developing in Europe. Germany was at war with Russia, France, and Great Britain. World War I had begun. Most observers thought it would be over quickly. In March of 1915, the German Imperial Board for the Olympic Games announced that the games would go on, but with athletes from only countries sympathetic to the causes of Germany. That was not a popular idea with the International Olympic Committee. There were several attempts to change the location of the Olympics, but none were found to be acceptable. The 1916 Olympics were canceled due to World War I.

D.L. Holmes was not going to the Olympics.

Due to his age and the nature of his employment, D.L. Holmes was never going to the Olympics.

3

RACING, STREETCARS, AND RACING STREETCARS

Interview with Gordon Hill, Class of 1926
Interviewed by Professor David L. Holmes Jr.

July 24, 1998

Professor David L. Holmes Jr.: You are the oldest Wayne track man I've had the pleasure to interview.

Gordon Hill: So old it wasn't Wayne yet. I went to College of the City of Detroit, or City College as we called it. In fact, when I started it was Detroit Junior College and then sometime in my first year, 1923, it became City College. We were the second graduating class.

Professor: Incredible! The second graduating class! And you were a farmer, so I assume going to college wasn't typical for farmers back then.

Hill: Well, in my family it was typical. My entire family went to City College. In those days the colleges taught a lot of vocations. Farming takes a lot of knowledge, and City College helped us learn what we needed to know on the farm in terms of soil, fertilization, entomology, and even equipment repair.

Professor: So, my dad didn't recruit you to City College. You didn't go to high school in Detroit, so he may not have known about you. You were a runner in high school?

Hill: Yes, yes. I grew up on the family farm in Mt. Clemens, MI. We lived about three miles from the high school. There was an interurban [streetcar] I could take, but my track practice was running to school and trying to beat it! [*laughs*] Mt. Clemens had a track team of sorts. It was a tiny school, about 275 of us, that's it. For track uniforms our mothers would cut underwear shirts and sew a red stripe across it. Our running shoes were whatever the school happened to have. Might be four sizes too big. We had to wait for someone to graduate that had our shoe size. [*laughs*]

Professor: If you were chasing the interurban, you must have been a distance runner?

Hill: Exactly, yes. In 1922, I came in second in the mile in a regional track meet. Track meets were strange events back then. This one wasn't just high schools competing against each other. Some colleges and athletic clubs were there, too. I came in second to someone who had already graduated from college and I was in high school! Then, in 1923, I won the state high school championship in the mile.

Professor: Excellent! State champion! And in the fall of 1923 you came to City College?

Hill: Yes. I remember walking into your dad's office and telling him I won the state championship. He was startled and excited. I remember exactly what he said. "My heavens, we're finally getting some good men!"

Professor: What do you remember about Coach Holmes? What was he like as a coach and as a person?

Hill: He was a rubber ball. He was always jumping up and down as if the house was on fire. If he had something to get excited about, he jumped up and down! And I remember he was a natural athlete, in every sport. Sometimes we'd take a break or just be horsing around with a football. He'd pick up that football and throw a perfect spiral to someone fifty yards away. And every track event he knew backwards and forwards. His depth of knowledge and ability was incredible.

Professor: Sometimes people describe Coach Holmes as almost saintly: no drinking, no smoking, no swearing, no unkind words of any kind. What was your impression?

Hill: [*laughs*] Those things are true, but he just went about his dirty work a different way. He was tricky. There was always a tremendous competition between Michigan Normal and City College. In any game, the competition became almost savage. Sometimes fights erupted. One year, the flu epidemic washed out our track team; all we had were twelve men. Coach Holmes came into the locker room, which was not much of a locker room—but that's a different story—while we were getting ready for the meet. He said that Lloyd Olds, the Michigan Normal track coach, had told him how he now had City College where he wanted them. His team had *not* been hit by the flu and Olds said he was going to keep Wayne from taking a single point in the meet. He and his team were going to keep City College scoreless. That made the team so angry; so angry we were ready to fight Olds ourselves. I was very angry. Practically all twelve men went out and won firsts in their events. I won the half mile and the mile. Olds put five or six men in each event, and City College usually only could put one. But City College almost won the meet! We only lost because of the relay. The team was all so tired out by that time, after they'd participated in so many events. Years later, though, thinking back on it, I doubt Olds really made that statement. That was just Holmes' way of motivating us to do well. It worked! He could be tricky.

Professor: You said it wasn't much of a locker room. I hear the program was usually broke.

Hill: He was a penny pincher because he had to be. He only got pennies. Every time the question of funding the track team or the entire athletic program came up, Holmes was in a dither. He was running around. The Board of Education wanted to cut track and all athletics. Music, art, drama, etc., they wanted to cut all those programs. They were offering a cheap education and they didn't want any frills. Athletics was seen as a frill. That's what he was up against. He managed to save athletics, but never could move it forward where it should be. He never talked about it, but you could tell he was raised a poor boy. We all were poor boys, but he avoided saying anything about it. Yet, I always suspected he was poor when he grew up. So, I think that's why he connected with his teams so well and why he understood the motivation of the college. His life was living with no money, so that's what he did at City College.

Professor: Any other memories about him?

Hill: My father died when I was fourteen years old. I had no dad. Coach Holmes was like my father. I loved him. But he was like my father in that he could be disappointed in me. One semester I became ineligible due to my grades. He was unsympathetic. I planned to be an MD. Here I was attending a little school that had no antecedents of intellectuality. It had just opened up. It gave the barest of educations. I had attended a country high school. But my mother thought I should be a doctor. In the pre-med courses, I got along fine as long as they were reading courses. When it came to math and science, I failed. Instead of the teachers telling me to leave pre-med, they tried to keep me in the program, thinking in the end I would get by. In those days, you only needed a couple years of college to be a doctor. I told Coach Holmes about it and he was angry. He felt like I failed him, and so did I. He went around to all my teachers, with me in tow, and practically got on his knees to beg and ask for new tests and extensions for me. I got some new tests, but it didn't do any good. That's when I went into the farming-related courses.

Professor: And you got back on track with your courses and with your relationship with Coach Holmes?

Hill: Yes. It was bumpy at first, but that was because of me. He was always full of pep; always on the jump. Some men you approve of for their intellect. Coach Holmes was not an intellectual. He was a farm boy. He did not have an intellectual attitude like you often found with college faculty. He inspired athletes. He could get 10 percent more out of an athlete than others would have. You did better than you thought you could because he expected it.

Professor: Did you ever travel to out-of-state meets with the team?

Hill: Oh, absolutely. I was on the mile relay. We would meet at Old Main early in the morning and load up in a car or two and drive to a meet in another state. On those road trips, we often didn't eat inside restaurants. Our meals would consist of the team sitting in the cars while Coach Holmes was inside the restaurant arguing the price of sandwiches with the owner. The team always ate together. He insisted on it, and so did we. If a restaurant owner said he wouldn't serve us because some of the team was Black, we would walk out. Same with hotels.

Professor: Did any of your fellow white team members have prejudices?

Hill: I never heard anyone utter one word against our team walking out of restaurants in such situations. We were teammates. We were friends. We all wanted to stay together. And Coach Holmes instilled that while we earned points as individuals in our events, we won meets as a team—all of us.

Professor: You came from City College and went to track meets at other universities. What did you think of the facilities?

Hill: Our facilities at City College were primitive. Really bad. We went to Michigan State and they had marvelous outdoor facilities, to us at least! We were agog when we went there. Kalamazoo College did not have a better indoor track than us. Western Michigan had a pretty good indoor track. They had a well-funded program. Hillsdale and Alma had even worse indoor tracks than City College. [*laughs*] Ohio Wesleyan's track was no better than ours. In general, we were glad to have what we had. We were working men's sons. Tuition the first year was about fifty dollars.

Professor: Fifty dollars? Incredible! Did City College even have any outside track facilities?

Hill: Yes and no. Yes we had them, but they weren't at the college. The team used Belle Isle for its outdoor track. We got there by ourselves. We just showed up. Practice started at 3:00 p.m. I had to go to Belle

Isle on a streetcar. I'd get off at the bridge then I would walk all the way across the bridge and to the track—and later walk back. Then I would take the Jefferson streetcar, cross over to Gratiot, go to the city limits, take the interurban to Mt. Clemens, then go milk a dozen cows. In the morning, I'd get up at 4:00 a.m. and milk the cows. My brother and I fixed the feed so my mother could feed the cows at noon. We had a dairy farm. Usually I had an 8:00 a.m. class, when I was in pre-med. I caught the 6:00 a.m. interurban and I wouldn't get home until 6:00 p.m. or later.

Professor: Sounds like you were a hard-working student! Tell me about your most famous race: the race against Paavo Nurmi.

Hill: I've received more attention for that 1,000 yards than anything else I ever did! Nurmi was referred to as "The Flying Finn." He won four Olympic gold medals and held six world records in distance events. Your father, Coach Holmes, along with Detroit's Finnish community, invited Nurmi to Detroit for an exhibition competition. It was a big deal! Nurmi first came to Washington, DC and was greeted by President Coolidge before arriving in Detroit. The race was originally scheduled for Olympia Stadium, but it wasn't big enough. Instead, it was moved to the State Fair Grounds which held fifteen thousand.

Professor: Apparently my father picked you to run against Nurmi!

Hill: Yes, exactly! Why? I wasn't even a miler that year. I ran the half mile. Your dad just told me to do my best.

Professor: If I remember the story correctly, Nurmi arrived at the State Fair and refused to run on the primitive track.

Hill: He said it was an amateurish setup. He refused to run a mile but, after much prodding, agreed to run 1,000 yards. But then, when we were called to our marks, Nurmi refused to run on the track until it was completely reconditioned. So, the fifteen thousand spectators had to sit and wait through getting equipment out, wetting down the track and rolling it again, and putting equipment away again.

Professor: And the race finally took place.

Hill: Yes, finally, we were back at our marks and the race began. Nurmi was fast, very fast. He was running at a pace I'd never run at before. It was killing me. By the second lap he was a good 60 feet ahead of me. My secret weapon, however, was a great kick in the last 220. I took off after him at full blast. I was pulling up on him and would have caught him if the race was 10 yards longer. The greatest sound I ever heard in my life was that huge crowd screaming its lungs out when they thought the local boy was going to catch Nurmi.

Professor: That's an exciting story. And you almost caught him. Very exciting. Congratulations on a race well run. I'm sure that was big news in the papers at the time.

Hill: Yes, sure was. My fifteen minutes of fame!

Professor: Any fellow teammates that stand out in your memory from your time at City College?

Hill: Absolutely. Ed Spence and Ken Doherty. Our track team could have beaten the University of Michigan in the 1920s. We had the best high hurdler in the United States. Spence held the low hurdle record. But the University of Michigan felt that running against City College was taking a chance. They did not want to be beaten by an insignificant school. So they would not compete with us, though Coach Holmes tried everything to get them to run us. We did beat Michigan State by about 38 to 20! And the City College basketball team was ranked fifth in the United States in the Spaulding Guide in 1925. Coach Holmes coached that team, too.

Professor: And Doherty?

Hill: Oh, yes, Doherty, after he graduated from City College, went on to medal in the decathlon in the 1928 Olympics. Great athlete and competitor. After I graduated, Coach Holmes continued to attract great track athletes. I graduated in 1926, so it was 1927 when John Lewis came to City College. Now *he* was a great runner.

4
ECSTASY AND AGONY

Detroit City High School League Track and Field Championships, Codd Field

May 18, 1924

It was like being on a beach during high winds; sand and other small particles whipping through the air with random pieces of paper floating through the sky like kites without a string. Except there was no beach and no ocean. They were at Codd Field, adjacent to Hutchins Intermediate School. It was the best track in the city, just upgraded during the 1922–23 school year. The gusty wind favored some athletes and frustrated others. It was a good day to throw the javelin, but not a great one to do the high jump, where the bar was swaying and falling off from the force of the wind. Tents that had been erected for officials and time-keepers were taken down so they didn't go flying through the neighborhood.

John Lewis stood with his back to the wind and raised his uniform shirt high to stop the sand from tearing the skin off his neck. He was only fifteen years old, and this was his first championship meet. He couldn't believe his eyes as he saw every Detroit track star right in front of him. The powerhouses of Detroit high school track and field were there: Northwestern, Cass Tech, Eastern, Central, and Southeastern. It was not lost on Lewis that he was from Northeastern, not Northwestern, and his teammates had scored no points yet in this meet. He watched Northwestern dominating race after race and waited for his time to shine in the 220-yard dash. He tried not to think about his competition. He was running against Jimmie Tait, from Northwestern, who held several Detroit high school records and was formidable. Then there was Leighton Boyd, Southeastern, who held any record Tait didn't hold. If there was a headline in the newspaper about track, Tait and Boyd were often in bold print.

Lewis had run against Boyd and Tait earlier in the week. It was the preliminary heat for today's championship races. Boyd, Tait, and Lewis were all in the same heat. Lewis came in third, behind both of the stars. Given that showing, he was lucky to be here today at all. But, fortunately for Lewis, Northeastern didn't have a very big track team, and he was the best runner they had. He was representing Northeastern no matter what.

The Detroit City Championships were not just a showcase for exceptional talent in high school track and field, they were also an opportunity for college recruiters to take a look at potential athletes for their teams. Scouts from Michigan Agricultural College, Michigan, Purdue, Michigan Normal, and other universities were always in attendance. These schools were big and would send a representative, not the main track coach, to watch and take notes. The College of the City of Detroit, on the other hand, was small, and Coach Holmes came himself. Holmes knew he wouldn't be able to match any scholarship offers and would lose the big stars to other colleges. But he had an eye for talent and could pick up some recruits who didn't realize the potential they had within. D.L. watched intently for those contestants who came in second or third, as they were the champions of the future.

An announcement was made for the 220-yard dash runners to get ready. Lewis braved the flying sand and made his way to the starting line. He stretched and prepared himself in the middle of the field. He allowed himself a few practice starts on the grassy infield. He tried to ignore his competitors, but it was hard not to notice Tait with his incredible quick start. Tait was small but had powerfully strong legs.

The 220-yard dash runners were called to the track. The wind had died down some, which would be one less thing to worry about. Lewis looked around and couldn't help but notice he was the only Black runner in this race. Out of the hundreds of athletes at the championship today, only a dozen or so were Black. It didn't matter to Lewis that much, but it seemed to matter to others, especially if he ever ended up in the newspaper. When Boyd was in the newspaper he was the "plucky little Southeastern sprinter." When Lewis was in the newspaper he was the "Negro runner."

Lewis had drawn the fourth lane, probably the best place he could be. He preferred Lanes One and Two, but that was when the 220 was run around a corner. The new Codd Field had a straight 220, so being in the middle would give Lewis the best chance to see other runners on either side of him. Tait was in Lane One, Boyd in Lane Five, and Bill Streng, a strong runner from Eastern High School, was in Lane Six. Those were the three Lewis had to watch. He wished he had Tait a lane or two closer to him, but he had Boyd right next to him, which was perfect.

"Runners, on your marks," said the official. Lewis dug small trenches in the dirt and cinders with the toes of his shoes. The track felt good and he would have plenty of resistance for his start.

"Set." The official pulled the trigger of the starting pistol and with a bang the runners leaped off their marks. From the very first step it was an intense race as all seven runners were about even at 25 yards. At 110 yards some runners began to separate and pull ahead. It was Tait, Boyd, and Lewis neck and neck. Streng was next, but about 2 yards behind. At 200 yards all three leaders were still together with Boyd just a half step behind. Tait, Lewis; Lewis, Tait; just inches apart, fighting for the lead.

The crowd at Codd Field was on their feet, especially D.L. Holmes.

The finish was the closest of the entire track meet, and officials had to meet to compare stopwatches and opinions of who hit the tape first. It was finally decided that it was Tait by a mere inch with Lewis a millisecond behind. Boyd was third and Streng fourth. Complicated by the wind, the winning time was 23.9.

A man wearing a suit, tie, and hat with a stopwatch around his neck came up to Lewis after the race and said, "Nice race, son." Lewis said "thanks" and went about his way. He asked another runner who it was. They told him, "That's Coach Holmes from CCD." At the time he thought nothing of it; he was too busy thinking about the race.

His second-place finish felt like first place to John Lewis. He was excited. He'd beaten Boyd, which was an accomplishment, and he was virtually tied with Tait at the tape. On top of that, a college track coach had told him he did a good job. It had been one of his best competitions, and he wanted to come back next year, a little older, and win it. When the championship meet was over later that day, Northeastern High School had accumulated 3 points—total—for the entire meet. Lewis felt especially proud that those three points were his.

One year later, Lewis was back at Codd Field for the 1925 Detroit City League Track Championships. He met his goal of soundly beating Tait in the 220-yard dash, but came in second to Eddie Tolan of Cass Tech. This year, however, he also placed second in the 100-yard dash, a race he had not placed in the year before. In a battle for the wire, Tolan beat Lewis by a hair to win it. Tait was a yard or two behind in third place.

Lewis was happy. He had doubled his point total from the year before. His team did better, also. One Northeastern teammate came in third in the 220 and another placed second in the javelin, bringing Northeastern's point total to 10, a far cry from the 51½ points earned by Northwestern, yet a huge improvement over 1924. Northeastern was poised for additional points in the half-mile relay, but one of their runners fell and they came in fifth. All in all, things were looking up for Northeastern and Lewis. They were slowly starting to make their mark within Detroit track and field.

In 1927, Lewis moved away from the short dashes. Tolan was dominating those races and Lewis' high school track coach thought they could capture more points elsewhere. Lewis started competing in the 440-yard dash. He beat the old 440-yard dash record in Detroit with a time of 50.8 seconds, and Northeastern came in second in the Detroit City League Championship meet with 35 points. At the State of Michigan Championship meet, Lewis came in first in the 440-yard dash and was recognized as the best quarter-miler in the state. His sweetest victory at that meet was beating Northwestern in the half-mile relay. Lewis received the baton tied with Northwestern and broke the tape 5 yards ahead. These were huge personal and team accomplishments, yet Lewis had no plans to do anything after high school, and this was his final year at Northeastern.

As one of the top high school athletes in the state, Lewis was ignored by the big universities. He had no offers, no scholarships, and no plans.

At his final track meet, Coach Holmes came up to talk to him. "How'd you like to run for the College of the City of Detroit track team, John?" asked Coach Holmes. "You have some great running skill, and I think we could make you even faster."

Lewis lowered his eyes and looked at the ground. "I wish I could, coach. I've heard about you. But we don't have that much money and there's no way I could pay for college. But, thanks," said Lewis. Holmes smiled and said, "How about I come by your house and talk with you and your parents about it. You'd be surprised what we can accomplish without a lot of money. I can get you a job at the college and you'll pay your own way. Your parents won't pay anything."

"I don't know," said Lewis.

"Well, it costs nothing to have me come talk to your parents about it," said Holmes. "You're already a champion. How'd you like to be an AAU or NCAA champion? How about an Olympian? I know some things I'd work on with you right away so we could get your 440 under 50 seconds. Give me an hour to work on your start and we can shave off a second right there. In fact, let me show you."

Holmes put his stopwatch in his pocket and took off his sport coat and hat and tossed them on the grass. He went onto the track and dug some starting holes with his dress shoes and began fifteen minutes of demonstration on how Lewis could improve his start. Lewis thought it was quite a sight! Here's a white man in a shirt, tie, vest, dress pants, and dress shoes crouched down on the track demonstrating starts. He shouldn't have smiled so quickly. D.L. then had Lewis try some practice starts. In just a couple of minutes Lewis could already feel the difference. All throughout high school he'd been pushing out of his start with his front foot. Coach Holmes taught him how to get more power with his back foot. He *could* be under 50 seconds. He couldn't help but be excited by the possibilities.

"Okay, coach," said Lewis. "How about tomorrow night? I'll let my parents know. Maybe 7:00?"

Holmes got the address, and the next night he visited John Lewis and his parents. The following day, Lewis filled out enrollment paperwork at Old Main. He was now a student at the College of the City of Detroit.

Just days after Lewis enrolled at CCD, one of the Detroit high school stars he remembered from the all-city track meets, Edwin Spence, became the NCAA 220-yard low hurdles national champion. Just another kid from a Detroit high school who was recruited by Holmes, went to CCD, and became a national champion. Lewis knew he had made a good decision.

In the fall of 1927, John Lewis started class, and track, in the halls of Old Main. He laughed to himself when he realized Jimmy Tait had also been recruited by Holmes and would be his teammate. His nemesis on the track might now be a friend. Eddie Tolan had been recruited by the University of Michigan.

Freshmen had a separate track team from upperclassmen. Lewis was on the freshman team and, due to college rules, was not able to participate on the varsity team. Lewis excelled as a freshman. At one outdoor meet in May of 1928, he came in first place in the 120-yard low hurdles, first in the 100-yard dash, first in the 220-yard dash, first in the shot put, and first in the discus, and his relay team won the half-mile relay.

D.L. recognized his talent and wanted to take Lewis to the Olympic Trials.

The June 1928 National Collegiate Track Meet in Chicago was serving as phase one of three events leading to competition in the Olympics. D.L. was there with three men from his track team and looking in on one former member of his team. Ed Spence, Bill Streng, and John Lewis were in Chicago preparing for their races. Ken Doherty had graduated from CCD but was there trying to qualify for the decathlon.

Spence could be described only as a phenomenon. He had won the 120-yard low hurdles the past two years. He held the national record at 23.4 seconds, which he set in 1927, beating his 1926 national record by 0.1 second. Spence performed well every time he came to Illinois. In 1926, he won the high hurdles championship at the National Relays at the University of Illinois. He was an All-American and was a sure bet to get an Olympic slot.

Streng was more of an outlier. He was an incredibly fast 440-yard dash man, bringing in a 48.5 at an event the previous week. But there was virtually no chance of him beating the runner from Stanford. If he placed in the top three today, he'd meet up with Fred Alderman, from Michigan State, in the next round. Alderman was the top seed in any 440 race in the Midwest. Streng had a tough road ahead.

Lewis felt a few butterflies in his gut. He saw athletes who were older and more experienced than he all converging on Chicago. However, he did hold the 440 high school title in Michigan. His entire senior year of high school, he never lost a 440-yard dash. In Chicago, however, he wasn't going to be competing against high school runners or college freshmen. He would be competing against the best track men in the Midwest.

D.L. loved the moment. It was a dream come true. He had been a track coach for almost twenty years, and he now had three athletes that could qualify for the Olympics. D.L. could hardly contain himself. Three strong runners. Three Olympic hopefuls. Three Detroit kids that could be going to Amsterdam. The competition would be fierce and thrilling.

Lewis made it through all three levels of preliminary competition, and on July 5, 1928, he competed at Philadelphia's Municipal Stadium for a spot on the Olympic team. His two CCD teammates, Spence and Streng, did not make it. Doherty, a CCD graduate, also made it to this level of the competition. The runners for the 400-meter dash had been determined through preliminary heats, and Lewis was not one of them. He was still in contention for a spot on the 1,600-meter relay team.

Two spots on the relay team had already been determined. Fred Alderman, the Michigan State sprinter, had been selected along with Emerson Spencer, of Stanford. Multiple qualifying heats had been run, and Lewis had made it to a special final heat. The top two runners in this heat would be part of the 1,600-meter relay team and go to Amsterdam to compete for the United States.

The weather had been extremely hot for a few days, with temperatures in the high eighties and low to midnineties. On the first day of the finals, the athletes were getting a bit of a break—but not the break they wanted. The winds picked up and it soon began to pour. It was raining so hard that several events were postponed until the second day. The weather, unfortunately, didn't cooperate on day two either. Conditions were very bad for running, as the track was picking up water quickly. It seemed just as rainy and windy as it was the day before, but there were no more days in the trials. Every race had to be run today. The finals of the 400-meter dash had been held in a downpour and into the face of a raging wind. The first four in that race were the competitors in the 400-meter dash in Amsterdam. Ray Barbuti, the powerhouse from the New York Athletic Club, crossed the finish line first with a time of 48 seconds flat; incredible considering the circumstances. The fifth- and sixth-place finishers took two spots on the 1,600-meter relay team.

The special final 400-meter heat was held in spite of the weather. Six runners were vying for the final two spots on the 1,600-meter relay. This was the moment of truth for Lewis. Three levels of qualifying competition to get to Philadelphia. Multiple heats of competition in Philadelphia to get to this final heat. He had not made the cut for the 400-meter dash, his specialty. Now he was fighting for one of those two last relay team spots. He prepared himself mentally and physically for the most important heat he'd ever run.

He was soaked to the bone, every inch of him wet from the pouring rain. He warmed up on the infield as other heats of other races took place on the track. Practice starts on the grass were very different from starts on the cinders, but he did them anyway. If he was going to win this, he had to have an excellent start. He thought back to Coach Holmes showing him how to get a faster start at the end of his high school track career. Lewis and D.L. had worked on that a considerable amount of time during the track season, and he felt ready for it today.

When the runners were called to the track, Lewis noticed how badly the track had deteriorated. The rain continued and there were no signs it was going to let up. He dug a couple of holes for his toes and found the cinders no longer had the resistance they once had, which meant the start could be sloppy, at best, and disastrous, at worst. He dug his toes in a little deeper to help counter the cinder collapse that might occur. As he waited for the starter to have them take their marks, Lewis pictured himself breaking the tape and coming in first like he had done so many times in Detroit.

"Runners, on your marks," said the starter.

Lewis could feel the rain pounding on his back as he crouched in his starting position. The holes he had dug for the toes of his shoes were filled with water, and water was running down the sides of his face into his eyes.

"Set."

Bang, went the starter's pistol, and the race was on. Lewis got off to a surprisingly fast start, but he was not in first. George Baird, of Iowa, was in the lead. At the 200-meter mark it was Baird in front with Lewis at his heels. The other four runners had dropped off and were 6 to 10 meters behind Lewis. The significance of that moment didn't hit Lewis. If he could just maintain his second place he would be going to the Olympics. Lewis wasn't thinking about that at all. He wanted to win.

Coming around the 300-meter corner, Lewis put on the burners. It was always his strategy to pace himself through the first 300 meters and then have a faster final 100 meters. Baird had that same strategy. Lewis shortened the gap between them but could not catch Baird. Baird broke the tape with

Lewis a fraction of a second behind. Pouring rain and soggy track, Baird still ran a 48.8.

All six runners walked around near the finish line, trying to catch their breath. Baird and Lewis caught each other's eye, congratulated each other, and shook hands. Both men were very happy to be headed to the Olympics.

The Olympic 1,600-meter relay team had been selected for the 1928 Amsterdam games. The four runners would be Spencer, Alderman, Baird, and Lewis. The Philadelphia qualifying events were covered widely in the newspapers. Once again, rather than describing Lewis as the State High School Champion 440-Yard Dash star, they called him the "colored youth from Detroit." Detroit, on the other hand, called him their next Olympic star. Lewis, along with Ken Doherty, who had qualified for the decathlon, had the hopes of the city riding on his shoulders.

There was not much time between Lewis qualifying for the Olympics and having to get on the SS *President Roosevelt* for the nine-day voyage across the Atlantic to Amsterdam. He and most of the other American Olympic athletes would leave on the ship from New York on July 11. Opening Ceremonies for the games were on July 28, and his event would take place on August 5. Lewis took a train back to Detroit and prepared for his Olympic competition and a trip that would keep him away from home for over a month.

Back in Detroit, his family, neighbors, and City College teammates were thrilled. Lewis was going to the Olympics! No person was more thrilled, than D.L. himself. Two of his track men were heading to the Olympics. Doherty, although a graduate, still had learned the ropes of the decathlon at City College. Lewis was a bright young star whose age was perfectly matched to see the possibility of multiple Olympic competitions. After the 1928 Olympics, he would enter his sophomore year at City College. For the 1932 Olympics, he would be in the same position as Ken Doherty was now. Like Doherty, he could be even better and faster four years from now.

The neighborhood where Lewis lived threw a block party for him. The Detroit Fire Department even opened up one of the fire hydrants so all the kids could enjoy the cool spray of water on a hot summer day. Lewis jumped through it once himself but was preoccupied with his mother, aunts, and other neighborhood women who wanted to fatten him up with incredible baked goods and scrumptious pies. He told them he needed to stay in shape for the Olympics, yet he did succumb to a rather large piece of his mom's apple pie.

The entire block was filled with fun and laughter as neighbors and friends came to wish Lewis well. There was a momentary swirl of whispers at the party as a few people noticed a white man wearing a suit, tie, and hat walking toward them. Someone tapped Lewis on the shoulder and asked, "Who is that?" Lewis looked up and broke into a big smile. He ran down the block to greet his coach. D.L. had stopped by to wish him well and congratulate his parents on their son's achievement. They welcomed him onto the front porch and moved some baked goods from a chair so he could have a seat. D.L. chatted about the incredible year Lewis had had as a freshman and talked about the one meet where he won every event he entered. Mrs. Lewis gave him a piece of her apple pie, which he happily accepted. He took a bite.

"Don't tell my wife," said D.L., "but this is the best apple pie I've ever tasted!"

If it wasn't for the obvious difference in skin color and attire, D.L. would have fit right in. He was comfortable being there, and they were comfortable having him there.

He could have stayed for hours, but after "just another sliver" of apple pie, D.L. made his way home. Before he left, he looked at Lewis and said, "John, come by my office before you leave for Amsterdam. I have something for you. Give yourself about forty-five minutes, too. We need to practice your baton passes." With that, he tipped his hat toward Mrs. Lewis and thanked her for the hospitality. He thanked everyone on the porch and made his way to the sidewalk, where kids were dancing in the rain of the fire hydrant. What happened next was not a surprise for those who knew him the best, but it caught many of those on the porch by surprise. D.L. walked to the edge of where the water was spraying, found a large puddle, and jumped with two feet into the middle of the puddle with a splash. The kids all laughed and he did, too. He turned and waved at the people on the porch—some laughing and some shocked—and then continued his walk down the sidewalk.

The time line for Lewis was quick. There were only a few days before he needed to be in New York. The first thing he needed to do was get down to the Fort Street Union Train Depot and get a ticket on the Red Arrow to New York. He needed to pack clothes for more than a month away from home. Then he needed to find some time to go see Coach Holmes.

The next several days were a blur as he prepared for going to the Olympics. The excitement of the event was tempered by the crunched time line to complete everything. Before he knew it, all the pieces came together and he was in New York walking out on Pier 86 toward the SS *President Roosevelt*. Lewis had never seen a ship this large. The only time he'd been on anything even close was taking the boat from downtown Detroit to the Bob-Lo Island Amusement Park on an island at the mouth of Lake Erie. He'd seen the *Tashmoo* and other large ships docked in the river but had never been on one of them. The *President Roosevelt* was even bigger, a vessel made for ocean voyages. It was so large, Lewis thought it must hold thousands of passengers.

He carried his trunk toward the huge ship through throngs of people. There were two bands on the pier playing patriotic songs and what seemed like ten thousand people there to wish the Olympic athletes bon voyage. It appeared as if every single one of them was waving a small American flag. It was a thrilling experience. His letter said to meet the concierge at the bottom of the gangway leading to the ship. Lewis wasn't sure what a concierge or a gangway was, but he followed others who also looked like athletes as they made their way to the ship. Several athletes were swarmed around a woman wearing an official-looking uniform. She had a clipboard and was giving athletes instructions. Lewis moved closer so he could hear. She was asking for last names, writing the names on tags, assigning room numbers, attaching the tags to their luggage, and asking the athletes to walk up the gangway, which turned out to be a long ramp that connected to the entryway of the ship. Several young men in similar uniforms were taking the trunks and other baggage up a different ramp. She said the trunks would be delivered to the rooms. Lewis made his way closer and gave his name, and she said he was in room 99. He left his trunk and started to slowly walk up the ramp. He looked around in every direction. There were thousands of people behind him waving flags and a huge ship in front of him with athletes waving from the balconies.

Once on board, Lewis found a spot by the railing so he could look back at the scene on the pier. He could hear the bands and see all the people with the incredible tall buildings of the city of New York rising behind. He wished his family and his teammates from City College could have been there to see it all. After one or two more hours of loading the ship with athletes, the SS *President Roosevelt* sounded its horn and slowly began to move away from the pier. Lewis stood at the railing, waving back to all those waving at him. It was a very special feeling.

John Lewis, a freshman at the College of the City of Detroit, was heading to the Olympics in Amsterdam!

As the *Roosevelt* made its way out to the ocean, Lewis saw an incredible sight: the Statue of Liberty. The eyes of the beautiful statue seemed to look right at him while the ship went slowly by as the band played "America." It was thrilling and made him proud to be representing the United States. The New York skyline got smaller and smaller until finally, Lewis was able to break himself away from the railing and go find his room.

He had never had a problem in Detroit with his City College peers. However, being one of just three Black athletes on the American Olympic track team made him wonder how accepted he would be in his stateroom. He walked with some trepidation and found the door marked 99. He could hear voices talking inside. He cautiously opened the door, not knowing if his reception would be positive or negative. Very slowly, he peeked his head around the door.

"John! Come on in! We saw your trunk here and wondered where you were," said one of the two men. It was Ken Doherty, the decathlete who had graduated from City College. His other roommate was George Baird, of Iowa, with whom he had competed to win one of the last two spots on the 1,600-meter relay team. "Were you already checking out the buffet?" asked Baird with a laugh.

Internally, Lewis sighed with relief. A huge weight had been lifted from his shoulders. This rooming arrangement was going to be fine. He had another Detroit kid and one of his 1,600-meter relay teammates as roommates. What could be better?

"No," said Lewis. "Just taking in the sights. Did you see the Statue of Liberty?"

"Yes. She's beautiful, huh? Quite a sight. And now we're on an ocean cruise. Unbelievable!" said Doherty.

"Well, not sure how much we'll be loving it a week from now when we're still on this boat. And this is our hotel while we're in Amsterdam. So, we better love it because we're on this thing for a long time!" laughed Baird.

Although the ship had originally been commissioned as a military vessel, after World War I it had been converted to a cruise ship. It was an elegant ship complete with staterooms, dining rooms, a spa, a casino, and even a golf range on the top deck. For the purpose of the Olympics, other features had been added, like a running track, a boxing ring, a gymnastics area, and a tiny makeshift pool. Normally, the staterooms would have each had two people in them. For the Olympics, it was three to a room, with four to six in the larger staterooms. They would arrive in Amsterdam in nine days.

In the meantime, all they could do was enjoy the trip. The sea was rough, and enjoying the trip was more difficult for some than for others. A huge dinner was served at 6:30 p.m., with a choice of chicken, turkey, or duck. Lewis was feeling a little dizzy from the movement of the ship but sat down to enjoy the amazing food. Others were downright sick and retired to their staterooms for the night. After dinner, Lewis stayed on deck and watched dolphins jumping in the sea and saw the most beautiful sunset he'd ever experienced.

That evening, an orchestra played until 11:00. Lewis enjoyed the music and listened to it along with the sounds of the sea. He felt much better when he was outside in the air. The journey ahead occupied his thoughts. He wanted to meet up with Alderman and Spencer to talk about the 1,600-meter relay.

Maybe they could practice some baton exchanges. Coach Holmes' "gift" when Lewis went to his office before the trip had been a baton for that exact purpose.

The next morning, Lewis went to breakfast with Baird and Doherty. They sat at a table with Macauley Smith of Yale, Arthur Sager of Maine, Lee Bartlett of Albion, and, to Lewis' delight, Fred Alderman of Michigan State College. Three of the four relay men were seated together. Lewis mentioned to Alderman that he'd like to practice exchanges. Alderman nodded and gave Lewis a sickly-looking smile, saying, "Yeah, sure, as soon as my head doesn't weigh one hundred pounds." Alderman ate about five bites of food, excused himself from the table, and went to his stateroom to close his eyes.

The breakfast was incredible: fruit, toast, eggs, cereal, waffles, meat, coffee, and a few things Lewis wasn't quite sure what they were. The waiter was Dutch and very neat and courteous. He spoke English perfectly, with just a touch of an accent.

All the Olympic coaches were also aboard the ship. While the athletic facilities were far from complete, coaches put together a workout schedule and shared times across the sports. The fact that there was a small track gave Lewis an advantage. It looked about the size of Old Main's track, and all he needed was a place to practice starts, baton exchanges, and sprinting. So far, he had been able to practice with only Baird. Alderman remained under the weather with seasickness, and he had yet to see Spencer.

Each day on the ship seemed to be about the same as any other day on the ship. Not that it wasn't nice; it was incredible. Meals were wonderful, like dining at a fine restaurant every meal of the day. The amenities like the spa, gambling, and golf were fun. The entertainment was fabulous, changing from the orchestra to movies to plays to comedians from night to night. The voyage, however, was getting long. Many of the athletes had been sick the entire time. Lewis felt fortunate all he had was the occasional headache when the seas got rough. He, like just about everyone else, was anxious to get off the ship and step foot in Amsterdam.

Finally, after eight days at sea, the ship entered the English Channel. Land! It was good to see.

Lewis watched the boxers practice that afternoon. He counted the other ships in the channel and had now seen twenty-two. That night, the ship docked in Cherbourg, France. Additional passengers were loaded, although Lewis had no idea where they were going to stay. Maybe there were some empty rooms he didn't know about.

On their ninth day at sea, the SS *President Roosevelt* made its way through the Netherlands. The land was beautiful, a low countryside with a checkerboard of green hues. The houses Lewis saw were small and pretty, and many of them had grass roofs. He didn't see many cars. Most people were riding bicycles. Alongside the green fields were fields full of colorful flowers. Many of the other athletes were also at the railing looking at the beautiful countryside and the unique people who lived there. Many people stopped to wave at the ship as it passed. It was hard to miss with huge letters on the side saying "American Olympic Teams." Others went about the business of their day. It was just about lunchtime when the ship anchored in Amsterdam. They did not yet have a space at a dock, so water taxis carried athletes from the boat to shore. As anxious as Lewis was to go see the Olympic facilities, he and his roommates stayed on the ship to eat a free lunch rather than venture into the unknown with an empty stomach.

No residential Olympic Village was constructed for these games. Eighteen ships that delivered athletes to the Olympics would stay in the port and serve as their hotels and home base. The SS *President Roosevelt* would remain Lewis' home for the next few weeks.

Buses were leaving every thirty minutes to take athletes to the Olympic facilities and into the central area of Amsterdam. Lewis, Baird, and Doherty walked on a small gangway from the water taxi to the docks where a huge sign said "*Haven van Amsterdam*," or "Port of Amsterdam" in English. Another large sign next to it said "*Welkom Atleten*" and Lewis saw the words "Welcome Athletes" and what must have been the same welcome in many other languages he couldn't identify. A guide of some sort was calling out instructions in English, so Lewis and his friends followed the crowd from the *Roosevelt* onto a nearby bus. There were many buses awaiting their passengers. A handwritten sign inside the window of their bus said "American Athletes," so they knew they were in the right place.

Ten days at sea and Lewis still had practiced the relay exchanges with only Baird. Alderman was sick and never up to it. Spencer was nowhere to be found. Lewis didn't feel as prepared as he wanted to be. But there was still plenty of time before their event would be held.

On the bus, Lewis was seated next to Ken Doherty, and they talked a bit. Even though they had roomed together, Lewis had never told him the story about Coach Holmes jumping into a puddle of water. He told Doherty the story, adding a few dramatic, yet fictional, elements that made it sound even better than it was. Doherty laughed and shook his head, but said he wasn't surprised. He told Lewis about a time during practice when Coach Holmes was demonstrating proper long jump form and the landing pit was full of water. He ran and leaped through the air and landed in the pit with a huge splash of water. He walked out soaking wet, never said a word, and acted like nothing at all had just happened. And it was actually a pretty good jump!

The two Detroit boys laughed. An ocean away from their city, stories of Detroit, Coach Holmes, and the College of the City of Detroit made them feel a little less homesick.

When they arrived at the Olympic facilities, Lewis and Doherty just stared in awe. They were magnificent, yet surprisingly unfinished. Both Lewis and Doherty had competed on tracks across Michigan and the Midwest. This was pristine and new; beautiful. It was also planned. Unlike so many tracks that were stuck into whatever space happened to be available, this one was set up perfectly. There was ample space for the track itself. Around the running track was a velodrome track for the Olympic bicycle races. The inner field was set up for soccer, or football as they called it in Europe. Inside the track, yet outside the soccer field, were large areas for each one of the field events. In all of the areas were workmen hurriedly trying to finish the stadium before the Olympics began.

For the moment, they would not be practicing on the track in the stadium. They would be working out in a nearby field. The conditions were less than ideal. Some teams who had arrived before the Americans were already out practicing. Lewis and Doherty just looked at each other and smiled. Less-than-ideal track conditions were nothing new to them. Hopefully soon, the track would be ready so they'd be able to give the facilities a try.

The track coach met with the athletes as they arrived. There was no set schedule for the day. It was Friday, July 20, and the 1,600-meter relay wouldn't take place until August 5. Doherty, however, was in the decathlon and had events or practice almost every single day.

The coach handed them a schedule with times when they would come to the temporary track to practice. Doherty and Lewis were on different schedules. There was considerable coordination necessary due to the need to share the limited practice fields with teams from forty-six other countries. Lewis had to be there every other day. On his off days he was free to do whatever he wanted.

Lewis took full advantage of that freedom. Each of his off days he did something different with one or more of the other athletes. One day it was the beach at the Zuiderzee; another day they went shopping on Kalverstraat. The most unusual day was when they rented bikes and went for a ride. The athletes were celebrities of sorts. When they looked behind them, another hundred or so bicycles were following! Lewis hadn't competed yet, but he had enjoyed every minute of being at the Olympics.

General MacArthur, chairman of the Olympics and in charge of the US team, however, was not enjoying the Olympics. The United States was expected to sweep the track and field events. Not just win but sweep. Expectations were not turning into reality. The Americans were beaten out of medal contention in the 100-meter, 200-meter, and 800-meter runs. MacArthur was feeling the heat and hearing the criticism of his handling of the Olympics. He was there to produce medals and make up for a poor American showing in the 1924 Olympics. It wasn't happening. In fact, it was worse than in 1924.

The group that Lewis ate with was grim, at best. Bartlett, from Albion, placed tenth in the javelin. He said he and the other American javelin throwers just weren't themselves. The group talked about Charley Paddock, almost assured of a gold medal, not making it to the 200-meter finals. He had won the 100-meter dash and placed second in the 200-meter dash at the 1920 Olympics. This was his third Olympics, and people whispered he was too old to compete. For the first time since the Olympics restarted in 1896, the United States had no medal winners in the 100-meter dash. Frank Wykoff, who had won the Olympic Trials in the event, placed a disappointing fourth. In the 800-meter run, Lloyd Hahn, who had set an unofficial world record in the event at the AAU Championships earlier that summer, came in fifth.

Thus far, only Doherty was seeing any hope in a sea of darkness. He had not placed in any of the decathlon events, but his point total was good in comparison with those of the other participants. He still had several events to go and was a solid fifth place heading into the pole vault, his specialty.

Now, all eyes turned to Ray Barbuti, the sprinter from New York, who was being counted on to bring in America's only medal in the sprints. Emerson Spencer, the world record holder in the 400-meter and Lewis' teammate in the 1,600-meter relay, had failed to make the cut in the 400-meter at the Olympic Trials. Quite a bit of pressure was riding on Barbuti's shoulders.

The moment of truth came for Barbuti on Friday, August 3, with the running of the 400-meter dash.

Lewis went to the track early so he could get a good vantage point to watch the 400. Most of the US track team went along with him. The pressure was on Barbuti, but the hope for some positive momentum for future races was felt by the entire team. Feeling an equal amount of pressure was General MacArthur, who had promised more medals than he had been able to deliver.

Up to this point, Americans had been beaten badly in the sprints and middle-distance runs. In addition to Barbuti, Herman Phillips was the only other American in the race. Both were talented runners, but their lane positions couldn't have been more dramatically different. Phillips drew the dreaded outside lane. Unless another runner was far ahead, there was no way for

Phillips to know where he was or get the benefit of the competition until he was in the final 100 meters of the race. Barbuti, on the other hand, had drawn the inside lane. Strategically, it was the very best spot. He would be able to see all the runners and know exactly when he had surpassed them. There is always that extra surge of energy when you can see the runner you need to beat.

The final heat of the 400-meter featured a cast of spectacular sprinters. In addition to Phillips and Barbuti, there were Storz and Buchner, both from Germany, Rinkel from Great Britain, and Ball from Canada. Buchner was particularly feared by the Americans. He was the German 400-meter national title holder and had run the 400 in 48 seconds flat.

You could cut the anticipation with a knife. Even General MacArthur settled into a seat to watch this particular race. Lewis watched intently from his vantage point on the infield of the track. The runners took their marks.

"Set!"

The runners leaped from their starting positions as the starting pistol fired. Phillips took the early lead. Not being able to see his competition, he was burning up the track trying to stay in the lead. For the first 200 meters it was Phillips all the way, with Buchner close on his tail. Phillips' 200-meter split was a lightning-quick 22.7 seconds.

It was Phillips in the lead followed closely by Buchner and his countryman Storz. Barbuti was in fourth with Ball and Rinkel close behind. The pace had been so fast that Phillips and Buchner were losing their energy. Barbuti made his move at the 300-meter mark. He passed the Germans and then passed Phillips. Barbuti was in the lead. He didn't realize that Ball from Canada was making a move as well. Ball passed the Germans and Phillips and was cutting down Barbuti's margin. Fifty meters to go!

Barbuti had 8 meters on Ball, but the lead was quickly shrinking. Phillips and the Germans had dropped back. The entire crowd was on its feet, yelling and screaming. General MacArthur was on his feet yelling as well. Lewis and his teammates were all cheering for Barbuti. Barbuti was near exhaustion as he headed for the finish line. The Canadian was at his heels. With 10 meters left, Barbuti still had a lead of 1 meter. His lead was cut to eight inches as both runners lunged for the tape.

The combination of Barbuti's lunge and his exhaustion placed him face down in the cinders at full speed. The pain of his cuts and abrasions was forgotten as the crowd cheered wildly. General MacArthur also cheered. Finally, a gold medal in a sprint! Barbuti sat on the sidelines getting medical attention as many other runners came by to congratulate him. Lewis was one of those who came by to shake his hand. Phillips, who came in last, was off standing by himself. Lewis went over to talk to him.

"It was your incredible pace that helped Ray win it, you know," Lewis told Phillips. "You burned Buchner right out of the race!"

"Thanks, thanks. I appreciate that. I burned myself right out of the race, too," Phillips said.

"Half that gold medal is yours," said Lewis. "You helped make that happen." Phillips nodded a thank you, but his head was still full of defeat.

In the stands, General MacArthur was receiving similar accolades for the win from other American dignitaries. The accolades had been few and far between, so MacArthur was enjoying the moment. To him, and most of the American public, the only measure of success at the Olympics was the number of medals won; especially gold. He started to think about how he could orchestrate some additional gold medals.

That evening, Barbuti and some of his teammates celebrated in their stateroom. They had picked up some alcohol in Amsterdam and were enjoying the moment. There were only two more days remaining of track and field competition, and Barbuti was done with his races. He had been very serious about his conditioning and thought other athletes had lost due to excess food, poor practice conditions, and not enough preparation. Now it was time to let loose. And he did.

Barbuti was feeling no pain when there was a knock on the door. Through the fog of his inebriation, Barbuti instantly recognized General MacArthur.

"Yes, sir," said a startled Barbuti. "What can I do for you?"

"First, I want to congratulate you on your magnificent win today. We were supposed to win all the sprints and you were the only one to do it. I thank you and America thanks you," said MacArthur. "Tomorrow, you'll be in the 1,600-meter relay qualifying heats. I'm pulling another runner in favor of you."

"Well, thank you for the compliment. But no. I won't replace someone who has worked hard to get to this spot. I won't do it," said Barbuti.

"I wasn't asking you. It's an order," said MacArthur forcefully.

"Sir, I'm not in the Army. I don't take orders from you and I'm not taking another person's spot."

MacArthur realized his tactics weren't working and changed his approach. "Ray, listen. You are the best sprinter America has. The sprints have been disappointment after disappointment from athletes we expected to win. I need you in this relay. America needs you in this relay," said MacArthur.

"Who?" asked Barbuti. "Whose spot am I taking?"

"Lewis. John Lewis. He was the final qualifier. Your times are better. You can tell him tomorrow," said MacArthur.

"No. I'm not telling him. If you're doing this, *you* tell him," said an angry Barbuti.

MacArthur summoned Lewis to the room and told him the news with Barbuti standing there. Lewis stood mute in disbelief and then broke into tears. His head was swimming with all the work and preparation he had put into the relay only to have it pulled out from under him at the last minute. So many obstacles he had overcome and now General MacArthur was taking his chance at a medal away. Lewis was crushed.

After delivering the blow, MacArthur left—consumed only with making himself look good by winning more medals and caring little about any work and sacrifice Lewis had put into earning the right to be in the relay.

"I'm sorry, John. This was not my idea. I said 'no,' I wouldn't do it," Barbuti said. He thought it was a terrible thing MacArthur was doing.

Barbuti's celebration party was over. He had preliminary heats to run the next day.

Lewis felt like his life was over. Everything he had worked for had been shattered in a moment.

Lewis didn't sleep that night. He never went back to his stateroom. He stayed on the upper deck and breathed the salty air while he pondered his future. How would he face his friends and family back in Detroit? Would he even be able to look at Coach Holmes? He was shaken to his core and he was embarrassed that his times suggested he was the slowest runner and the one to lose his position. He didn't know what to do. There was still a week left in the Olympics, and he was a man with no reason to have ever been there.

Lewis was still sitting on the deck when the sun rose and breakfast service began. He had no appetite for food or anything else. He was angry at MacArthur and still crushed by his lost opportunity. If he had only beaten Baird in the special qualifying heat for the 1,600-meter relay. If he had only placed in the top six in the 400-meter qualifying heats. If he had only . . .

He wondered if he was the only person on that ship who came to Amsterdam and didn't compete. Sure, some came and lost, yet they still were able to compete and lost on their own abilities, not because the general pulled them out.

Lewis was adrift in his own thoughts. He reran every qualifying heat in his head over and over. The brand-new track at the stadium wasn't the best, but he couldn't use that as an excuse because everyone ran on the same track. He was unsettled; he didn't know what to do, what to say, or what to think. The disappointment was consuming him. It hadn't occurred to him how long he sat there until the sun began to set. He decided to go back to his stateroom and get some sleep.

During his time on the deck Lewis heard that the American 1,600-meter relay team, with Barbuti rather than him, won their qualifying heat and were set to compete in the finals the following day.

On the day of the 1,600-meter finals, Lewis woke up hungry. Baird and Doherty were in the room and gave Lewis looks of compassion but didn't know what to say, so they didn't say much. The silence spoke volumes. Later, Baird walked up to Lewis and patted him on the back and said, "I'm so sorry. This shouldn't have happened. It's not right."

Lewis could only give a nod of appreciation.

The three of them went to breakfast together. There wasn't much talking, but Lewis wished Baird good luck in the 1,600-meter relay and Doherty good luck in additional decathlon events. Baird and Doherty needed to leave quickly due to their events. Lewis stayed behind and thought about whether or not he'd go watch the relay.

It was General MacArthur with whom Lewis was angry, not Barbuti, and he wanted to see his friend Baird do well. So, Lewis put on his USA sweat suit, took a water taxi to the dock, and hopped on a bus to the stadium. News about his removal from the relay team had spread like wildfire across the American team. Everyone offered Lewis conciliatory words, and a few offered disparaging remarks about MacArthur. Lewis liked hearing the latter best. He kept his anger below the surface, but he was still seething.

His emotions remained mixed as the 1,600-meter relay was about to begin. He wanted to root for his teammates, but he also wanted his absence to be missed on the relay team.

General MacArthur's emotions were not mixed. All he wanted was another gold medal. With a gold, his decision to pull Lewis would be forgotten and he would get the accolades he thought he deserved for masterminding another gold.

The 1,600-meter relay athletes were Baird in the lead-off position, Alderman second, Spencer third, and Barbuti as the final runner.

Lewis felt a knot in the pit of his stomach. He knew it should have been him out on the track. A flood of cheers was showering down from the crowd upon all the athletes getting ready for the relay as they were introduced. American flags of all sizes were waved from the stands. Lewis had pictured this moment—but not from the sidelines. He struggled with the outcome he wanted to see.

Lewis did not place himself in the front row to watch the race. Instead, he wandered around looking half interested and half occupied with other thoughts. Every now and then he'd get a pat on the back from a knowing teammate. Runners had taken their marks and the race was about to start. Lewis glanced at the track just as the starter's pistol fired.

Baird, his roommate and new friend, got the team off to a great start. By the time he exchanged the baton with Alderman he had taken the lead. Alderman maintained the lead and handed off to Spencer. It was Spencer who changed the race. He had one of the best 400 meters of his running career. His time was a blazing 47.7 seconds and he took a 5-meter lead and turned it into a 9-meter lead.

Lewis felt some consolation in the 400 meters Barbuti ran. Barbuti received the baton with a 9-meter advantage. Engelhardt, of Germany, was the last runner for his team. With every 100 meters Engelhardt shaved off 2 meters of Barbuti's lead. In the final 100 meters of the relay, Engelhardt had cut the lead down to 2 meters and he was coming on strong. Barbuti summoned all the strength that he had to stave off the competition. He found some hidden energy and finished strong, but with just a 3-meter margin over the German.

The Americans won the 1,600-meter relay with a world record time of 3:14.2. The American spectators were going wild! Cheers of "USA" filled the stadium. General MacArthur wore his biggest smile of the games. Only one person in the stadium was filled with a sense of sadness: John Lewis from City College in Detroit. He so wanted to be on that track. He walked onto the track and congratulated all of his 1,600-meter relay teammates. Barbuti gave him a huge hug.

Later he went back to the SS *President Roosevelt* but avoided all the celebrations and activities that closed out the Olympic track and field competition. There was still another week of the Olympics. He greeted almost all of it with a sense of detachment, making only small exceptions to watch Johnny Weissmuller win two gold medals in swimming.

Lewis was offered and accepted an invitation to compete in an international track meet held in Ghent, Belgium, near the end of the final week of the Olympics. His reasons for accepting were twofold. First, he had come to Europe to compete and he still wanted to compete. Second, the novelty of the SS *President Roosevelt* had worn thin, and he was ready to be anywhere but there.

The two-day Ghent track meet turned out to be a satisfactory consolation prize for Lewis, as he won the 200-meter and the 400-meter races and was on the winning 1,600-meter relay team and the winning 800-meter relay team. While not nearly as satisfying as an Olympic medal, the wins helped heal some of the pain of being pulled from the Olympic race.

Lewis arrived back in Amsterdam the morning of August 13, missing the closing ceremonies of the Olympic Games but in time for the 12:30 p.m. departure of the cruise ship. Nine days later, the ship docked in New York. Due to rain, the city had a modified celebration for the return of the Olympic athletes. There was no big ticker-tape parade as planned, but there were still several celebrations honoring the athletes. Lewis felt out of place.

The following day, he and several other Michigan athletes boarded a train headed for Detroit. Lewis and Doherty would end their journey there, while others would board connecting trains to get them back home.

Lewis' head and heart were filled with emotion. He was happy to be back home. Even happier to be away from the reminder of the abrupt end to his Olympic medal bid. The other members of his Olympic relay team were all going home with gold medals. Lewis was going home empty-handed.

As he and Doherty left their train car and looked for their luggage, which had been unloaded and placed on the concrete boarding platform, Lewis could hear the screams of his family welcoming him home. He had been gone over a month and, other than a few letters back and forth, there had been no communication between him and his family. Lewis summoned a smile as his family surrounded him with hugs and good wishes. Upon their insistence, he pulled his medals from Ghent out of his bag and enjoyed the adulation and high-pitched fawning over the only thing he had to show for a month in Europe. Doherty, on the other hand, was receiving much the same recognition, but had an Olympic bronze decathlon medal to display.

Waiting by the exit from the train platform in his usual vested suit, tie, and hat was D.L. Holmes.

There was no one wearing a bigger smile than D.L.

He let the families have their time with their sons and patiently waited until each group made their way toward him. Doherty's group was first. D.L. shook hands with everyone and gave Ken a hug. He invited Ken and his family to a big Olympic celebration they were having at Old Main the following Friday night. All the athletic teams and their families had been invited. "I wouldn't miss it," said Doherty.

When John Lewis and his group came by, D.L. did the same thing. But Lewis, much like the first time he'd met the coach, didn't make much eye contact and looked mostly at the ground.

"We want to celebrate you going to the Olympics and give you a Detroit welcome," said D.L.

"I'm not sure, Coach," said Lewis. "I've been gone a long time and there's a lot I need to do."

Lewis' mother chimed in, saying, "Of course we're going to be there! What are you saying, John?"

Lewis pulled D.L. off to the side so he could have a private conversation. "Coach, you know I didn't participate, right? It's not like I came in fourth; I didn't run at all!"

"I know, son. I know," said D.L. quietly.

"I don't deserve an Olympic welcome. I did nothing," said Lewis. "It just doesn't feel right. I'm not an Olympian."

"Well, John, I have to disagree with you on that," said D.L. "You know my Olympic story, right?"

"Yes, Coach. You tried out but didn't make it."

"Right. At the time I was ranked one of the best running broad jumpers in the country. I was sick, not at my prime, any number of excuses. But, bottom line, I didn't jump far enough. I didn't make it past Chicago," said a sullen D.L.

Now, Lewis looked D.L. in the eyes. He could see the tears in his eyes and knew the pain was still fresh, as if it had happened yesterday, not in 1912. It reminded him of the burning pain he still vividly felt at being removed by MacArthur in favor of Barbuti. Looking at D.L., Lewis wondered if the pain would ever subside. The Olympics brought glory for many, but pain and anguish for many more.

"Sorry, Coach. You should have been there," said Lewis.

"But I wasn't. You, on the other hand, were there. You went through three different levels of qualifying to make it to the Olympics. You were a freshman, a *freshman*, competing against athletes who had already graduated from college. In fact, you're still a freshman. You won't be a sophomore until next month. And you made it! You, John Lewis, on your own merit and own abilities, made it to the Olympics. Tell me who else qualified from the College of the City of Detroit?" asked D.L.

Lewis knew there was no one. Spence and Streng hadn't made it through all the levels of qualification.

"That's right," said D.L., not waiting for the answer that both of them already knew. "Three men started this process and just one, you, remained."

D.L. put his hand on Lewis' shoulder and looked him in the eyes with an intention that went right into his soul. "John, you think you don't deserve the recognition because you didn't run. Well, let's switch places, you and me. You be the guy who didn't jump far enough in Chicago. See what recognition that gets you. And I'll be the guy who qualified for the Olympics, went to New York City, saw the Statue of Liberty, cruised the Atlantic on an ocean liner, met every Olympic star of the 1928 games, toured the Netherlands, went to Belgium and other places in Europe, helped my Olympic relay team prepare to win a gold medal and break a world record, and then won two individual and two team gold medals in Ghent. I'll be that guy, who, yes, is also mad at General MacArthur. But I'd much rather be that guy than the guy who never had any of those experiences representing his country."

D.L. paused and kept looking at Lewis. "You qualified for the Olympics, John. You *went* to the Olympics! You helped your relay team win gold by practicing with them and making them better. Barbuti didn't work with them for weeks before the competition. You did. You've done well. You've done what most other athletes can only dream about doing. You are an Olympian."

Tears had welled up in Lewis' eyes, but he did not break the eye contact with D.L. He thought about what D.L. said and began to nod in agreement. It seemed like several minutes had gone by, but it had probably been less, as a conflicted Lewis contemplated all D.L. had to say. "Thanks, Coach. I'll see you Friday."

"Hey, Mom! We have a party to go to on Friday!" shouted Lewis as he turned and ran to his family.

John Lewis was named captain of the varsity track team for the 1929–30 school year. He was the first Black captain of a varsity team in Wayne's history. Lewis was inducted into the Wayne State University Sports Hall of Fame in 1978.

5

ALWAYS A HUSTLER

Interview with Richard "Dick" Brown, Class of 1949
Interviewed by Professor David L. Holmes Jr.

June 9, 1997

Dick Brown: We were very poor. We lived on Tireman, and I was on the track team at Northwestern High School. I was a long-distance runner; one mile and two mile. Coach Holmes got me to come to Wayne. He came and talked my parents into it. He got me a job in the cafeteria, things like that. Coach Holmes looked out for me in different ways. I came up poor but went to Wayne and finished. Then I went into the Army. I tried to duck the draft by going into grad school. I worked all the way through after I graduated from Northwestern in '46. We came up in poor times on the old west side; that's what we called it. Everybody was poor.

Professor David L. Holmes Jr.: You were a good runner at Northwestern?

Brown: Just so-so. I was better at cross-country. I ended up being the captain of the cross-country team. When I was in high school I was working downtown at Russeks on Woodward. It was an exclusive women's store that Blacks didn't even, you know, they didn't even want them to try on clothes in there. I was a porter and then I wrapped packages and things like that. I worked there for several years. I would work out in the morning with the cross-country team and then go to school. After school I'd go to Russeks. They had an afternoon practice, too. But lots of guys worked so we did our practice in the morning.

Professor: What caused you to choose cross-country? Did you place well in the city competition?

Brown: Not real good. Actually, I don't even remember city races in high school. College I remember. I had it in my mind that I was going to college, and Wayne was where I was going. There was no thought about any place else. There was no money. At Wayne I was the number one cross-country runner. Let me show you my plaque here. I think the time in the NCAA meet is a minute off. I think it was probably 21.32. But I don't want to claim I was better than I was!

Professor: Where was that championship?

Brown: East Lansing. I placed thirty-seventh out of a couple hundred runners over four miles. Not bad for state competition. My cross-country coach in high school used to tell us Black boys can't run distance. [*laughs*]

Professor: And white boys can't jump?

Brown: Right! I'll never forget him ingraining that in us. But, you know, we can run anything just like anybody else. There was Aaron Gordon; he came to Wayne from Miller High. He was one of the first Black distance runners to make a name for himself in Detroit. He's a friend of mine. We became buddies in the Army Reserve.

Professor: Army Reserve? So, you ended up being drafted?

Brown: Yeah, I had finished my bachelor's and enrolled in grad school. But one semester I lightened up on my credits and, bang, I get drafted. After basic training they sent me to counterintelligence corps school in Maryland. Then I applied for Officer Candidate School, OCS, and went down to Fort Benning. I did a little running for the Army, too.

Professor: OCS is not easy.

Brown: No. But, you know what really helped me? Being on a track team. I was in good shape. And then I pledged a fraternity, Alpha Phi Alpha, which is the largest, oldest Black fraternity. So, I knew they weren't going to beat me down at OCS because they used to beat us when I was going through the fraternity! So I said, I know I can make it. Even if they did beat me, I knew I was going to make it. I came out as a second lieutenant and got sent to Chicago, in counterintelligence. I was on civilian status for a while and worked there doing background checks. Then, I was sent over to Japan. I was over there for a year during the Korean War. I never went to the war, I was in Tokyo. I had a nice plushy job over there. [*laughs*] When I came back, I applied for teaching jobs and I met up with Pete Petross. We were teaching at the same school. So, anyway, long story, Pete was in the Air Force Reserve so I joined the Army Reserve. I stayed in the reserve and made my rank and went all the way up.

Professor: Oh, that is excellent. Congratulations on that. Let me back up a little bit. You were a college kid in a poor Black neighborhood in Detroit. Were Blacks who went to Wayne considered the "cream" of the Black neighborhoods? Were you highly respected because you went to Wayne?

Brown: I don't know if we stood out. Only a few of us from Northwestern and from Miller would go to Wayne. Once in a while somebody from Northeastern would come along. But other high schools didn't have any, or many, Blacks. There was Miller, Northwestern, but other than that on the west side there were no other schools where there was a large number of Blacks.

Professor: Wilbur Wright High School?

Brown: Might have, but they were strictly a technical school at the time. I don't even know if they had sports teams. I really don't think they did at the time.

Professor: Were your teachers, on the whole, white or Black at Northwestern?

Brown: I never had a Black teacher until I got to graduate school at Wayne State. It was, I believe, Aubrey McCutcheon, who was an attorney and taught a class.

Professor: So, in undergrad, you ran cross-country and track? You ran the mile and two-mile?

Brown: Yes, the mile and two-mile. I won most of the dual meets and I'd win both races. In cross-country I won most of the time until my last year. Chalmer Alexander, I think, he beat me most of the time.

Professor: Was it common to run both the mile and two-mile in the same meet? Or did you do it on different days?

Brown: I think it was fairly common for distance runners to run both races, yeah.

Professor: What about at bigger schools like Michigan and Michigan State? Did they generally have a different set of runners for each race?

Brown: They probably ran both races. I'm not sure. Back in those days we had so few meets with Michigan and State that I really don't know what they were doing.

Professor: Tell me about the integrated status of the Wayne track team. Was it different from what you saw or heard about other schools?

Brown: Completely integrated, everything. That's why I admired Coach Holmes so much. I mean, he didn't care. Black, white, Jewish, whatever, he didn't care. You lived on Faust, right? I've been to your house. Other coaches would not have done that. He took us all up to Georgian Bay to "train," but we did a lot of fishing, too. No other coach would do that. He went out of his way to keep us all together. I remember once in Ohio we went to a restaurant and they didn't want to serve us, or maybe they wanted us to walk around to the back door. We got in the car and left. He was like that; everybody or nobody.

Professor: I know he had a list—whether it was in his head or he carried it in his pocket, I don't know—but, he had a list of places that he knew where they wouldn't be turned down. It took him many years to develop that list. Then, when they'd have a meet in a new area he had to write letters or take a chance. He told me one time that he signed up for a hotel and they looked at him and asked if he was Jewish? He said no. He probably should have said yes and walked out. But he said no and they let the team stay. The discrimination wasn't just against Blacks; it was Jews, Eastern Europeans, Asians, and even Catholics. If you weren't a WASP—White Anglo-Saxon Protestant—you had some degree of discrimination against you. Oh, and male. WASP females still had discrimination. Please reflect on how this all ties together: Coach Holmes, Wayne University, your career as a teacher.

Brown: Being on the track team gave me the chance to work and earn some money. I pushed myself because my parents didn't have enough money. I can't remember them, maybe once or twice, even buying me clothes. I bought most of my clothes with what little cash I had at the time. But I was always neat. I got a friend, in fact, Pastor Hill, he was pastor of Hartford Baptist Church, one of the outstanding Black churches of Detroit, anyway, Pastor Hill would call me "Prosperous Brown." Going to church I always wore a tie and, you know, neat clothes. There weren't any expensive clothes back in those days. I'm saying all this because working my way through in track gave me some stability. Maybe other people thought I was in good shape financially, but I really wasn't. Another friend of mine from the cross-country team, Peyton Hutchinson, was a go-getter type of guy. My last year at Wayne he sold me a car, a 1941 or something. No, you know what it was, a 1936 Dodge with a 1940 motor in it.

Professor: And this was in 1949?

Brown: Right, right. I was able to drive to Wayne instead of taking the bus. One of my friends still tells me to this day he remembers me driving him to graduation ceremonies at Wayne. I don't even remember doing it.

Professor: Did you drive your car to track meets?

Brown: Oh, no, no, no! Always wanted to keep it close to home just in case it stopped working. [*laughs*] So, I didn't have a lot of money, but I wasn't in bad shape. I had that little hustle, working at the store downtown, and I was always a hustler. I mean, I always had more than one job. When I started teaching I started refereeing, too. I refereed football and basketball. It was a great little bit of extra income. I enjoyed it. I refereed for more than twenty years, and I got a little plaque from the state for officiating. I used to start track meets, too.

Professor: And your two jobs when you were at Wayne were the store downtown and the cafeteria?

Brown: Right, right. I worked in the Wayne cafeteria a couple hours a day and then went to the store for the late afternoon and evening. Then, track or cross-country practice took another hour and a half every day. I was busy!

Professor: What about going to an away track meet? How did you get there and where did you stay?

Brown: Most of our meets we would go and come back the same day. They were close enough, either Ohio, Indiana, or even Chicago—I don't know, wherever Illinois Tech used to be. I can't remember staying in hotels or motels at all. I never got to go to the Penn Relays or the Drake Relays. In fact, the only ones who did go were the sprinters. Lorenzo Wright, being a broad jumper, went too, but that was all they'd let go to the relays. We'd leave early in the morning from Old Main.

Professor: In cars?

Brown: Yes, always in cars. Never had a bus. There would be two or three cars; five or six people in each car. Coach Holmes always driving one of the cars. We'd eat in the cars, get to the meet, change clothes, compete, shower, change clothes and drive back to Old Main.

Professor: Late at night?

Brown: Yes, late in the evening.

Professor: Was the radio on in the car? I ask because I could never have the radio on with him. He didn't like youth music. So, you could drive all day with no radio.

Brown: [*laughs*] No, don't remember. There was a lot of talking and chatting. Don't ever remember there being any silence.

Professor: Any other reflections on Coach Holmes?

Brown: I remember seeing him run around that indoor track, you know, showing us how to kick up our legs and get a good hop, and stretch out. He could do it himself, at his age. Just a person that I looked up to, that inspired me in those days. He inspired me more than any other person I knew, Black or white.

Professor: And why was that?

Brown: Because of the way he looked out for us, encouraged us to do our best, and just stood for uprightness. I didn't know anything about him and religion, but I knew that he was a religious guy. I attribute much of my success in life to him, I really do.

Professor: Did others feel the same?

Brown: Oh, yeah. Those who came along same time as me did. Back in those days, most of the Blacks who had good jobs were in the post office. Another thing, even back in the '50s, there were hardly any Blacks in the school system—working, I mean. When I came out I was turned down for teaching before I was drafted. I tried to get a placement and couldn't get it. When I came out of the Army and went to see somebody down at the Physical Education Department, he said, "Why don't you apply?" I did and sailed right on through.

Professor: You got the job this time.

Brown: Right, right. I started out as a substitute. I got out in '54 and got placed in '55. Yeah, I went right through without any problems. Taught physical education for thirteen years. Then I got promoted to a job they called elementary staff coordinator, which was really another assistant principal. It was an attempt to put another Black administrator into a lot of schools because they really didn't have many Blacks at the time. And then, I had that job for a year and then officially became an assistant principal. Spent twenty-one years as an assistant principal.

Professor: Excellent. That's a tough job. When did you retire?

Brown: 1989. I enjoyed the school system. After I retired I went on to finish my doctorate. Retiring enabled me to finish it. Took me nine years; had to get extensions. But that got me into this conflict resolution I've been doing for the Detroit school system. I love it, but it's getting to be too much for me. I'm seventy-three now and lugging books around and having a schedule; think this is my last year.

Professor: Lugging books! Don't even get me started! I lug a lot of books, too! [*laughs*] Coach Holmes invented or improved so many things for track, like starting blocks and hurdles. But you were long-distance, so I'm guessing you didn't use any of them.

Brown: Oh, no. Long-distance runners had to use the lap timer machine. In Old Main, it took us twenty-two laps to make a mile on the inside track! Forty-four for a two-mile! It was so monotonous running around in circles I needed that lap timer!

6
TINKERING WITH TRACK

January 30, 1949

HOLMES INVENTS "PACE-SETTER"
It's Big Aid for Runners, Swimmers

Genius Dave Holmes is at work again. Do not disturb, for the gentleman is trying to revolutionize the ancient and glorious sport of running.

David L. Holmes is recognized as Wayne University's athletic director. He is noted, however, as the Tartar track coach who has tinkered with gadgets of all sorts in an effort to produce the maximum speed afoot.

His latest creation is the result of a 10-year experiment. It's a compact little metal box which, when called upon to do so, can set off such warning devices as bells, buzzers, gongs, lights, etc.

These signals are not meant to scare the laxity out of a runner and send him after world records. The gadget, known hereafter under its patented name, The Pace-Setter, has a far more noble purpose.

The Pace-Setter's distinguishing feature from ordinary warning or alarm devices is that it is repetitive. It is a trackman's answer to the musician's metronome.

An indicator is turned to any time interval—say 10 seconds. At the end of each 10-second interval a bell will ring, or a buzzer will buzz, a light may flash, or a camera may snap. In the world of track and swimming, where pace is a key factor, it's a wonder no one came up with the automatic pace-setter long ago. Practically all training for runners and swimmers alike embodies the mastery of pacing.

Runners are prepared for events like the 440, 880, mile and two-mile by constant runs at established paces. Through repetition, they begin to "feel" their speeds. Swimmers fall into the same pattern.

If the Pace-Setter goes off before the runner completes a lap, then he knows that he is behind the prescribed pace. The reverse is true, naturally, of the fellow who is stepping along too rapidly. For swimming, lights above and below the water line can be attached to the Pace-Setter.

Holmes has two big problems in adapting the Pace-Setter to wide use. First, it can't be used in competition unless all participants agree to its presence. Secondly, present production costs are too high.

Holmes, a grey-thatched coach of 65 who has spent 35 years as a track mentor, says he cannot market the instrument for less than $75. "This means that only coaches in the larger schools would have budgets which would permit them to buy the Pace-Setter," he says.

Faster times, he says, are sure to come when the Pace-Setter comes into its own.

Meanwhile, Holmes has no plans for commercializing his product. He has agreed, however, to turn out a number of the instruments and place them at the disposal of coaches who ask for them.

Holmes first produced his Pace-Setter in 1939. It was a huge cumbersome affair. The latest model was finished in 1946, but he still is planning some intricate changes.

—George Puscas, *Detroit Free Press*, January 30, 1949

(© *Detroit Free Press*, USA TODAY NETWORK)

D.L. finished reading the *Free Press* article with a grimace. "Genius"? "Grey-thatched"? He didn't truly see himself as either. He thought he should give the *Free Press* a call because they got his age wrong. He was sixty-one, not sixty-five. He'd also been a track coach for forty-one years, not thirty-five. Surely that should be publicly corrected. He looked in a nearby mirror. His hair was thinner and almost completely grey. The wrinkles on his face seemed deeper than in years past. "Hmmpf. I can see why he thought I was sixty-five," D.L. said to himself dejectedly. He was a gentleman, and he decided it wasn't necessary to make a phone call to the paper. After all, the article's purpose was to get some attention for the Pace-Setter, not for D.L.

He went back to the mirror. Maybe he could look less like sixty-five and more like sixty-one by straightening himself up a bit. He looked at his white shirt in the mirror and pressed away a couple of wrinkles to the right side of his tie. This morning he had decided to wear a long tie instead of a bow tie. He liked both types. But he had to admit he had a favorite tie and he wore it more often than all the rest. From ten feet away it looked like stripes, but every third stripe was actually a locomotive followed by other train cars. It was a bit ironic, seeing as how Wayne track teams could never afford to travel by train, but he thought it looked good with his light-brown vest and dark-brown sport coat. His white shirt had French cuffs, and he pulled at them a bit to draw them down about a half inch beyond the sleeve of his sport coat. He had his locomotive tie, so he wore his locomotive cuff links as well. He pulled his pants up and tucked in his shirt. D.L. never wore suspenders; he always wore a belt, and he always had his pants tailored so that they had a nice one-inch cuff at the bottom. He checked the knot of his tie. The top button of his white shirt was always buttoned, and his tie was always tight around his neck. He thought having a loosened tie and an open top button was unprofessional and unkempt. On a January day like this, it also helped protect his neck from the cold drafts that found their way inside of Old Main.

Quickly checking his pockets, he was relieved when he noted he had five stopwatches with him today. Four just never seemed to be enough. There would be indoor practice later, and he needed to be prepared. For D.L., wearing a vest was less about style and more about having enough pockets for the multiple stopwatches he almost always carried.

If the day was cold, like it was today, he would add a long tan trench coat as his top layer. Normally, it was unbuttoned so he could access his stopwatches. In his photo for the newspaper, D.L. had worn no eyeglasses. He inconsistently wore dark-colored plastic-framed glasses for distance vision, but often forgot about them and left them on during closer encounters. When outside, you would never find him without a hat. D.L. liked a hat called a "fedora," although he wasn't really familiar with the term. It seemed he wore the type of hat most coaches wore, with a large brim and a piece of complementing trim material circling the base of the crown. It looked good on him.

The entire ensemble fit his personality perfectly. From 1908, when he started coaching, up until this day in 1949, suit, shirt, and tie styles had changed. Yet, the basic elements of his wardrobe were very consistent. So consistent that, on a relaxed summer Saturday out fishing on a lake, he may have left his sport coat folded on a chair on the shore, but he still wore his white shirt, tie, and hat in a rowboat in the middle of the lake.

His attire was really not so different from that of most American men. If you went to a ball game over at Briggs Stadium, it would be full of men wearing white shirts, ties, and hats. Even couples canoeing at Belle Isle dressed as if they were going to church. It was the norm for D.L.'s generation.

Yet, he also held himself to a higher set of expectations than most. He never swore, never drank alcohol, never smoked, never told off-color jokes, and couldn't understand why anyone would.

He also had a disdain for asking people for money. He loved the coaching part of coaching but wasn't very fond of the political part of coaching. While this was an admirable quality, it was a quality that did not serve him well. His teams never got the facilities they needed and deserved. And his inventions never quite hit the commercial market in the way that they could have with someone less adverse to pulling strings, calling in favors, making demands, and making money.

He actually *was* trying to make the Pace-Setter commercially viable, but the newspaper didn't need to know that. D.L. hoped the *Free Press* article would get the attention of track coaches in the metro Detroit area. Although modest to a fault, even D.L. had to admit it was a great invention.

It had been an excellent training tool for Wayne runners for a dozen or more years. He had come up with the idea in the early 1930s and had tinkered away on it for years, trying out various iterations of it year after year. If there was one story told more than others by the men on his track teams, it was the story of a very consistent hate for "that" machine! But, boy, did it ever work! Consistent split and lap times are essential in track, and the Pace-Setter produced them.

The Pace-Setter wasn't D.L.'s first foray into entrepreneurship. His first contribution to the track and field community—beyond coaching—was "Movies on Paper" in 1932. D.L. attended the 1932 Summer Olympic Games in Los Angeles, California. He had already made a name for himself as a coach and had produced Olympic athletes. As a result, D.L. was allowed access to places most other attendees couldn't go. He was able to get very close to the top Olympic athletes and film them as they competed in their events. His films then became a study in form; more specifically, Olympic medal–winning form.

D.L. did two significant things with the movies he filmed. First, he made the movies themselves available to track coaches to use as training. Showing a bravado he didn't normally show, D.L. called them the "only good movie films of the Olympic Games." You could rent them, all 1,200 feet of event film, for ten dollars or purchase a copy of them for twenty-five dollars. D.L. himself often used these films when he went recruiting at Detroit high schools. "I can make you a champion," he would tell high school track athletes. "Just like this," and he'd show them some Olympic track stars in action. Second, D.L. studied the films intently, frame by frame, and created his book, "Movies on Paper." What is "Movies on Paper"? One of his own sales brochures explains it best:

> "Movies on Paper" is literally what the title implies—movies transferred into black and white—actual motion analysis of the world's great stars as they did their stuff in the 1932 Olympic Games. Every important movement of each contestant is shown as the athlete makes a jump, vaults, puts the shot, etc. This affords an opportunity to SEE how the record-smashers actually "turn it on."
>
> —David L. Holmes, "Movies on Paper" sales brochure, 1934

The drawings of the Olympic athletes in each split-second movement of their competition allowed coaches and athletes to see championship form step-by-step and determine where their form broke away from world record form. The shot put, for example, had separate pages for each of the top three finishers, and each page had twelve to fifteen drawings showing each phase of the athlete putting the shot.

The illustrator for the intricate drawings was none other than David L. Holmes. In addition to all of his other talents, D.L. was also an accomplished artist who drew satirical cartoons for his college newspaper. His drawings of athletes in action were accurate and impeccable. The same sales brochure quotes an unnamed track coach from a small northern town as saying: "My boys won first and second in the vault. Now I'm the vaultinest coach in the woods, and I weigh exactly 255 pounds! Your book did the trick."

"Movies on Paper" was a success financially and critically. It was the first time anyone had studied winning form in multiple Olympic events and published it for coaches. D.L. published the first edition of it in 1933. Demand was high enough that he published "bigger and better" editions in 1934 and 1935 as well. At $2.50 a copy, profits were good, but not huge; there were no Cadillacs in the driveway on Faust. And, D.L. being D.L., none of the profit went into his pocket. He used it to send his athletes to compete in out-of-state track meets.

D.L. was always tinkering with something or other. He was working on the Pace-Setter while he was drawing the "Movies on Paper" book. The Pace-Setter was almost ready for commercial production and sales, so D.L. was tinkering with his next idea—the folding hurdle.

Hurdles were not something new. D.L. wasn't inventing them, he was improving them. At Old Main, there was no space to jump hurdles, much less store them. They needed to take up less space. Hurdles had become better in his lifetime. He was only nine at the time and not paying any attention to technological improvements in track and field, but he now knew that it was 1896 when hurdles became lighter and portable. Prior to 1896, if you hit a hurdle, it didn't move. He couldn't even imagine how it felt to hit a hurdle and have it not move.

It was not the "movement" that D.L. thought needed work. In fact, the height and weight of the hurdles and the pounds of impact necessary for a hurdle to move were all prescribed in the rules. If he was going to tinker with hurdles, he still had to ensure they had four heights—two for men and two for women—and had a resistance of eight pounds to pull them over, not knock them over, at each of those heights. They also needed to be heavy enough that they didn't bounce into another lane if a hurdler hit them.

D.L. was adamant about hurdle weight and construction. Hurdles originated as barriers. In the days prior to 1896, that's exactly what they were: immovable barriers. In 1949, if you hit one, they were intended to slow you down. NCAA and AAU rules said that if you knocked over a hurdle that didn't meet the resistance specifications, any record you might have set would not be recorded. D.L. remembers well when he was at the 1932 Olympics watching Bob Tisdall's record-breaking 400-meter hurdle run. Tisdall knocked over a regulation hurdle, won the race, and was disqualified. That was the rule at the time: knock over a hurdle, even accidentally, and you're done. D.L. thought any athlete *purposely* knocking over hurdles should be disqualified. And he also wanted hurdles heavy enough to slow down the hurdler who was trying to cheat the rules.

He was working on a twenty-six-pound hurdle. It would have all four heights, it would have resistance weights that could be removed if it was being used at the high school level, and it could be folded to take up less storage space. He had a target date of 1951.

He had enough prototype folding hurdles available that he decided to use them at an invitational meet Wayne was hosting at Redford High School. It was 1950, and Redford had just installed a beautiful new track. Local high school tracks were still better than Wayne's facilities, so D.L. jumped at the chance to hold his meet on a brand-new track surface and put his new hurdles to the test.

It was the sixteenth running of the Wayne University Invitational Relays. Every excellent high school runner from Detroit and near Detroit would be there. Track men from Cooley, Redford, Miller, Northwestern, Ferndale, Denby, Central, Dearborn, Mackenzie, Highland Park, Pershing, Cass Tech, Northeastern, Western, Northern, Southeastern, St. Joseph, Southwestern, East Detroit, and Eastern would be running. The opportunity was prime for D.L. to test his hurdles and pick out his recruits for the following college semester.

Everyone was excited for the competition on the new Redford track. Just one week prior, the Detroit Public School League one-mile run record had been shattered on this track by a Northwestern distance man with a time of 4:24.9, trimming 1.5 seconds off the old record.

This was a blazing track, and D.L. was looking forward to trying out his new hurdles on it.

The day of the relays, D.L. and a carload of Wayne track men were the first to arrive, hours before anyone else. They walked out onto the track to admire its beauty and its "newness." No one from Wayne had ever seen a new track before—not in Detroit, anyway. There were a couple of wisecracks intentionally made within earshot of D.L., saying, "so this is what a track is supposed to look like." D.L. heard them, winced internally, but smiled, and went about his own admiration of the track. It was a sight to behold. Each one of them bent down to feel the cinders. It wasn't just ash; it was the perfect combination of ash, cinders, and clay that formed a porous yet stable track surface. D.L. knew the feelings he had at that moment were not appropriate, yet he could feel envy churning in his gut. "How could a high school have a better track than Wayne University?" he thought to himself.

A few of the Wayne men were testing the track by running some short sprints. So, prior to setting up the events for the day, they decided to take the opportunity to give the track a "real" test run. Three of the Wayne men who rode with D.L. were 440 runners. "Let's do a quick 440 and check this baby out!" one said. And so they did.

After some stretching and warm-ups, three starting blocks were set on the track within the proper 440 staggered intervals. There would be three runners. D.L. served as starter and timer with another Wayne man removing the starting blocks and yet another Wayne man in charge of the third stopwatch. It was 7:08 in the morning, so there would be no starting pistol. The neighbors would appreciate that.

"Runners, on your marks," said D.L., softly but loudly.

"Set. Go!"

D.L. started both of his stopwatches simultaneously. The other Wayne man started the third stopwatch. The three track men were off and flying around the track. There was a bit of inner-team rivalry at stake, so this was not a consolation race; this was a run for bragging rights. They were running full out.

At the 220-mark, D.L. looked at the split and couldn't believe the pace. It was hot, very hot. All three runners were on fire.

They came around the final turn with runners one and two in a tight race and runner three about 6 yards behind. D.L. stood at the finish line with thumbs ready to stop the clock and record this run on an amazing new track. Ten yards, 9 yards, 8 yards . . . like bullets from a gun they passed through the finish line as D.L. stopped his watch. He looked at the times. He looked again. He walked over to the other Wayne man with the third stopwatch. "What did you get?"

They compared the stopwatches a bit as the three runners laughed and joked back and forth about the win; the third-place runner jokingly complained he was cut off from his lane and was lodging an official protest. They slowly made their way back to D.L., who was still puzzled while looking at the stopwatches.

"What's up, Coach?" one asked.

"I knew this track was good," said D.L. "But I didn't know it was this good. You two just beat the Wayne record, and you," he said, pointing to the runner in third place, "beat your own best time by 2 seconds!"

"So we're going in the record book, Coach?"

"Sorry, no." said D.L. "Not a sanctioned race. But I know you already know that."

"Wow! This is an amazing track. The one-mile record broken last week, we broke the Wayne 440 record today, you got your best time, this track is amazing!" one said.

D.L. rubbed his chin, deep in thought.

"Coach?"

"Yeah, this track certainly is *something*," said D.L. "Where's the bag with my long jump tape? We're going to measure this thing," said D.L.

They started at the 440 finish line and went all the way around the track, picking up and putting back down the tape measure, which only went 30 yards at a time. D.L. wrote down the results on his pad of paper. "Let's do it again in Lane Two," he said. He wrote down the results again. It was the same number.

"Well, men, sorry about your records crumbling so quickly. This track is 432 yards long—8 yards short of regulation. No wonder so many records have been beaten here this year."

The Wayne University Invitational Relays still took place that day, but with many heads shaking at the discovery by D.L. Holmes. The next morning the *Detroit Free Press* called it a "$25,000 blunder":

They discovered that their new Redford track, constructed by the Board of Education, may be almost worthless, as far as track meets are concerned. A hunch check by David L. Holmes, coach at Wayne University, revealed that the layout does not measure 440 yards as intended or believed.

—George Puscas, *Detroit Free Press*, June 4, 1950

(© *Detroit Free Press*, USA TODAY NETWORK)

Cooley High School won the event with 72 points. Northwestern followed in second place with 56 points, while Miller was third with 47. Still an exciting day, but a day when times in any long-distance event meant nothing.

D.L. moved up another notch or two on the hierarchy of legendary track coaches that day. Many other track coaches had been to that track during the season and thought nothing of it. D.L. was there about five minutes before he knew something was wrong.

He momentarily had celebrity status, being congratulated and patted on the back for figuring out something so quickly. With the exception of the members of the Detroit Board of Education, who were probably not overly happy with his discovery, everyone else involved thought he was a star. The crew he brought with him from Wayne was equally impressed. "How does he know this stuff?" one asked.

When the award ceremonies were over and the participants and their families had headed home, D.L. and his crew loaded his car back up for the drive to Wayne. He would drop off each of the Wayne students at their homes, then take the track supplies to Wayne, before he would go back to his house on Faust.

D.L. Holmes had captured all of the attention at the Wayne University Invitational Relays. Even Cooley, although placing first, received less attention than the famous Coach Holmes. Even his new invention, the Holmes Folding Hurdle, was overshadowed by his discovery of the incorrectly made track.

The hurdles had been used for the shuttle-hurdle relay and performed perfectly. However, the spotlight was shining so brightly on D.L. himself that his invention wasn't even noticed.

It was one of those bittersweet moments in his life. Everyone was talking about him, but for the wrong reason. He wanted to talk about his new hurdles.

On May 29, 1951, David L. Holmes applied for a patent for his Holmes Folding Hurdle. Throughout the 1950s they were widely used in high schools, colleges, and competitions across the United States.

Tested! Accepted! The NEW Holmes Folding Hurdle

Professionally designed by a coach who has spent his entire life in this field. Designed to fill an urgent need; a need thoroughly understood by every track coach and every athletic director.

Exclusive features that save time, money and storage space:

1. Easy to handle
2. Saves 90% storage space
3. Simple one-second height adjustment
4. Rugged steel construction—Can't break
5. Meets all official rule demands—NCAA, AAU, High School Federation, etc.
6. The ideal practice hurdle with removable weights

—Holmes Folding Hurdle sales brochure, 1951

7

ANOTHER SHIT HOLE

Interview with Paul Pentecost, Class of 1948
Interviewed by Professor David L. Holmes Jr.

May 23, 2001

Professor Holmes was already caught up in a conversation with Paul Pentecost before he turned on the tape recorder. Pentecost began as a student at Wayne in 1944. He was a high jumper for Coach Holmes. When he graduated in 1948, he became the athletic publicity director for Wayne. In 1957, he was promoted to assistant director for university relations. He went on to oversee many university publications. He retired in 1988.

The conversation that had already begun was about McGregor Bay in the Canadian part of Lake Huron and fishing trips with Coach Holmes. Fishing was one of Coach Holmes' favorite things to do. The conversation was going well when Professor Holmes remembered to turn on the tape recorder.

> **Professor David L. Holmes Jr.:** Hang on, hang on. Forgot to start this darn thing. It's 23 May 2001. We are at the home of Paul Pentecost. So, there's a camp up there, Smith's Camp. I went up and visited . . .
>
> **Paul Pentecost:** The Cabins.
>
> **Professor:** Yes, Smith's Cabins in Little Current.
>
> **Pentecost:** Yeah, the cross-country team went up there my senior year and chartered a boat. Went up into McGregor Bay.
>
> **Professor:** And it was Dan Fields who kept claiming that the pike were as long as the table. He had his hands out as far as they would go! [*Professor Holmes extends his arms their entire width, smiling*]
>
> **Pentecost:** Well, we had more than enough fish to eat. Most of it was caught off the end of the dock. Of course, that was a while ago.
>
> **Professor:** [*looking at a photo*] Who is this guy right here?

Pentecost: Hmmm, Bob Tilsey. No, Ray Durben. Wait, no, that's Mac and that's Alex Stradkowski.

Professor: Alex Stradkowski, there's a name.

Pentecost: Last I heard he was on the dental school faculty at Johns Hopkins.

Professor: It's a great photo. There's a number of things I want to talk to you about, in no special order. I wouldn't mind hearing you reflect on the other track coaches at the time, like Lyle Bennett.

Pentecost: Oh, at Central. Bennett was at Central Michigan. Well, there was Lloyd Olds at Michigan Normal, which is now Eastern Michigan. He was a great rival of your dad's.

Professor: How was their relationship?

Pentecost: It was a good relationship. Friendly enemies. Their teams were very competitive. I always thought that if we beat them it was because your dad outcoached them.

Professor: Olds was a very good coach.

Pentecost: Yes, a great coach. They had way better facilities than we did, too.

Professor: They had a fieldhouse, did they not?

Pentecost: Yes, they had everything! Not everyone did, though. There wasn't much of a track program at the University of Detroit. They had Butler, who was also a trainer, for what track they had. At Michigan State there was Carl, ah, can't remember his last name.

Professor: I'd be interested to know whether they had integrated teams. Did they keep their teams together on trips, you know, with Black and white kids together?

Pentecost: We wouldn't go someplace if we couldn't stay together. I don't remember the team ever being split. Coach always had an itinerary. If we were going to the Penn Relays we would eat lunch at the Y in Pittsburgh. Other times it was places like the Greyhound Post restaurants at the Greyhound depots.

Professor: Because they would take your Black runners?

Pentecost: Right. And along the Pennsylvania Turnpike there were only Howard Johnsons. Occasionally we'd go into a place, you know, no Greyhounds in the area, just out in the boonies, and there'd be a huddle in the back room while they decided whether to serve us or not. Most of the time they did. But, once down in Wilberforce, Ohio, we had two Black runners in a race against Central State at Wilberforce College. We went down and they wouldn't serve us. Well, we didn't eat. We all left. We thought if there was any place we could get fed it would be there because it was right on the edge of campus.

Professor: Oh, man.

Pentecost: That's southern Ohio in those days. Even at Wayne some of the teams your dad didn't coach would split up the players by race. He wouldn't. Your father had no qualms about it, going way back to the 1920s with John Lewis, who was Black. He actively recruited Black players. Other colleges didn't want Black athletes. And even if they had Black athletes they would leave them at home rather than deal with it. If they were playing at Vanderbilt, for instance, Dan Magugan was Yost's brother-in-law, and he told Yost to leave his Black players at home, which he did. But never your dad. It was always all of us.

Professor: Big part of his legacy. During your association with Coach Holmes, how was Wayne viewed by other coaches when the Wayne team showed up?

Pentecost: With great respect. We ran University of Chicago at Bartlett Field House. Your dad never had any problems getting track meets scheduled. Everybody knew he'd bring a good team.

Professor: But rarely did he bring any weight people, right? Very seldom a shot-putter or discus person.

Pentecost: I don't think we had any that were real outstanding during my years. And we were quite handicapped in the pole vault, too. You just couldn't get a good run in that old gymnasium.

Professor: Tell me about that run.

Pentecost: Well, you started out against the wall in the hallway. Then you'd start your run through a set of double doors, turn a corner into the gym, run as far across the gym as you could, put the pole in the box, and jump. Crazy! [*laughs*] Shot put was a padded shot and you had to land it on mats. There were classes down below the gym, you know, and if we were practicing. . . . [*Pentecost bangs on the table a few times, laughing*] It was particularly disturbing to the chemistry department because they had weights, you know, and scales for measuring compounds and so forth. But . . . [*more banging on the table*]

Professor: They'd come up to protest?

Pentecost: Oh yeah, yeah. [*laughs*] And we practiced sprints in the front hall on a tile floor. Practice would be 8:00 or 9:00 at night. Why? Well, because the college had night classes and coach would use a starter's pistol. They would have to tell the students to not be alarmed if you hear a gun go off. It's just the track team. Today, wow, the whole building would empty!

Professor: That's a great story.

Pentecost: The starting blocks were on a plywood base. We had to bring those down all the way from the gym to the front hall. There were elevators so we could take elevators down. We'd set it up in the hallway and if it was a sprinted finish, you had these swinging doors down at the far end of the hall in Old Main. You could go right through the doors—you were outside then—and go down the steps. We'd always have to be careful because if you went into the street a streetcar might come by. We didn't want to lose anybody to a streetcar.

Professor: So these guys would be screeching and slowing up as much as they could, but they still might go through the doors. Hopefully there was a rail to hold.

Pentecost: Yes, there was a center rail outside. But it was an improvisation. Coach, he did what he could with the equipment he had. The building was designed as a high school; Old Central High School. It wasn't built as a university facility but it was adapted over the years. It had an elevated indoor running track; twenty-two laps to the mile!

Professor: Almost everyone mentions that indoor track.

Pentecost: You could train distance runners on it if they could learn how to take the curves and not develop shin splints. Your dad had this secret formula for treating shin splints. It was called "Hot Stuff." That's what he called it, and boy was it ever hot. He'd put that on and it was hotter than the pain, I guess. So, you'd just continue to run.

Professor: [*laughing*] I'd never heard that story before.

Pentecost: We had a cross-country meet one time. It was an AAU meet, and Longines, the watch company, had developed a photo timer. It was going to be used at this meet. The finish was so close we had to wait five minutes while they developed the film to find out who won. Of course, the new-fangled photo finish got us coverage all over the country!

Professor: I remember that! I was there. They've been running forever; six miles, right? Anyway, they've been running forever and then there's a photo finish. It seemed so dumb to have a photo timer there because you assumed they would come in all spaced out. But no, they came in side by side.

Pentecost: Your dad had a cross-country course over at Villa Rouge, remember that? He had four or five places on the course where he'd be waiting and reading off times as you passed. Then he'd drive his car to the next spot. He'd start honking his horn, which meant speed up, you're too slow. Then he had this chart, he did it weekly, everybody was on the chart and it said what you were expected to do that week in practice. Not sure when he had the time to do those things.

Professor: He would go down in the basement every night and work on those things. Every night after dinner he would go downstairs. He was trying to figure out how to budget the next track meet, too.

Pentecost: Track barely had enough money to get by. We traveled in cars to meets. Your dad would sometimes drive ahead of us. He'd say he needed to see a former student or something. Mostly athletes didn't want to drive with him! But, anyway, he gave me money to feed the team along the route to the Penn Relays. It wasn't much money and I said, "I can't . . ." and he said, "Oh yes you can. Just tell them not to eat too much. I don't want them all bloated and fat." Well, we didn't eat too much, not on that budget. The next year, we took sandwiches from home. Don't eat too much! [*laughs*]

Professor: Did you leave early in the morning for the Penn Relays?

Pentecost: Oh, yes. We'd pull out from Old Main about 5:00 in the morning. We would drive straight through to Philly. That was an achievement considering the roads at the time. We had just two-lane roads, one each direction. We'd get a little bit of the turnpike in Pennsylvania.

Professor: So you'd have five or six guys in each car?

Pentecost: Normally we'd have five. I remember one time we went to Penn, I was driving. In addition to me there was Watanabe, Karolionok, Stroia, and Simons. Stan Simons was Black. Stroia was Romanian. Karolionok was Russian. Watanabe was Japanese. And I, representing the Pentecosts of Brunswick County, Virginia, since 1750, was the only WASP [White Anglo-Saxon Protestant]. So, it was really a United Nations of a track team.

Professor: Was Wayne unique in that regard? This was the mid-1940s and it seems like most athletic teams across the United States were largely WASP.

Pentecost: Yes, that was generally true until teams started discovering the Jamaicans. They could run!

Professor: What can you tell me about the recruiting of Detroit high school track stars to universities other than Wayne?

Pentecost: One time your dad had Charles Fonville, who was a great shot putter, all locked up for Wayne, or so he thought. University of Michigan coaches walked in and talked him into going to Ann Arbor.

Professor: Fonville had Leroy Dues as a coach in high school.

Pentecost: Yes. We got a lot of help from Leroy Dues and some of the other former Wayne track guys.

Professor: Wayne did well recruiting from Pershing High School?

Pentecost: Absolutely. Carl Holmes, your uncle and D.L.'s brother, was track coach there and was a great help. Some of the recruiting wasn't all that tough because track kids like Lorenzo Wright, Buddy Coleman, and the Wingos all felt better at Wayne because they really weren't accepted in East Lansing or Ann Arbor.

Professor: I realize you were the WASP member of the team, but what obstacles did your teammates experience?

Pentecost: I remember we pulled up to one of the "dive" establishments where we were going to eat on the way to a meet. The coach went inside to see if we could eat there. One of the white teammates asked why we always had to go to such "shit holes" to eat. He wondered if Wayne had no money for a decent dinner? One of his Black teammates pulled him aside and said "We can only eat where we *all* can eat and usually it's a shit hole." The white kid didn't realize what Coach Holmes was doing. He thought he was saving money, not ensuring the entire team could go inside.

Professor: I don't know if that was good or bad that they didn't know what the coach was up to. Maybe it's a credit to him that he just tried to make everything about the track meet and sidestep as much discrimination as he could along the way. It always sounded to me like Coach Holmes had his own sort of Green Book to know where you could eat and sleep with Black team members.

Pentecost: Oh, he absolutely did! I don't know if he wrote it down or just had it in his head. But he knew where to go. Of course, it always depended on who happened to be working that day, too. Some trips a restaurant would be okay and other trips it wouldn't. He always went in to check first.

Professor: Let's get back to the Penn Relays. You stayed with the team at a hotel in Philadelphia?

Pentecost: That's right. The Sylvania.

Professor: What was it like?

Pentecost: Coach Holmes got some type of special rate there. It could have been through the Penn Relays. When a big relay would come to town they'd recommend hotels for you to get a college or business rate. And what we did was sleep four, five, or six of us all in a big room that would have been used for a hospitality suite. There was a bedroom with a couple beds, but also a larger room. They would put four or five cots in there. It had a bathroom and shower and everything. We slept dormitory style. Just down the block was Horn and Harter's, the cafeteria. It was the first automat most of us had ever seen. You would put in a dime and a little door would open and you'd pull out your piece of pie or a sandwich or whatever. And that's where we ate. It was right on the streetcar line and we could take the streetcar over to the stadium for the meet. Franklin Field was where we went. It was an economical way of getting there. Wayne did very, very well over the years, too. One year, you might remember, we won the 440 relay. Then, that same year, Lorenzo came in second and Buddy third in the hundred. Lorenzo won the long jump. Overall, we took fourth or fifth in the meet.

Professor: And people were surprised Wayne did that?

Pentecost: Oh, yes! They'd refer to us as "Little Wayne University." The big schools didn't like losing to us.

Professor: I still have plenty of questions for you. I've been asking people what made Coach Holmes tick?

Pentecost stopped for a minute to consider the question. He had known D.L. for almost twenty years and was involved with the entire coaching staff at Wayne. There were so many unique characteristics about him. He was one of the first coaches who analyzed the events to see exactly what motions were successful and which ones were not. He knew pacing and strides and was very precise about how he trained athletes for specific races. He knew track equipment better than anyone. But none of those things made the top of the list in describing D.L.

Pentecost: He cared about people. He could make the slowest guy on the team feel important just because he was on the team. Another thing—and I don't know if this was a plus or a minus—we never really got beaten. Not according to the coach. There was a bad track or a bad call at the finish. He was always so kind. He didn't want any of us to feel beaten. No matter how bad you did, he had his arm around you, talking you up.

Professor: And he invited everyone on the team to our house, too. It wasn't just the great performers who showed up.

Pentecost: Right. The track team was at your house every year. Coach would put a cooler of pop down in the basement, and your mother would put out a great spread of food. It was the first time some of the kids had seen life outside of Black Bottom.

Professor: That's right. Black Bottom was the east side but downtown?

Pentecost: It was where a lot of the Detroit Medical Center is now and down where I-375 was built. It was the area primarily south of Gratiot near Miller High School.

Professor: My mom and dad loved that party. They loved having the team over.

Pentecost: And we all loved going to it. There aren't a lot of coaches who would have you over to their house. Coach Holmes did it all the time.

Professor: I remember it very well. My life was shaped by his sense of inclusiveness. One last question. Over Coach Holmes' career, is there anyone that stands out in your mind as maybe an unsung hero? They didn't break any world records or go to the Olympics, but they did well and represented Wayne successfully?

Pentecost: Hmmm, well, there were many. But the one who stands out most in my mind is Leroy Dues. He was a shot-putter and discus guy. He became a track coach and teacher at Miller High School after Wayne. He was the first Black athletic director in Michigan. And he helped out Coach Holmes for decades after he graduated. Leroy Dues.

8

THE ELUSIVE 49

Indoor Track and Field Practice, Old Main, College of the City of Detroit

September 10, 1929

"Too wide, too wide. Your hop is taking up nearly four feet. It's just tape you're stepping on inside the gym here. When we get outside, you're going to be landing on the toeboard. That's a foul—and maybe a broken ankle," said D.L. "We've got to get you closer to three feet."

"And mind your elbow. Did you notice how the shot went over to the left? That's because your elbow is coming too far away from your body. Keep it close," instructed D.L.

Leroy Dues had been a shot-putter and discus thrower in high school. And he had been very successful at both. Just prior to his graduation from Pittsburg High School in Pittsburg, Kansas, Dues won the Southeast Kansas Conference shot put with a 47′6½″ heave of a twelve-pound shot. He broke a high school conference record that he had set the year before.

Now the entire Dues family had relocated to Detroit. It was a bit of a culture shock. Pittsburg had a population of about 18,000. Not a small town, but nothing like the metropolis of Detroit with a population of 1.5 million. The biggest city Dues had known was Kansas City, Missouri, about two and a half hours north, that boasted 400,000 folks. Detroit was huge in comparison. Route 66 was the biggest highway of his youth. He marveled that Detroit had Woodward Avenue running right through it that was just as big. The hustle and bustle of the big city excited him.

He had always planned on going to college to get a teaching degree. Dues was happy to discover that the College of the City of Detroit offered a teaching certificate. He immediately enrolled for the fall term of 1929. He walked into the athletic office to find out about the track team. He wanted to continue his shot put and discus competition in college. A secretary showed him into the athletic director's office, and that's when Leroy Dues and D.L. Holmes met for the first time.

"Nice to meet you, young man," said D.L. "You look like a football player. What position do you play?"

"Actually, I'm not a football player. I throw the discus and shot put," said Dues.

A sly smile came across D.L.'s face. Discus and shot put. D.L. rarely had any good weight men.

"How far can you put that shot?" asked D.L.

"Well, this past spring I won the conference with 47′6½″."

D.L. quickly stood up from his desk. "Really! My goodness! Over 47′ in high school!" D.L. began pacing back and forth in his small office space in a converted house on Putnam Street. He had his hand to his chin, thinking through all the possibilities for the future. About fifteen seconds went by before he said anything else, but it seemed like longer.

He grabbed Dues' hand in a two-handed handshake and said, "Well, welcome to Detroit. Very excited to have you on the track team. Freshmen practice with the varsity squad, but I can't take you to the same competitions. There are some competitions for track men your age, they call them junior competitions, where I think you'll do quite well. And I know you're not a football player. But just think about the football team. I was the football coach until this year. I coached everything. We're getting some more coaches in here now. I think you'd be very good at football. You are built perfectly for the game."

"I'll think about it, Coach," said Dues.

"My secretary will give you the practice schedule, a track suit, and warm-ups," said D.L. "Do you have track shoes?"

"Yes, I have some from high school."

"Good, good. We run on a tight budget here and that's one of the things that's the toughest to get. Now, feel free to stop in here anytime. If you have extra time between classes to practice, you let me know and we can spend an hour together. While the weather is still nice, we can get some outside practice in almost anytime. Inside practice is a different story," explained D.L.

"Okay, thanks, Coach," answered Dues.

"Very nice meeting you, Leroy. I can tell just by looking at you that you're going to be a champion!"

Dues wasn't quite sure what to make of D.L. The coach hadn't even seen him do anything yet. And what was this football idea all about? Yet, it was very reassuring to be welcomed so excitedly into the college track team. D.L. was the most enthusiastic coach he'd ever met. This was going to be great.

"Nice meeting you, too, Coach," said Dues. "See you for practice soon."

"You know, it occurs to me that I have nothing pressing going on right now. Have you seen the gym at Old Main?" asked D.L.

"No. I was in the building to register, but didn't look around," answered Dues.

"Well, if you have the time, let's take a walk. And let's take a shot with us. The semester hasn't started yet, so there are no classes. Science classes are right below the gym and, not sure why, but seems as though the shot landing on the floor kind of stirs those folks up a bit!" chuckled D.L. "I'd like to see your form."

"All right, sure. I don't need to be home until dinnertime," said Dues.

And there it began. Dues and D.L. went directly to the gym at Old Main. On the way out of the house that served as the athletic department offices, D.L. stuck his head in the office of Coach Norman Wann. This was his first year as head coach of the City College football team. D.L. introduced Dues to the coach, saying, "I have a great prospect for you here, Norm. This is Leroy Dues and he's a state champion shot-putter. He says he's not a football player but look at that build. He has football written all over him. Best part is, you get to start from scratch. No bad habits. This young man is going to win you some football games!"

The following week, Coach Wann met with Dues and he became part of the freshman football team.

Back at the Old Main gymnasium, D.L. had a makeshift shot put circle taped on the floor. He had forgotten the cushion for the shot, but he had a few mats in the gym and laid them out where he thought Dues might be able to reach.

"You're going to have more power with a shorter gap. Four feet is too big and you're wasting energy," said D.L. as he continued coaching Leroy Dues.

Dues was one of the best prospects D.L. ever had in the shot put. A sixteen-pound college shot, however, was a different animal than a twelve-pound high school shot. Dues found the additional four pounds and larger diameter required some work on his form rather than more arm strength. He had plenty of strength.

D.L. and Dues spent hours and hours working on form. When classes began for the semester, all track and field practice took place outside. At first, Dues had to ration his time between the football team and the track team. He was having a successful football season, personally, and was considered one of the best freshman linemen they'd ever had. As a team, football wasn't going very well. After the football season ended, Dues could concentrate on shot and discus full time. When the weather turned cold, they had to move inside, and inside shot put accommodations were limited at best.

The straw-filled mats D.L. set up inside the gym at Old Main to cushion the landing of the shot on the gym floor were not very adequate or effective. The shot itself had a padded leather cover laced over it to add to the cushioning effect. A sixteen-pound shot, however, was equivalent to the weight of a professional-sized bowling ball dropping onto the floor. There wasn't much you could truly do to eliminate the sound and power of its impact.

More than occasionally, the shot missed the mats entirely and came crashing onto the oak floor. It may have been an errant put or it may have been an excellent put that caused it to miss its mark. A loud bang was always an opportunity for additional instruction. Even on an excellent put, D.L. reviewed what Dues had done right to make it so powerful.

There was a feeling of excitement that D.L. hadn't experienced in field events before. Dues had the potential to be one of the top shot put men in America. As a freshman, Dues couldn't compete in all the places D.L. would have liked to take him. There were a couple of competitions coming up at the end of the indoor season where D.L. could take Dues to compete. In February there was a YMCA competition using a twelve-pound shot, and later that same month the National Junior AAU competition using a sixteen-pound shot was being held in Baltimore. It was a meet meant for freshmen and high school seniors.

Attendance at the Baltimore trip was questionable. It was November, and something bad was beginning to happen in America. The stock market had crashed just a few weeks back and there was a great deal of fear about money. D.L. didn't have any extra money to invest in the stock market, so the drop of the Dow Jones Industrial Average by nearly 50 percent didn't impact him. But people were uneasy. D.L. was uneasy. He had read in the newspaper that Winston Churchill was looking out the window of his hotel while visiting New York for a United Nations meeting on the day the market crashed and saw someone leap out a window to their death. No one understood what was happening, but fear was gripping the nation. Rumors abounded concerning multiple suicides due to huge losses in the stock market.

D.L. also worried about his budget at the college. All athletics at the College of the City of Detroit operated on a shoestring budget before the stock market crash. What would happen now? Would students drop out because they didn't have the money for tuition? Would the reduction in students mean a reduction of athletic funds? Would out-of-state competition be impossible? Would the trip to Baltimore to showcase Leroy Dues be canceled due to lack of funds?

It was always a mixed blessing that the College of the City of Detroit was part of the Detroit Public Schools. Funding came through them. That meant a

Board of Education more focused on K-12 education often treated CCD as an afterthought. Yet it also meant there was more stability in funding because it wasn't solely based on the tuition and student activity fees assessed to students.

The uncertainty gnawed at D.L. He didn't know what the future would bring, but he knew it wouldn't be positive. For the moment, he planned like it was just another year. Everyone could feel that it wasn't.

They made it past the Christmas holidays and New Year's Day. It was 1930, but it didn't look like they could put 1929 behind them just yet. Programs had not been impacted at the college so far. D.L. set his sights on the YMCA competition in February. While it wasn't a college competition, it was a good venue for him to test out the promising young shot put star on a competitive stage.

Eighty-five athletes from five different YMCA units within Detroit met at the downtown YMCA branch gymnasium on February 8. D.L. liked competing at the facility because Old Main's facilities were better. He couldn't say that very often, so he relished the chance. At the Y, it took twenty-four laps to cover the distance of a mile. At Old Main, it was only twenty-two laps.

The Adams Avenue YMCA was the defending champion of the meet. The Northern branch and Fisher branch both had chances to steal the bragging rights that night. Hannan Memorial branch had only three entries so was considered a noncontender. The St. Antoine branch was in their first meet of the season and was an unknown. D.L. had arranged for Dues to become a member of the St. Antoine branch some months ago so he could participate in this meet. The Y system was segregated, and St. Antoine was the only Detroit YMCA branch that accepted Black members.

The shot put competition took place using a twelve-pound shot because this was not a college competition. Yet, Dues still incorporated the new form that D.L. had been teaching him. When he went to the circle he thought about keeping his elbow in and his jump gap smaller. His first of three puts was a 46′8½″ distance. D.L. was thrilled. Not quite the 47′6½″ he had heaved in Kansas, but still very good. His second put improved on that with a 47′2¾″.

D.L. and Dues talked a bit off to the side before his third put. D.L. was as animated as always, acting out the perfect shot put technique he wanted. Dues tried to pay attention to the instruction but it was difficult not to smile when a white man dressed in a suit and dress shoes was gyrating with a phantom shot. And if once wasn't enough, he did it four times in a row.

"Got it, coach," said Dues. "Glue that elbow to my side."

Dues got into the shot put circle. "Elbow in, shorter hop. Elbow in, shorter hop," he thought to himself. He faced away from the landing mats. He began his move with a glide and a hop as he extended his muscular arm out toward the ceiling of the gymnasium. Before the shot had hit the apex of its flight he heard D.L. exclaiming "Oh, my. Oh, my!" off to the side. The shot almost missed the outermost portion of the mats that had been set up. It was an excellent heave. Dues not only won the event, he set a new Detroit YMCA record with a put of 50'3". His nearest competitor was 10 feet back.

Even with Dues' incredible performance, the St. Antoine YMCA branch came in second with twenty-eight points. Adams Avenue clinched another victory with forty-three points and remained the reigning champion of the Detroit YMCA units.

Neither D.L. nor Dues cared about the point totals or who won the meet. All they cared about was the amazing distance by a City College freshman. D.L. was thrilled, and Dues was even more excited. It had been his longest shot put distance ever. The time to celebrate was short, as they needed to prepare for the National Junior AAU Track and Field meet coming up on February 22. This was also a meet for high school seniors and college freshmen; however, it was officiated with college rules. That meant a sixteen-pound shot. In an unexpected move of good fortune, the location of the meet was changed from Baltimore to Detroit. It would take place at Olympia Arena.

Although it was now a local event for D.L. and Dues, athletes from around the United States were on hand to participate. This meet was a national competition. Dues prepped for using a heavier shot for this event.

The night turned out to be electric. Four National Junior AAU records were broken and another tied. Three of the new marks were set by Michigan athletes. Herold Oliver, formerly of Highland Park and now a freshman at Michigan State Normal, won the pole vault and broke the Junior AAU record with a jump of 12'6¾". An athlete from Ypsilanti Normal, William Menold, came in first in the standing high jump with a height of 4'10¼". The third new record was set by Leroy Dues.

Dues took a sixteen-pound shot and heaved it 46'1⅝" to win the event and break the Junior AAU record, which had been 44'4". Dues had been a state champion in Kansas and was now a national champion in Detroit.

With several more important competitions ahead of him between February and June, Dues was already having an excellent year. The United States, however, was not.

The toll of collapsed banks had reached five thousand, and the value of stocks was continuing to plummet. Agriculture was hit hard. Many small farmers were unable to compete because they couldn't afford the machinery necessary to cultivate crops. With the money supply tightening, demand for food went down. Families had to decide where to cut their budgets to make ends meet. The dinner table became meager just so electric and gas bills could be paid. Only larger, more mechanized farms could survive. Car sales were also hurt by the tightened money supply. Workers at automobile plants were laid off as demand fell, and it took a dramatic toll on Detroit. Without car sales, steel production waned, as did house construction. Unemployment numbers nearly tripled from 1929 to 1930. The United States, and the world, was entering a new economic reality.

That new reality hadn't quite hit college athletics. The fourth annual Michigan AAU indoor track and field event was still taking place on March 22, 1930. Over two hundred athletes from eighteen organizations, including six colleges, were slated to compete. This was a state-level meet, and the junior division had their own events in which to compete. Dues had another successful evening. He hurled the sixteen-pound shot 45'7" to win the event and set a new meet record for the Michigan AAU junior division.

In the outdoor season, Dues continued to do well, winning the shot put almost everywhere he went. In April he celebrated a decisive win over Michigan State freshmen, coming in first in the shot and second in the discus.

At the outdoor YMCA Interbranch track meet held in June, Dues broke the outdoor shot put record for the meet with a heave of 46'1½". He also threw the discus 127'6", winning the event and breaking the meet record. He followed up on those records in July at the State of Michigan Track and Field Championships, which were held on Belle Isle. Dues erased one of the oldest records on the books by hefting the shot 47'6", beating the old mark by over 2 feet.

D.L. was in awe. He didn't want to get too far ahead of himself in his dreams, but he couldn't help thinking about the 1932 Olympics. He would need to get Dues consistently beyond 49' to qualify for the Olympic Trials. He had two years to do it. It certainly seemed realistic. Just a year ago Dues had been heaving a twelve-pound shot 47', and he was now heaving a sixteen-pound shot the same distance. His improvement was impressive. Just think what he could be doing in two more years.

When football season began for the 1930–31 season, Dues was now on the varsity squad. He was stocky and strong, weighing 195 pounds and packing a wallop on the defensive line. If you were on the receiving end of one of his tackles, you knew it for weeks.

The football season, however, turned out to be a disaster. The opening game was against Notre Dame. It was an outsized matchup, and ND dominated the play and the score with a 51–0 outcome. Teams from much larger colleges decimated the Tartars each and every weekend. Michigan State, Western Michigan, Central Michigan, Toledo, and Bowling Green all rolled over the College of the City of Detroit. The only fair competition was the game against

Hillsdale College. City College lost, but only by a score of 13 to 12. Over the nine games in the season, City College scored just 37 points. Their opponents scored 238 points. At least Dues had shot put and discus to look forward to.

The indoor track season looked like it would be spectacular for Dues. He had accomplished so much during his freshman year, and now he could attend more significant competitions across the United States. In mid-January, Dues suffered a back injury that kept him out of any competition for more than a month. Finally, at the end of February, Dues was able to compete at the annual Michigan State College indoor track meet.

In addition to the hosting college and the College of the City of Detroit, athletes from Western, Eastern, the University of Detroit, Grand Rapids Junior College, Flint Junior College, Albion College, and others participated. The number of athletes per school was lopsided, at best. MSC had forty-two Spartans participating. Western was bringing a squad of thirty, while the University of Detroit entered eighteen. CCD had eighteen athletes under the direction of D.L. Holmes. Leroy Dues was there attempting to break a meet record of 44'7" that was set back in 1927. Given the distances he had been throwing, a new record seemed well in hand.

The meet took place on Sunday, March 1, 1931, in East Lansing, Michigan. The shot put record was broken, but not by Dues. During the warm-ups for the event Dues felt the same pain in his back that had kept him away from competition for all of February. D.L. felt it best to give him more rest. There was no sense in reinjuring it and setting him back another month. There were important competitions ahead. Dues was a scratch that day.

Barnhill of Western won the shot put, and broke the meet record, with a heave of 46'2¼". The College of the City of Detroit did manage to score some points in the meet. They had a first place in the 330-yard dash, a first in the 440-yard relay, a first in the 880-yard relay, a fourth in the 40-yard low hurdles, a second in the mile relay, and a second in the 40-yard dash.

It wasn't until the outdoor State Championship meet in May, also held at the Michigan State College campus in East Lansing, that Dues was back in form. In the Friday night preliminary competition, Dues broke a meet record set earlier that day with a heave of 46'9⅜".

At the Michigan Collegiate Conference Track Championship meet later in May in Ypsilanti, Dues did not push the iron ball as far as he had a week earlier, but he still won the meet. His winning distance in the finals was 45'10¾". That distance was good enough to set a new record for the meet.

D.L. could see that Dues was feeling better and getting back to his successful form. His back could still be tender if he moved it the wrong way, but

D.L. thought he was ready for national competition. He made the decision to send Dues to the National Collegiate Track Championships meet in June.

Stagg Field in Chicago was the location of the National Collegiate Track Championships meet. Dues was feeling healthy that weekend with no lingering back problems. He had been winning meets, but he was not satisfied with his distance. The best he had done since his back injury was a 46′9⅜″ heave at the outdoor State Championship meet. That distance might have been good enough to win the State of Michigan, but he knew it wasn't enough to win nationally.

D.L. was thinking a little further down the road. The following year was the Olympic Trials, and Dues had to be heaving over 49′ in order to be eligible. Dues had some of the best shot put form that D.L. had ever seen. He had the perfect build for the event, with great arm strength. But his back injury had set him back. He knew Dues was being careful to not injure his back again. In holding back, he wasn't making the distances he had previously achieved, much less increasing those distances.

D.L. and Dues had worked for hours on form and distance at Old Main for the week leading up to the Chicago meet. He had some good heaves in practice. It was just a matter of putting all the pieces together at exactly the right moment in Chicago.

There were preliminary elimination heats and field events on Friday, June 6. In the shot put event, eleven athletes would qualify to move on to the Saturday finals. Dues and D.L. studied the form of Bob Hall of Southern California, who had heaved the shot the furthest with a distance of 49′9″. That was exactly the territory where Dues needed to be. While his back felt fine, he couldn't help but review his distances since his injury. He needed to break that 49′ mark.

Dues did not break 49′ during the Friday preliminaries, but he did become one of the eleven qualifiers for the finals.

The University of Southern California won the meet by a landslide. Among those wins was Bob Hall's first place in the shot put. Leroy Dues came in fifth place. While he wished for a higher spot on the winner's board, he was pleased with his toss of 47′7″. It was his best since his back injury.

D.L. was also very happy. The imaginary threshold had been broken. It looked like Dues was back on the road to success. A fifth place nationally wasn't a bad place to be as a sophomore.

As summer began, D.L. took his annual trip up north to the Georgian Bay for fishing. He had often taken some cross-country athletes along with him for practice and camaraderie. This summer was different. The impact of the stock market crash in 1929 was still strong, and the economy was getting worse, not better. Most of D.L.'s athletes couldn't afford the trip, and their families needed them to stay in Detroit and work. Jobs were scarce. The unemployment rate had reached 16 percent, and the economy deflated by nearly 9 percent. There was no sign that either of these economic indicators would be slowing anytime soon. Many of the athletes' fathers were out of work. Whatever odd jobs D.L.'s college boys could pick up were a lifesaver for their families. The administration of the College of the City of Detroit was talking about changes for the 1931–32 academic year. D.L. cut his vacation short so he could return and tend to the needs of his teams and his college. Budgets were going to be even tighter than normal. Athletics were at risk.

The timing could not have been worse for Dues' prospects of becoming an Olympian. D.L. had two main objectives for the year: get Dues over the 49' mark and find the funds to get him to the Olympic Trials.

The fall of 1931 began with another dreadful football season. The only game of the season not in the loss column was a 0–0 tie against Wilmington on November 21. The sole points the Tartars scored in the seven-game season were the result of one lonely touchdown against Defiance in a 26–7 losing effort. They were shut out by every other team.

Worse than the scores and the dismal win-loss record was the injury to Leroy Dues.

In the season opener against Albion, Dues sustained a serious ankle injury while making a tackle. He had to be carried from the field. The injury was so intense that he did not see another minute of football the entire season.

He was done with football for the year. Would the injury also mean he was done with track and field?

Dues still supported his team by attending all of the remaining games. D.L. worked with him regularly to help him regain some mobility. By the end of October, Dues no longer needed crutches in order to walk. He was able to put weight on his ankle. By the beginning of November, D.L. had him jogging around the elevated indoor track at Old Main.

At the end of the football season, Coach Wann was hopeful that Dues would be well enough to return in the November 14 game against Olivet. His recovery was going well and his ankle had healed nicely. All Dues would have to do was make sure one of the assistant coaches wrapped his ankle tightly so that it couldn't be injured again. But D.L. stepped in and prevented it from happening. Having Dues return to football would not save a season that was already hopeless. All it could do was injure him further.

In fact, the season was so bad that D.L., in his role as athletic director, was forced to remove Coach Wann from football, and he hired Joe Gembis as the new head coach.

D.L. knew that this would be a very special year for Leroy Dues. Dues needed to be at his healthiest for the indoor track season, which would help him qualify for the Olympic Trials. The back problems he had had the previous season had not returned. A healthy ankle was just as important to increasing his shot put distance and creating a successful season.

The first indoor meet of the 1932 season was against Western State Teachers College on February 13. The Tartars had the advantage because it was being held at Old Main. D.L. always had a slight grin on his face as he welcomed visiting teams to the elevated track in the small gymnasium. Even if the opposing team was faster, they wouldn't know how to negotiate so many turns. Sprints and hurdles were held on the wood and tile hallways. The shot put took place on the main floor of the gymnasium.

The meet would be Dues' first time to perform in competition since his ankle injury in football back in early October. Western had a good team, and D.L. knew the Tartars needed the points from the shot put in order to have any chance to win the meet. D.L. talked to Dues off to the side of the gymnasium.

"This isn't the Olympic Trials, son," D.L. said. "Get your five points, but don't hurt yourself doing it. I've got you throwing last, so you'll always know how much you need to give to win. We don't need to break any records today. Just get back in the game. That's all I want from you. Just feel good about being back in the circle."

Dues always gave everything he had to everything he did, and it was very out-of-character for D.L. to ask him to hold back. But Dues understood all of the reasons. His back could easily be injured again. And he could still feel the injury in his ankle if he moved the wrong way.

Prior to the indoor season beginning, D.L. had had Dues come to his office for a long talk. They talked about fishing and families and how his studies were coming along. But the largest topic for the day was the fact that D.L. wanted Dues to start preparing for the Olympic Trials.

"I believe in you, son. You have the strength. You have the talent. You have the disposition. You have everything it takes to be an Olympic contender. I'd sure love to see you be an Olympian," said D.L.

Dues wanted nothing more than to go to Los Angeles and be part of the Olympic Games. It would be one of his wildest dreams come true. He had won the state in Kansas as a high schooler. He had won the nation in Detroit as college freshman. Could he win on the world stage as a college junior?

Dues found a space to be by himself in the tiny gymnasium at Old Main to get his thoughts straight. *Do well enough to win, but don't go so hard you reinjure yourself,* he thought to himself. He floated through his stance and delivery several times, remembering back to how funny it looked when D.L. did it. Dues didn't care what other people thought now. He saw himself in slow-motion hurling the shot through the air. He let his arm reach for the ceiling of Old Main and he watched an imaginary shot break the lights and head toward the rafters. He found it difficult to concentrate on the task at hand. His mind was in Los Angeles, not in Detroit. Although the trials were months away, today was an essential first step.

Even though it was February, the gymnasium was hot and humid. There were too many people in a too-small gym, half of them sweating athletes and the others coaches or spectators wishing they weren't wearing suits and ties. Dues already felt uncomfortable as his first test of the 1932 indoor season was upon him. The heat and humidity pushed against him like a blanket. He had trouble filling his lungs with air. He stepped out into the hallway for some fresh air. The pressure he was feeling wasn't just about this dual meet. It was about his recovery and his ability to not only return to his previous distances, but surpass them.

Could he do it? Coach Holmes was counting on it. More importantly, Dues wanted it for himself.

The Western team had two good shot-putters. Kenneth Barnhill was consistently heaving the shot more than 46 feet. Henry Harper, the only Black member of the Western track team, was putting out distances consistently in the 44' range and often over 45'.

When the time came for the shot put competition, Barnhill was scratched. D.L. wasn't quite sure of the reason, but he let Dues know that his main competitor was Harper. He was the man to beat.

Hare, of City College, was up first. He heaved the shot 38'7". Harper, of Western, was next. He beat Hare's heave but wasn't close to his best at 39'6". A few other contestants were ahead of Dues. D.L. reminded him to be careful. Do well enough to win, but don't reinjure yourself while doing it.

Dues stepped up for his first attempt of three heaves of the shot. He had stretched quite a bit more than usual getting ready for this competition. His muscles felt good. He was ready.

He took his place inside the circle with the shot under his chin. His most effective style had him start with his back to the landing area, and he made a half spin as he turned and hopped to launch the sixteen-pound shot to the matted area of the gymnasium floor. The throw of 42'4" was not close to being his best distance. But it was good enough to beat his teammates and, more importantly, to beat Henry Harper. If no one beat that distance, that was the only heave necessary tonight.

His ankle felt fine. His back had no pain. Harper did not have a good night and could not beat Dues' 42'4". Harper had to settle for second place. Dues landed himself in first place with just one throw.

The victory was exactly what D.L. wanted to see. They would take the five points and move on to the next competition. By the end of the indoor track season, Dues had come in first in every single competition. He beat the City College indoor record with a heave of 47'4". He also beat the state of Michigan collegiate record at 47'11¾". He went on to beat the Central Intercollegiate Conference record with a distance of 47'9⅞"—which simultaneously set a Notre Dame gym record.

He had an incredible indoor season. Dues was back in prime form, but a 49' heave still remained elusive.

D.L. and Dues had work to do. The Olympic Trials were coming up on July 15.

The outdoor season started in earnest in April. Michigan State College badly defeated the College of the City of Detroit by a score of 110 to 21 in a dual meet. Leroy Dues, however, set a new MSC stadium record with a heave of 47'2⅛".

In May, Dues was scheduled to go to the Penn Relays. Normally, D.L. would send a relay team or two. But not this year. Dues was the only athlete from CCD to attend, due to funding issues caused by the ongoing financial difficulties gripping the United States. The college couldn't afford to send him, so D.L. reached deep into his own pocket to fund the trip.

At the Penn Relays, Dues beat the defending champion but came in second with a toss of 47'10¾". Charles Jones, of New York University, won the event and set a new Penn Relay record with a heave of 50'. Dues was still working on attaining 49'. A heave of 50' would be truly elusive.

Later that month, Dues finally hit his target distance with a throw of 49'2" in a dual meet at CCD. It was a new field record. In June, CCD had a dual meet at Michigan Central, and once again Dues tossed a 49'2".

The two puts of over 49' meant Dues could go to the regional Olympic competition in Evanston, Illinois. Regional qualifying competition was being held on July 3.

D.L. took Dues and one other athlete to Evanston. Each athlete needed to place in the top three in their event at this regional event in order to qualify for the final phase of the Olympic Trials in Palo Alto, California.

The best athletes in the Midwest were attending this competition, all with Olympic dreams. Dues was putting the shot further than ever. He was feeling good with no lingering issues in his ankle or his back. The timing was perfect.

He was breaking his own distance records every time he heaved a shot. And his body was cooperating, allowing him to put his full effort into every single competition.

D.L. had given him the green light. It was time to give it all he had.

On July 2, D.L., Dues, and another athlete arrived at Dyche Stadium at Northwestern University in Evanston, Illinois. It was a huge stadium that could seat forty-seven thousand people. It was also new, built in 1926. The feeling of walking into a massive college stadium was nothing short of awe-inspiring, especially considering the College of the City of Detroit didn't have a stadium at all. The track was an immaculate cinder masterpiece that looked absolutely perfect. The shot put area was the nicest Dues had ever seen.

They picked up the schedules for practice times, warm-ups, and approximate event timing for the following day. Dues was more excited than he had ever been for any event. If he was successful here, he would be going to the final phase of Olympic qualification.

The next morning Dues woke up with a huge sense of anticipation. He was ready to make this day a success. The competition was very difficult. One of the athletes he would be facing was Alfred "Hippo" Howell, the university record holder from Oklahoma University. Howell, however, lacked consistency and was coming to the semifinals with a most recent heave of 46'10¾". Dues was coming with two throws of over 49'.

D.L. spent a great deal of time with Dues making sure he was limber enough for the competition. Although he had performed well with no lingering back or ankle pain, one wrong move could change it all. It seemed like hours of stretching took place before D.L. would allow Dues to have his first shot put practice.

As the field events began, D.L. put his hands on Dues' shoulders.

"You are the best weight man I've ever had the pleasure to coach. You know exactly what you need to do. Go show 'em what you've got," said an excited D.L.

Dues soaked up the moment. An almost capacity crowd was here to watch the Olympic semifinals. Every event was met with huge roars from the crowd. Even the field events, which often took a back seat to the running events, were being watched closely, and the athletes could feel the crowd's anticipation for their performance.

Dues was on deck for his first heave. So far, no other athletes were hitting the 49' mark.

Out of the corner of his eye, Dues could see D.L. watching intently. Dues was called to the circle.

He picked up the sixteen-pound shot and raised it in the air several times to further warm up his arm and shoulder. He placed the shot in his right hand and brought it up under his chin. His back was facing the area where the shots landed. With a quick movement, he raised his left arm and left leg into the air, balancing all his weight on his right leg. His right leg launched his body forward for his hop, which landed his left leg perfectly at the toeboard.

D.L.'s coaching was evident, as the shot never moved from its placement under his chin. Dues would be able to get the most power for his heave by keeping the shot tucked away there.

As his left foot came down to the ground, Dues let out a huge grunt as he pushed his right arm up and out toward the landing area and shifted his weight back to his right foot. The momentum created by this movement wanted to take him out of the circle, but he was able to control it. It felt like a very good put.

Dues and D.L. watched as the shot flew through the air and landed just before the circle of chalk that indicated 50′. It had been the best heave of his life! Leroy Dues put the shot a distance of 49′8¾″. D.L. was quite literally jumping up and down. He was already hugging Dues when the measurement was called out loud for the scorekeeper. No other athletes came close that day.

Dues took first place in the event. That first place would take him to Palo Alto, California, for the Olympic Trial Finals.

The AAU also gave Dues, and other first place winners at the semifinals, $105 to cover the expenses of attending the finals. This turned out to be essential, as the college had no money. The Great Depression had finally hit the heart of college athletics. Budgets were cut and many competitions eliminated from the schedule. Any Olympic expenses D.L. would have to figure out on his own.

Once back in Detroit, D.L. and Dues sat down to determine a schedule. The Olympic Trial Finals were July 15. It would take a few days to drive all that distance. D.L. would also need to figure out where they could eat and where they could spend the night. Racism was always an obstacle, but especially in unfamiliar territory.

It was Leroy Dues who came up with the best suggestion. The only possible route was to drive Michigan Avenue from Detroit to Chicago and hop on Route 66 all the way to California. Route 66 went right by Dues' hometown in Kansas. They could eat one of their meals and spend one of their nights there.

D.L. loved the idea and looked forward to meeting some of Dues' relatives who had remained in Kansas. D.L. sent a couple of letters letting some city personnel know their local athlete would be in town for a visit on his way to the Olympic Trials. Dues let his relatives know so they could have a warm meal and a place to sleep prepared.

Both D.L. and Dues were totally unprepared for the reception they received. It was like a crowd for a parade, except there was only one car—the one D.L. was driving. The high school marching band played some songs and the mayor was there to personally welcome Leroy Dues back to Pittsburg, Kansas.

Swarms of people surrounded Dues and D.L. as they attempted to walk through the small downtown area and meet some of the relatives. Dues was nothing short of a celebrity that day. A hand-painted banner had been hung up that said "Welcome Leroy Dues. Our Olympic Hero."

It seemed as though just about everyone wanted to see him heave a shot. The mayor asked. Relatives asked. People who Dues had never seen before in his life asked.

Neither D.L. nor Dues thought it was a good idea. But it looked like they weren't going to be able to get the meal or night's rest they came for without a demonstration.

The high school football field wasn't far away, so the huge crowd all walked over to watch the demonstration of Dues' Olympic skill. They would not hold the demonstration in the shot put area, as it was far too small. Instead, they set up in the middle of the football field.

As the crowd made its way into the football field area, D.L. helped Dues do warm-ups and stretches.

"This is not Palo Alto, Leroy," said D.L. "They don't need to see a 49' put."

The townspeople were still pouring in. The small bleachers were filled and folks were standing all the way around the football field. Someone started chanting, "Le-roy! Le-roy! Le-roy!" Very soon, the entire crowd had joined.

D.L. looked at Dues and smiled.

"All right, champ. How are you feeling?" asked D.L. "Remember, this is just a demonstration. It's not the Olympic Trials."

"I'm feeling good, coach," said Dues. "I'll take it easy."

The mayor got on a megaphone and reintroduced Leroy Dues to the crowd. The noise level was deafening. The chant of "Le-roy" started all over again. Dues waved to the crowd.

Once the chant died down, the mayor told Dues' story: first place in every competition he had this year. Dues was now headed to California to get his place on the Olympic track team.

Dues picked up the 16-pound shot and raised it in the air several times. He went through all his normal preparation as he placed the shot in his right hand and brought it up under his chin. The football field was now eerily quiet, as the anticipation of the demonstration held the attention and breath of everyone in attendance.

As he always did, he raised his left arm and left leg into the air, balancing all his weight on his right leg and launched his body forward, releasing the shot with incredible power and distance. It was an excellent put.

D.L. ran after the shot as the crowd went crazy. Once again, Dues was swarmed by people chanting his name and congratulating him on his Olympic journey.

Everyone was ecstatic—except D.L. He knew something was wrong. Dues had given him a look right after the heave. It was a look D.L. had seen too many times before. Dues had hurt himself.

After the hubbub of the night calmed down, Dues and D.L. retreated into the calm and comfort of a relative's living room. This was the house where they would have a bite to eat and be staying that night.

"How's your back, Leroy?" asked D.L.

"I tweaked it a little bit," said Dues. "I don't think it's too serious. I just need to stretch it out."

That night, D.L. helped Dues go through his stretching ritual. The next morning before they hopped in the car for the next leg of their journey, they did the stretches again. This was repeated several more times before they reached Palo Alto, California.

They reached their Olympic destination on July 14, one day before Dues was to compete. D.L. spent the rest of the time working on Dues' back. Dues was not 100 percent, but he felt good enough to compete the next day. He had to compete the next day. The Olympics were on the line.

July 15 was here. It was the date D.L. had been waiting for since he met Leroy Dues three years previously in the athletic offices of the College of the City of Detroit. Dues was the best weight man he had ever had. Today was his chance to make the Olympic team.

Only the three top finishers would make it on the team. Dues had to be one of those.

Dues went through all of his typical preparations just like it was any other track meet—except it wasn't like any meet he'd ever been in before. This was competing for the Olympics. He was nervous, and he knew his back wasn't at its best.

D.L. worked with him to get him ready, but he also gave Dues some space. He understood this was the biggest stage on which Dues had ever competed.

The best shot-putters in the United States were all there. Herman Brix was there. He was the world record holder in the shot put with a record of 51'2½". Leo Sexton was there. Sexton held the 1930 collegiate shot put title.

There were fifteen competitors in the shot put, and every one of them was a champion somewhere.

After what seemed like an eternity, Dues was on deck. His confidence was rattled by Harlow Rothert's heave of 50'11½" just before him.

D.L. put his arm around Dues. "Just do your best, son. There's nothing I can coach you on right now. Just go do what you came to do."

Dues went to the circle with his shot. He raised it up in the air several times, as was his custom. He positioned himself like he always did and with a grunt heard hundreds of feet away, he hurled the iron ball into the air.

As he did so, he could feel the weakness in his back. He didn't have the power today. His heave was 44'5⅜". It was his best of three attempts.

Dues came in fifteenth of fifteen athletes in the Olympic shot put finals.

Rothert, with his put of just under 51', came in third. Leo Sexton won the trials with a heave of 52'8", a world record.

It was a quiet drive back to Detroit. Although they retraced the same route on their return, they did not stop in Pittsburg, Kansas, opting for a night at a YMCA instead.

Leroy Dues still holds the Wayne State University indoor shot put record with a heave of 49'10⅞". He became the first Black athletic director in the State of Michigan in 1944. Dues was inducted into the Wayne State Sports Hall of Fame in 1977.

9

MY GOODNESS

Interview with Jim Coulter, Class of 1951, and Ray Morgan, Class of 1956
Interviewed by Professor David L. Holmes Jr.

May 24, 2001

Professor David L. Holmes Jr.: What year were you at Wayne, Jim?

Jim Coulter: I graduated in 1951.

Ray Morgan: I started in 1951.

Professor: So, Ray, you're Class of 1955.

Morgan: Well, my eligibility ran out in '55. I graduated in 1956.

Coulter: I graduated in '51. I only ran for the coach for two years. I was a transfer from Alma College. That was the same time George Gaines was at Alma.

Professor: What were the track facilities like at Alma? Were they better or worse than Wayne?

Coulter: Worse!

Professor: Worse?

Coulter: If it rained, the Alma track couldn't be used for three days. At Wayne, if it rained we could use the track the next day.

Professor: I see. Did Alma have an indoor track?

Coulter: No. No indoor track and no indoor track team.

Professor: So, you transferred from Alma to Wayne and were on the track team.

Coulter: Yes, track and cross-country. It was a great decision all around. It cost less at Wayne. I could live at home, so no room and board cost. And I got to be coached by your dad. He was way ahead of his time in coaching techniques.

Professor: Well, I would love to hear some stories about him. What do you remember?

Morgan: [*laughing*] I have a story! Your dad was not a great driver! He had a little guardian angel that followed him around. One time we went to the Penn Relays and we got third place in the mile relay. This is not about your dad's driving, but I have to tell you. The reason we got third place in the mile relay was some idiot from Manhattan University got the baton—anchoring—and threw it away. Maybe it was his first time running a relay, but he didn't know he was supposed to finish with the baton. They were disqualified.

Professor: He threw the baton away coming into the finish line?

Morgan: No. He got it, ran about five steps and threw it away. Which was, you know, the most stupid thing. Worked out well for us. [*laughs*] Anyway, the next day we ran the half-mile relay and your dad took us to New York City that night. He just wanted us to see New York. We stayed in New York for the night and drove back to Detroit on Sunday. Well, that was all before freeways. It's just two lanes with one lane going our way and one coming at us. So, it's nighttime now and we've been driving all day long. Your dad would never let anyone else drive. I'm watching and your dad is driving in the left lane—the oncoming traffic lane—passing everyone in the right lane. He liked passing other cars. Did it all the time. All of a sudden we see headlights coming at us. We're driving in the oncoming lane! I'm in the back seat in the middle. I looked over at Cliff Anders sitting to my left. His eyes are getting bigger and bigger. He's grabbing the back of the seat in front of him. I look over to my right at Tim Blank. His eyes are as big as saucers. He's a white kid, but now he's quite a bit whiter than I've ever seen him. And, all of a sudden Boom, Boom, Boom! Holy shit! What happened? No one could say anything. He cut in. Didn't hit anyone or anything. Just cut in quickly to get back in the right lane. All us guys were just watching those headlights get closer and closer. But, your dad was absolutely confident he was going to get in front of one more car . . . and he did! His little guardian angel!

Professor: Oh, my! And he taught me how to drive! [*laughs*] If you went to a meet in more than one car, did people try to get in a different car?

Coulter: I can answer that. We would drive to Lansing for meets. I had a '37 Chevrolet, which was a piece of junk. I would drive to the Lansing meet. Your dad's Hudson was relatively new. But my car filled up first. Then driving back, again well before the freeways were built, it was a two-lane road. I'd take the lead and straddle the center line so he couldn't pass me. When an oncoming car approached I'd just pull over into my lane and then pull back out over the line after they passed. I got all sorts of thanks from the people who were driving with him!

Professor: And you had a full car?

Coulter: Yes, usually five and sometimes six.

Professor: And everyone knew what you were doing?

Coulter: Oh, yes. It was only about a ninety-minute drive back from Lansing, maybe a little bit more. But, it kept us all safe.

Professor: Oh, my, my, my.

Coulter: But you know, other than his driving, there isn't one negative thing I can say about the man. I remember one thing that really impressed me about Coach Holmes was at a dinner we had to honor him. It was either for his retirement or his birthday, something like that. Anyway, it was at Jacoby's Restaurant in downtown Detroit and everybody got up to say something about him. I remember the things said about indoor track practice where the shot-putter had to aim for a mattress on the gym floor so it didn't bang too loud for the science class on the first floor under the gym. The pole-vaulters had to run down a hall, make a left turn when they got to the gym, and go through a set of double doors before they could vault. But every one of those people said something about him that indicated when they went to practice he dropped everything else to pay attention to them. This was said six, seven, eight times that night. For example, he'd take the shot-putter and show him how to put the shot and then he'd get up on the track and run beside Lorenzo Wright. He'd be running alongside Lorenzo, hitting him in the tail, saying "come on, get going." Every one of those guys thought he spent 100 percent of his time with them. Think about that. It's impossible. But they really thought that way. They thought he was completely devoted to just them at practice. That's always impressed me. They're all working out at the same time, so how could he give 100 percent of his time to anyone? He couldn't. But he did it in such a way that everyone thought they were special.

Morgan: Your dad was the most caring, patient, loveable coach and person that I've ever met. I mean, he was just unbelievable. I don't think I ever saw him mad. I saw him irritated, but not mad. I don't think I ever heard him swear. The worst thing he ever said was "Heavens to Betsy."

Coulter: Or he'd say "My Goodness."

Morgan: [*laughs*] That's right. "My Goodness." Then there was some stupid joke he used to tell. Something about fertilizer on a field. The farmer said . . . ahhh, I can't remember how to tell it. He would tell it about every two weeks.

Professor: [*laughs*] I don't think I ever heard that joke.

Morgan: You'd think after hearing it so many times I'd remember. Sorry. But, for sure it was a clean joke. Never anything off color with him.

Professor: What do you think made him tick?

Morgan: I think his background. He went to Oklahoma A&M and was a sprinter and jumper. He knew track from actually doing it. Seems like he came out of a tough background; poor, you know.

Professor: His grandfather was a minister and his father ran a music store in Stillwater. His father moved there so that all the kids could go to college. It was tuition-free at the time. His father was very gentle, very kind, absolutely radiated kindness.

Coulter: You know, he always demonstrated things to each of us. But he was never trying to show off his strength. Yet, you knew he was strong. I remember one time we were inside for practice and he said he had a good exercise for pole-vaulters. There was a set of parallel bars in the gym. He grabbed one of the bars with both hands and slowly lifted his feet up over his head, bending himself into the shape of a V. Then he started to do pull-ups in that position. He was explaining how it helps simulate the action of grabbing the pole and pushing off it as you vault. So I thought, well that looks easy. I'll just go up there and do that myself. I couldn't get my feet over my head, much less do a pull-up like that! He had amazing strength.

Morgan: He stayed in that position?

Coulter: Yes, and this was 1950. So, he's in his sixties. I couldn't believe it when he did it without even a quiver in his arms. He just held himself and talked and very slowly moved himself up and down. That was the same day, of course, that he demonstrated proper hurdle form.

Morgan: In street clothes.

Coulter: Yeah, well, his street clothes. A white shirt and tie. And dress shoes. He's running around the track in dress shoes.

Professor: [*laughs*] Must have been a sight. Did you ever see him work out?

Coulter: No. I never saw him work out, other than to show somebody else what to do. Like, no exercises, and we didn't have any weights at that time, of course.

Morgan: Oh, this just popped into my head: the Holmes Hurdle! Every time we went to a track meet he had a little scale. The hurdles were supposed to fall over at so many pounds of pressure. They had high hurdles, low hurdles, and you flipped the weight and moved it up or down. Every time we went somewhere he went "ewwwww" because it wasn't tipping over at the right time.

Professor: I went to a track dinner where they had a photo of him with a Holmes hurdle. I wish I had that photo. So, what do you remember about meets at Wayne or meets elsewhere?

Morgan: Well, I didn't realize how much he cared about winning because he was always so easygoing. I'll tell you one time I saw him angry. Well, maybe not angry, but perturbed. We were running a cross-country meet at Western Michigan. The football field at Western had a kind of steep hill that had stands on it. The other side had no slope with freestanding grandstands. So you ran the race by starting out on the track about three-quarters of the way around the football field and then up the side of the hill through the gate and out of the stadium. Western had two really good runners who we knew would come in first and second. We thought we'd have a chance for third. There were some checkpoints along the route. The last checkpoint was about a half mile from the finish. I don't remember the exact position, but I do remember that if we just maintained our positions we would have won the meet. One of our runners, Owen, was not the brightest light on the board. He was running in front of me. So, you're literally running through the woods on a path. You run down a straight path and I could see him in front of me. He would get the points we needed to win the meet. Then you made a little turn and I didn't see him, but I knew I was following him. There were flags on the trail to give you directions. White was turn right. Blue was go through. Red was turn left. Somewhere in this last half mile we came to a straightaway and no Owen. I don't see him. I finished, but not in third and went onto the track to see what happened. I still don't see Owen. Coach Holmes says to me "What happened to Owen?" I don't know. About twenty minutes later over the side of the football field, there's Owen climbing over an eight-foot fence all beat up, cut and scratched. He'd taken a wrong turn. Missed a flag or something. He had to be running through the woods where there was no path. Coach was just exasperated. Absolutely out of joint. I don't think he ever said anything to Owen or to anybody, but his body language said everything. You know, unbelievable.

Professor: How did Owen take it?

Morgan: Owen was clueless. I still know him today. He still claims he didn't go twenty minutes out of his way. But, who knows where he went. I'm not sure Owen knows where he went. [*laughs*]

Professor: Did you travel out of state for cross-country meets?

Coulter: Oh, yes. I remember one meet in Toronto, Canada. I have the article someplace. We took five men to Toronto to run against a team that was the Canadian champs. They had the best team in Canada and a tough five-mile course. Our cross-country courses were primarily four or sometimes three miles. It was up hills and down hills, it was tough. And it was sleeting so bad we couldn't walk the course like we normally would do to check it out. They took first and second place, but we took third, fourth, fifth, and sixth. And then came me. I finished something like ninth. We beat them 28–27. It was a big thing because they were the champions of Canada at the time. And we only had five men.

Professor: Aren't seven men allowed to run?

Coulter: Right, but we only had room for five in the car. [*laughs*] Actually, I think we only had five on the team! I'd get this side pain every time I ran. Every single time I would get the pain and want to quit. I'd say "Coach, I quit. I'm not going to do this crazy race again." And he would always say, "I don't blame you. If I hurt like that I'd quit, too. But, do me a favor. Come in Monday and we'll make arrangements and see what we can do." So, I go in Monday and, of course, I wasn't hurting anymore. He'd say, "Do me a favor and find somebody to take your place. We have four good runners and we need a fifth runner to finish." So, obviously, the next Saturday I'd be running again. I finished out the season. Your dad was a con man!

Professor: [*laughs*] Yes, well, I often hear stories about his very polite and gentle arm twisting.

Coulter: [*laughs*] On the other hand, he was good at seeing things you didn't see yourself.

Morgan: Right, like Mark Smith.

Professor: I want to hear this. Tell me about Mark Smith.

Morgan: Coach saw Mark standing in a gym class. He was 6'3" or something. Coach went up to him and asked if he'd ever high-jumped. He hadn't. So, coach tells him to come out for track and he'll show him how to high-jump. Mark gets on the team, learns how to high-jump, and ties for first at the NCAA Championship meet the next year! Coach picked him out of a gym class!

Professor: I remember him. He should have gone to the Olympics but he was off-cycle. The timing was off.

Morgan: Well, when you—and I'm not sure what year it was—when you jumped you landed in a sand pit. They just had sand. The best pit would be when they put this foam rubber stuff in there. But Mark used to jump, land in the sand on one foot, turn, and then land on his ass. He hurt his tailbone. Ever after that he was apprehensive, particularly at places like Central Michigan where it wasn't state-of-the-art. It was just a sand pit that they spaded up.

Coulter: Same thing with the pole vault. You had to land on your feet. These days they're going over and landing practically on the back of their head—on the back of their neck. And you couldn't jump, even at nine feet that I jumped—which wasn't very good—you can't go nine feet and land on the back of your head in a sand pit and expect to jump again. Now the landing mat is big and soft and makes the jumper confident. They jump and have no fear of the landing. Back when we jumped, we feared the landing.

Professor: So true. Sometimes people look at the old height records and comment about how low they were. Well, it wasn't the jump or the vault height that mattered. It was the distance down to a very unforgiving surface that mattered. That eleven-foot vault was an eleven-foot drop to the ground. It's like jumping out of a second-story window and landing on your feet. What would the difference have been in training for pole vault or high jump at Michigan State or the University of Michigan?

Morgan: Well, first of all, they would have had a coach specifically for the event.

Coulter: Then they would have the top-of-the-notch materials. Whatever was best for landing, they would have it. Instead of gym mats indoors, which were almost as hard as landing on the floor, whatever was available they would have it.

Morgan: The high jumpers and the pole-vaulters at Wayne used to take mats and they would roll the mats and then take bleacher boards and put bleacher boards on top of the mats, and then mats on top of that. It created a higher platform for landing your jump and less chance to hurt yourself on the drop. We had to do that every day. And then, after practice, we had to put them all back where they belonged. At those big schools they had a high-jump pit and it was just there. Always there. Jumpers didn't have to set up anything. And like I said, they'd have a specific coach or tutor for that event. Coach Holmes would come down and spend some time with the high jumpers, spend some time with the pole-vaulters, the hurdlers, and then go back up on the track to work with the guys running up there. He did everything. Every event.

Professor: And outdoors, did you have a sand pit?

Morgan: Yeah.

Professor: Who would take care of it?

Coulter: I don't think anybody took care of it. I think we did. High jumpers and pole-vaulters would spade our own landing pits. I don't recall ever seeing a maintenance man on the track.

Professor: Do you think the bad condition of the facilities was the reason you were short on track and cross-country athletes? Wayne was a working-class school, so people had other things to do, so they didn't run track.

Coulter: Well, that is correct. A lot of them didn't run track. Most of us went to Wayne because it was inexpensive. When I was there tuition was sixty-two dollars or maybe sixty-eight dollars a semester. Then there was an eight-dollar student activities fee. Coach would get us jobs to pay for it. Running track was just something to do while we were there. Wayne had a good education department, and a lot of these guys were going into education, some into physical education. So, running track was logical.

Morgan: I don't know how many students Wayne had at the time. But I'd say the great majority of students came to class and then went home. Students didn't live on campus. So, some of the extracurriculars suffered because the students left campus.

Coulter: That's why they called it the streetcar college. Everybody hopped on the streetcar after class and went home. All the classes were at Old Main, and our indoor track facility was the hallway. It wasn't very conducive to someone who wanted to make a career out of track.

Morgan: But you could go to Wayne and everything was there. If you wanted to make a social activity out of it, which we did, we ran track, we joined a fraternity, we went to football and basketball games. It was all there for you, if you wanted to take advantage of it.

Coulter: I think the biggest challenge for Coach Holmes was attracting students. You think of the big universities and they're good in every subject and every sport. They're big enough to command people's attention for athletics and education. Students came to Wayne because it was a good education that was cheap. I don't think many people came to Wayne for the athletics. Coach just had to do the best with what came to him.

Morgan: Why did he come to Wayne, anyway? Seems like he could have gone almost anywhere with his skill.

10
KANSAS TO DETROIT

September 12, 1894

"I don't understand, Papa," said D.L. as he sat next to the crackling fireplace in their Carlton, Kansas, home. The chill of the fall morning air seeped through the walls while the warmth of the fireplace tried to push the cold back outside. "Why did Grandpa do that?"

"He didn't want to do it. He wanted to stay with his family. But he had no choice," answered D.L.'s father. "He was just a little bit older than you, nine years old I think, when his mother sent him away."

"Why would she do that?" D.L. asked with great concern.

"Her husband had died. She was left with seven children to care for and she couldn't do it. She had no job and no income. She had no way to support all those children. So, she bound over her boys to other families. That way they'd be taken care of and be educated in a trade. My father went to the home of a shoemaker," said D.L.'s father.

"Grandpa made shoes?" asked D.L.

"Well, only while he was with the other family. Your grandfather became a minister."

"He didn't like making shoes?"

"No," said D.L.'s father, "he didn't like the situation at all. He missed his family and wanted to be with them."

"Why didn't he leave?" asked D.L.

"He couldn't. He'd been bound over by his mother."

"What's bound over?"

D.L.'s father tried to explain it in seven-year-old terms. "It was a contract, a written agreement, where my father would be taken care of in a home, fed, educated, and would learn a job. He started when he was nine, and the agreement was intended to last until he was twenty-one. However, he was twenty-three before he could leave."

"And he didn't want to be there?" asked D.L.

"No."

"And he wasn't allowed to leave?"

"No."

"And he didn't like the work he had to do?"

"No."

"Did his mother sell him to that other family?"

"Well, we don't know for sure. But probably yes. She had no money," D.L.'s father said sadly.

"Was he a slave? Did President Lincoln free him when all the other slaves were freed?" asked D.L.

D.L.'s father was taken aback by the question. He took a moment to compose himself and gently answered his son. "First, this happened some twenty years before Lincoln was president. My father's release wasn't about emancipation. Second, being 'bound' had an end. Being a slave did not. I'm sure some of the boys who were bound over had horrible experiences much like the slaves. But they knew when they were twenty-one they would be released. Slaves often lived their entire lives under the control of other people."

"But, Grandpa was under the control of another person and he didn't want to be there. They didn't let him leave."

"That's true, son." D.L.'s father thought carefully about what he was going to say next. He didn't want to paint his grandmother as a thoughtless and uncaring person. He had never met her and had no idea what she was like. He didn't want his son to have negative thoughts about his ancestral background. "The difference is my grandmother agreed to it. Slaves were taken against their will."

"Grandpa was taken against his will, too!" said an increasingly agitated D.L.

"Yes, but he was nine years old and not old enough to make those kinds of decisions. Think about his mother. She had seven children, no job, and no money. She wanted her children to have the best life possible and she didn't have the resources to provide them that life. What if she kept the family together and they died because they didn't have food or shelter? I'm sure it was the hardest decision she ever had to make. And I'd guess it haunted her all the days of her life. She did what she thought was best to do for her boys."

D.L.'s father sat back in his chair, feeling pleased with his explanation. In his heart he did not believe his grandmother was an uncaring mother. He had just spoken the same words to D.L. that his father had said to him. In an impossible set of circumstances, she did the only thing she could to help her boys. She was compassionate.

The opposite interpretation of the events was still swirling in D.L.'s mind.

"So her best was selling her boys?" asked D.L. as his voice cracked from the tears about to pour down his face.

Tears also welled within D.L.'s father's eyes, but he did not acknowledge them. He looked lovingly at D.L. as he sat on the floor in front of him. He had had the exact same thoughts as D.L. when he was younger. It was only with the passing of years and the making of difficult decisions that he was able to shine a new light on what had happened to his father.

"Son, it's easy to judge the decisions people make after we have seen the result. It is much more difficult to make the decision when you don't know the outcome. We must assume people want the best, even when it doesn't turn out that way."

D.L. could barely choke out the next question through his tears. "Papa, are you and Mother going to sell me when I turn nine?"

D.L.'s father picked him up and held him tight. "No, no, no. We would never, ever do that. We love you and we love your brothers and sisters. We will always be a family."

"But what if you die and Mother can't take care of us?"

D.L.'s father wiped his tears and held him tighter to comfort him. "We are blessed, son. We have something my grandmother didn't have. We have family. I don't plan on dying anytime soon, but if I did your mother would take the whole family to stay with one of your aunts or uncles. You'd all be together there. You would be just fine."

"Did your papa go back to his family when he was released?"

"He tried. He went back to the house where he grew up, but there was a different family living there. He asked many people where his family had gone. All they knew was they thought they had moved to Ohio. He had so little information, he knew it would be a futile search. He stopped looking. He never found anyone in his family, and they never found him. He was always sad about that."

D.L. looked into the fireplace at the fire now desperately in need of another log. Red embers glowed like a beautiful sunset. Grey smoke wafted upward, pulled through the flue by the outside air as the sweet smell of the burned maple logs filled the house. The heat of the fire was waning, but he felt the warmth of his father still holding him tightly.

"Why do some people do bad things to other people?" D.L. asked faintly.

"That's an excellent question, son. Why indeed? My grandmother was desperate. She thought she was doing the right thing. But some people think they're better than other people. Some people see a difference and think they're better because of that difference."

"What kind of difference?" asked D.L.

"My father was a minister. Religion has always been one of those big differences to some people. They think their religion is better than others'. Within Christian religions people think their form of Christianity is better than another very similar form of Christianity. But then, as a group, they'll treat Jewish people poorly. We're Irish. Some people don't like Irish folks. Others don't like Italian people. Even within the Irish, some people from the south don't like the people from the north. Then there's the African people. They have a different skin color, so some white people think they're better. Remember this, son. We're all the same inside. We all want to be loved and we all want a chance to succeed in this life. No one is better than anyone else. Some people with money think they're better than those of us without. They're not better. No religion, no nationality, no level of wealth, no skin color is better or worse than any other. We judge people on their character. Always be a person of great character. Always do the right thing and always treat other people the way you would want to be treated."

"You say that every day, Papa." D.L. said as a faint smile began to appear.

"And I always will. I'm going to fix this fire and it's time to do your chores, son. Laddie is waiting on you. Now get along."

D.L.'s father watched him as he walked out the door. Such big questions for such a small boy. Yet he could not have been more proud. At seven years old, D.L. had empathy beyond his years and could sense how events in life impacted other people.

D.L. walked out to the barn to start his chores. He was still sad about the stories his father had just told him. He couldn't imagine having to leave his family. Fortunately, his mood would soon change. Any chores that had to do with Laddie, his horse, he loved. He couldn't wait to open the barn doors.

Laddie was a beautiful, muscular horse with gorgeous deep brown hair and a long black mane. D.L. wished he could grow up to be that strong. Laddie was a bit large for a boy seven years of age to ride fast, but D.L.'s father allowed him to saddle up and take Laddie for walks or trots through their Kansas farmland. The two had a special bond. It was a bond sweeter than the sugar cube treats D.L. gave him every time he came into the barn.

There were two other horses, but D.L. loved Laddie the most. He went to the shelf where he kept the sugar cubes and pulled one out for Laddie. The stallion knew exactly what was coming and excitedly gave his head a nod and made a sound that could only be described as a laugh, if a horse could do such things. D.L. unlatched the swinging door to Laddie's stall and gave him a hug before offering the sugar cube from his open hand.

"You're not going to another family, Laddie. You're my horse forever," D.L. said, reassuring Laddie just in case the horse had any doubts about D.L.'s love.

Laddie lowered his head toward D.L. and gave him a friendly nudge with his nose to let him know the treat was appreciated. D.L. took Laddie outside of the barn and brushed him down, which could be especially hard, given his beautiful black mane was often tangled. Laddie sometimes rebelled when his mane was brushed because it could hurt if it was brushed too hard. But D.L. had a special and gentle touch, and Laddie never flinched during his brushings. Among D.L.'s other chores were refreshing the hay and refilling the water. Anything that was for Laddie was a joy to do. D.L. worked hard as his favorite horse explored the fenced area outside the barn. As D.L. did his chores, he always looked back at his good friend.

This ritual went on day after day; the hug, the sugar cube, the walk outside, the brushing, and the chores.

One day, D.L. went out to the barn and the sugar cubes were gone. He couldn't understand it. There had been plenty there the day before. He went inside his house to tell his father.

"There were at least ten in there yesterday," D.L. said, concerned.

"Probably just some mice finding a nice treat," said D.L.'s father. "Go get some more from your mother."

D.L. replenished his sugar cube supply and went back to his daily ritual with Laddie.

The next day, D.L. went back to the barn and the sugar cubes were gone again! Those darn mice! D.L. wasn't happy about it. He was going to get just one sugar cube from his mother this time. And, as he did every day, Laddie loved the treat.

The following day, D.L. got another single sugar cube from his mother and went to give it to Laddie. But his father asked him to do an extra chore first. So, D.L. put the sugar cube on the shelf in the barn and told Laddie he'd be right back to get him out of his stall.

When D.L. returned to the barn, there was Laddie, out of his stall, eating the sugar cube off the shelf. It hadn't been mice after all! Laddie had figured out how to open his stall door, go eat all the sugar cubes, and get back in the stall and shut the swinging door!

Laddie was not only beautiful and strong; he was also smart!

One of the other two horses was named Daisy. She was the horse the family used on special outings to church or to visit nearby friends. They would hook up a small nondescript wooden carriage to Daisy and she would take them to their destination.

Daisy, however, was not a patient horse. If the sermon ran a little too long or if they added an extra song, Daisy had an internal clock that said it was time to go home, and she would leave. The family would emerge from church to find that Daisy and the carriage were gone. Sometimes they would catch a glimpse of her far down the road. It was D.L.'s job to run after her and bring her back. More often, the Holmes family walked back to the farm to find Daisy innocently waiting by the barn with the family carriage attached.

Neither Laddie nor Daisy were D.L.'s main means of getting places. He mostly walked or ran where he wanted to go. Whether it was to school, to a friend's, or for a piece of penny candy at the country store, D.L. used his feet to get around.

In 1895, when D.L. was eight years old, he and his family moved from their Kansas farm to an area near Carlton in the Oklahoma Territory. D.L.'s father was a teacher in addition to being a farmer. Moving to the new territory meant D.L.'s father could have more land and would be able to establish a new rural school to serve the other pioneers who had moved there. The Holmes family loaded up their wagon, hitched Daisy to it, and made the long journey across the plains. The Holmes children all took turns riding Laddie along the route.

Their new home was a small, one-story, wood-sided structure with two bedrooms to shelter the Holmes family. With four children, there was not a lot of space. The quarters became even smaller in 1898 when another daughter was born and in 1900 when another son was born.

Money was tight. The land was rugged, and the crops were barely plentiful enough to feed the family and their animals. The teaching pay was meager. In 1901, D.L.'s father took a job at an abstract company in Stillwater, Oklahoma. It was a good job, paying forty dollars a month. The family packed up once again and moved to Stillwater.

The primary reason for the move was not the job, although that was important. D.L.'s father wanted all of his children to get a college education. Oklahoma A&M was located in Stillwater and was tuition free. It offered a college-prep high school as well as the college itself. Living in Stillwater gave them the opportunity for a free college education because the children would all live at home while attending.

D.L. was fourteen years old now and enjoyed the excitement of the big city. Stillwater's population of almost 2,500 made it a much larger city than the Carlton area, which didn't have quite 300. When the eight members of the Holmes family moved away, the population went down by almost 3 percent.

One of the things D.L. loved most about Stillwater was Stillwater Creek. He loved to fish and never had much chance to do it anywhere else he lived. In Stillwater, he could walk to one of the many tributaries of the creek running through the town. He would catch bass, perch, pickerel, and sunfish. If they were big enough, he'd bring them home to his mother to cook for dinner. If allowed, D.L. would spend all day fishing by the side of the creek. In between school and chores and spending time with Laddie, D.L. always seemed to find some time to go fishing.

He had favorite spots where he caught the best fish. In order to get there he had to walk into town and cross the bridge over the creek and then walk a mile back up to his fishing hole. D.L. couldn't be troubled with all that fuss. Parts of the creek were only ten to fifteen feet wide. D.L. would toss his fishing pole to the other side, put the worms in his pocket, get himself a nice long runway, sprint to the edge of the creek, and jump right over it.

When he went fishing with his friends, they couldn't believe it. There was no way they could jump that far. D.L. had another method for them. He had fashioned a nice pole from the trunk of a slender pine tree. He showed his friends that they could run with the pole out in front of them, quickly put the end of the pole into the water, hold the pole, and go flying over the water to the other side.

When D.L. did the demonstration it looked easy. When his first friend tried it he ran with the pole, quickly put the end of the pole in the water, and swung up to the highest point before realizing he didn't have enough momentum to push the pole to the other side. Instead, he teetered for a minute until gravity took hold and brought the pole down—with the friend still holding on tightly—into the middle of the creek. The loud "splash" was drowned out by the laughter of all the other friends watching.

D.L. demonstrated again and again, each time pointing out what he was doing to get a successful crossing to the other side of the creek. He would watch his friends' attempts and coach them on how to have more success and more distance.

By the end of the first couple weeks, D.L. had all of his friends vaulting over the creek without getting wet.

His jumping skill was used wisely by his high school track coach. D.L. was always entered in the running broad jump, and was often in the pole vault as well. While he loved the sprints the best, he excelled in jumping. No one in Stillwater could jump as far as D.L. Holmes.

Even when he entered Oklahoma A&M, it was tough to find anyone who could beat D.L. He was an all-around athlete there, playing football, basketball, and track. Athletics were a huge part of his life.

Just prior to D.L.'s college graduation, his father had the opportunity to purchase a music store. The amount of money was huge: eight hundred dollars. But he was able to get a loan from the local bank. He was already paying his ten-dollars-a-month mortgage payment at the bank and had never missed a payment. They thought he was a good risk. D.L.'s father now did abstract work, real estate sales, and ran a music store in addition to farming.

He had given up his teaching position when the family moved to Stillwater. His mother gave piano lessons out of the store.

The family was musical. Many of them had good singing voices, and several played piano quite well. D.L.'s father had hopes the music store would become a family business and pass down through the generations. D.L., however, had other plans. His music professor at A&M was also pressuring him to enter a career in music. Instead, D.L. chose athletics as his career. Earl Holmes, the oldest of the Holmes children, entered the music store business.

D.L., immediately upon college graduation, went to work as a coach. His first stop was Bethel College in Russellville, Kentucky, where he taught history and coached athletics from 1908 to 1912. He moved to the State Institute of Technology in Tonkawa, Oklahoma, as athletic director and coach from 1912 to 1914. He had only completed the 1914 track season at DePauw University, in Greencastle, Indiana, when he was contacted by David Mackenzie of Detroit. Mackenzie was starting the Detroit Junior College and wanted to have an athletic program. He wanted D.L. to come to Detroit even though the college wasn't quite ready for athletics. So, D.L. came to Detroit in 1914 and worked at Cass Technical High School as basketball coach, baseball coach, football coach, and track coach. In 1917, Mackenzie had D.L. transferred to Detroit Junior College.

D.L. kept copies of newspaper articles from the short period between college graduation and his arrival in Detroit. He had success in every sport he coached. A January 27, 1911, article from the *Democrat*, in Russellville, Kentucky, reads:

The fast basketball team of Bethel College swamped the much-touted Southwestern Presbyterian University team Saturday night to the tune of 29 to 7. After three weeks of hard practice Coach Holmes seems to have rounded out a team that can hold its own with almost any in the south. A decided improvement was shown in teamwork since the game with Peabody, of Nashville.

Although he was in DePauw for only a very short time, the *DePauw Daily* reported:

Coach Holmes started his first afternoon with the track squad by pulling off his coat and showing the boys some of the fine points. Things went off with a bang, and then he kept things banging all the evening. From now on practice will consist of hard work, with special emphasis on individual coaching by Holmes.

On May 6, 1914, the *Indianapolis News* reported:

DePauw took the dual track affair with Rose Poly here yesterday afternoon in a walk, scoring a total of 103 points to 23 points for the Engineers. The Old Gold thinly-clads took first in every event but one, and took all nine points in the 220-yard dash, mile run, high hurdles and broad jump.

D.L.'s reputation was well known and widely reported by 1914, so it is not surprising that Mackenzie would have heard about him and wanted him in Detroit. As fate would have it, Cass Technological High School was a magnet school bringing the best teachers and best students from across Detroit together to create an excellent learning environment for high-achieving students. A bright female mathematics teacher from Marquette, Michigan, was among the staff at Cass Tech in 1915. Her name was Hazel Madden. D.L. took quick notice. Both young, both smart, both enjoying the field of education, they began to date. Holmes, a strict nondrinker, would take her on the Woodward streetcar to grab a Vernor's ginger ale at the famous soda fountain near the Bob-Lo boat docks on the Detroit River. A trip to the Vernor's soda fountain was one of the more popular things to do for dates in Detroit. D.L. and Hazel did it often.

It was also in 1915 that Mackenzie began assembling the staff for Detroit Junior College. David L. Holmes was finalized as athletic director and coach of everything. It would be two more years before Mackenzie could get his junior college idea off the ground.

But D.L. didn't mind staying at Cass Tech. He enjoyed the close proximity it gave him to his favorite math teacher. The year 1917 turned out to be an auspicious one. The Detroit Junior College was opened, and David L. Holmes married Hazel Madden. They bought a house in Detroit and began their life together.

In the Detroit Junior College days, everything was a blank slate. Mackenzie had assembled a small team of capable individuals to build the junior college from scratch. Enrollment that first year was 100 students. The junior college was operated inside Central High School. Mackenzie was both high school principal and junior college dean. The high school and the junior college ran simultaneously inside the same structure.

The building itself was beautiful.

D.L., and everyone else, fondly referred to her as "Old Main." She was an immense, multi-gabled, impressive yellowish-brick school building at the southwest corner of Cass Avenue and Warren in the Cass Corridor area of Detroit. By 1894 standards, when construction began on the high school that would become Old Main, it was a massive structure complete with every convenience a school building could have—almost. It was built as a citadel of academics, not athletics. As a result, it was built with no athletic facilities whatsoever; no gymnasium, no locker rooms, no natatorium, no gridiron, no track, nothing.

The architectural firm Malcomson & Higginbotham designed the large three-story building, which, prior to several additions, occupied almost half a city block. The building looked much larger than three stories, as the lower level had outside windows and was about a half story above the ground. The lower level also did not use the same yellow brick. Instead, it used large gray rough-hewn blocks that gave it the feel of a medieval castle. The design had the gray blocks rising above each entrance to the building, as if the drawbridge over the moat was lowered to welcome you inside. The roofline was built containing high peaks and steep slopes, adding to the impressively large look and feel. The most recognizable feature was a four-faced clock tower soaring upward an additional three stories above the center entrance on the Cass Avenue side of the school. Four huge ornamental cupolas with massive spiked tops graced the roof to the sides of the clock tower, adding to the castle-like aura. The style was known as Romanesque Revival. The original T-shaped building had 103 rooms and could educate 1,600 students. The auditorium was large, holding 2,000. The floors were maple and the doors oak, the drinking fountains surrounded in individually handcrafted Pewabic tile. It was an impressive school for its era, and now, in 1917, it was still an architectural gem.

Old Main was called Central High School when it opened in 1896. Principal David Mackenzie instituted high academic standards, and Central High quickly became known as one of the top high schools in Detroit. In 1908, an addition including boy's and girl's gymnasiums and science laboratories was completed. Old Main's footprint eventually grew to almost an entire city block.

All of the additions happened before D.L. arrived. While having the gyms was certainly better than not having any, it wasn't the athletic facility D.L. had in his dreams. Both gyms were small, even for its original intent when the building was Central High School.

The facilities would have to do. They were all D.L. had. Mackenzie had promised when he recruited D.L. that he would be able to take the athletic program to great places, and the facilities would grow with him. D.L. couldn't wait for that to happen.

In the interim, D.L. hung mats against the walls so sprinters and hurdlers could end their runs strong—and crash into the padded wall. Mats were full of hay or straw, and not entirely better than crashing into the cinder block wall itself. Pole-vaulters, when D.L. was lucky enough to have one or two, ran down the hallways through two sets of double doors and then turned left, traveling down the length of the gymnasium before they vaulted—landing on two or three of those same unforgiving straw mats piled below.

Then there was the indoor track. The boy's gymnasium had an elevated track that required twenty-two laps for a mile. The gymnasium was small, so the turns were tight. The corners were pitched like a velodrome, and the running surface was slick. As poor a track as it was, it was D.L.'s best facility. He loved hosting indoor track meets there. His athletes always had an advantage because they knew how to run the track.

In 1919, two years after D.L. and Hazel were married, they had a daughter, Jean. Thirteen years passed before they added another child to the family, David L. Holmes Jr. Somewhat remarkably, David L. Holmes, the coach, and David L. Holmes Jr., the son, shared the same August 28 birthday.

The Holmes family lived in a modest, but very nice, brick home on Faust. It was in the Rosedale Park area of Detroit, near Southfield Road and Grand River Avenue. Every Wayne track athlete was in that house at one time or another.

Everyone was welcome at their home on Faust: Black, white, Jewish, Catholic, Serbian, Finnish, All-American athlete, or the athlete who never scored a point. Everyone was respected; everyone valued; everyone included. Other than being Detroiters, which was a strong bond, they shared a bond of their station in life. Almost everyone was poor, including D.L., who was always trying to market a new track innovation to make an extra buck. Few, if any, ever had plans to attend college until they met the coach.

Every summer D.L. and Hazel threw a celebration party for the track athletes. A "United Nations" of college boys would descend on the home on Faust. It was not a scene regularly occurring in this normally white area of the city. But everyone knew Coach Holmes and his boys and welcomed them to the neighborhood, many neighbors shouting "Go Tartars"—the strangely named Wayne mascot—as they walked to the house from where they had parked.

D.L. and Hazel embraced each and every one of them as they arrived.

D.L.'s son always watched this procession intently.

When D.L. noticed his son's amazement, he bent down and whispered in his ear. "Son, we're all different somehow. Some people can run fast, some people can sing well, some people are taller and some shorter. None of those differences make people better. No religion, no nationality, no level of wealth, no skin color is better or worse than any other. We judge people on their character. Always be a person of great character. Always do the right thing and always treat other people the way you would want to be treated."

D.L.'s son just smiled. He had heard that same thing from his dad many, many times.

There were always some alumni who came to the party. A few were from Detroit Junior College and a few more from the College of the City of Detroit. Most were from Wayne University, which is what it was called after 1934. The stories often turned to the lack of money and lack of facilities.

For a serious athlete of any kind, Wayne was hardly the school to attend. Its football players practiced on an unkempt field and played home games on borrowed fields. Its tennis team worked out on a high school court three miles from Old Main, and the swimming teams trained in high school pools. Its basketball teams played home games on high school courts and in armories. And indoor track meets were held in the hallway.

Despite all of these challenges, D.L. still produced great teams and great athletes.

He remembered back to his first meeting with Mackenzie as he was being recruited to Detroit Junior College. Yes, he would be the director of all athletics. Yes, he would personally coach football, basketball, and track. Yes, his salary would be considerably improved over what he made at DePauw University.

The most attractive carrot offered in the recruiting package, however, was what Mackenzie said about Michigan.

"I hear you're a fisherman," Mackenzie said. "In Michigan, you're never more than six miles from water. We have sixty-five thousand bodies of water ranging from ponds to four of the Great Lakes. You'll catch pike, muskie, salmon, trout, bass, perch, sturgeon, catfish, and more. You could go fishing someplace different every single day for the next fifty years and not come close to fishing all the possibilities in Michigan."

A twinkle appeared in D.L.'s eyes and a big smile came across his face.

"This sounds like a great opportunity, sir," D.L. told Mackenzie. "I accept your offer."

Mackenzie quickly stood and with great excitement extended his hand.

"Coach Holmes, welcome to Detroit!"

The Holmes family in about 1903. Standing: O.W., Earl, Pearl, and D.L. Seated: D.A. Holmes (D.L.'s father), Carl, Neta, and Lura (D.L.'s mother). Photo credit: Jean Holmes Wunderlich Estate.

D.L. practicing long jump, 1904, in a field in Stillwater, Oklahoma. Photo credit: Jean Holmes Wunderlich Estate.

CLARK - HOLMES - WRIGHT - WOOD
June 1907

1907 Oklahoma A&M mile relay team. Recorded a time of 3:28.4 on a dirt track. D.L. Holmes second from left. Photo credit: Jean Holmes Wunderlich Estate.

D.L. in his room at the Harley Hotel where he stayed while working in Russellville, Kentucky. 1909. Photo credit: Jean Holmes Wunderlich Estate.

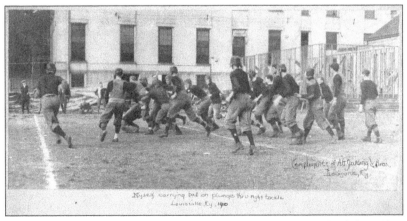

D.L. coaching and playing football in Louisville, Kentucky, 1910. Photo credit: A.G. Spalding & Bros., Louisville, Kentucky.

The Bethel College football team went undefeated in 1911. That's D.L. standing in back on the far left, dressed to play. Photo credit: Jean Holmes Wunderlich Estate.

D.L. enjoying a ride in the wagon in Oklahoma Territory, 1911. Photo credit: Jean Holmes Wunderlich Estate.

D.L. riding his horse, Laddie, in 1913. Photo credit: Jean Holmes Wunderlich Estate.

Always the fisherman, D.L. returned to Stillwater to visit his parents in 1913 and couldn't resist trying to catch some fish. Photo credit: Jean Holmes Wunderlich Estate.

D.L.'s 1916 Cass Tech basketball team. This team won the Detroit City Basketball Championship that year. Photo credit: Jean Holmes Wunderlich Estate.

D.L. and Hazel on Belle Isle in the spring of 1917 before they were married on June 16, 1917. Photo credit: Jean Holmes Wunderlich Estate.

11

HITLER'S OLYMPICS

Interview with Allan Tolmich, Class of 1941
Interviewed by Professor David L. Holmes Jr.

April 18, 2003

Professor David L. Holmes Jr.: Hello, Allan. I'm very excited to talk to you today about your days in track at Wayne. Thank you for agreeing to meet with me. You may have been one of the least likely people to be successful in track, especially hurdles, and yet you were a world record holder, held ten national indoor track records, were a four-time national AAU champion, and were an All-American. Incredible! I know your background, but for the benefit of this tape recording, can you give us some background on how you ended up running track at Wayne?

Allan Tolmich: Right, right! When you say "least likely," I assume you're talking about my height. I'm 5'10". Well, I was 5'10" in college. I've probably shrunk some since then. [*laughter*] That was considered too short for hurdles. Forrest Towns, who held the world record in the high hurdles when I competed, was 6'2". Prior to Forrest, Percy Beard held the world record and he was 6'5". Most coaches thought there was a perfect height for hurdles, which allowed the athlete to glide over the hurdles, not jump them. Not me. I jumped them.

Professor: Yes, too short for hurdles. You started at Wayne in 1934, so you had another disadvantage, too. You were Jewish.

Tolmich: I still am Jewish. [*laughs*] But, exactly, it wasn't just Hitler that didn't like Jews. Anti-Semitism was rampant. There was a lot of discrimination. I wouldn't have been able to be on most track teams. But Coach Holmes didn't care and Wayne didn't care. He just wanted me to be fast.

Professor: In one of my interviews with Keith McClellan, writer of the great book about the early track days in Michigan, he told me about a conversation he had with a track team member from the 1920s, who described Coach Holmes as:

One of the greatest motivators of young men of all time. There's no question in my mind. His sincerity, his belief in people, his willingness to accept people regardless of their ethnic or racial background. He accepted people from Eastern Europe when they were considered scum. He accepted them in the 1920s! He accepted African Americans when it was unheard of. He accepted Jews when the city and state governments were rife with anti-Semitism. Fielding Yost in his whole career at U of M never allowed an African American to try out for a team he coached. His father had been a Confederate general. He didn't like Roman Catholics. He single-handedly kept Notre Dame out of the Big 10. But Coach Holmes had Jews, Eastern Europeans, African Americans, Catholics on his teams in the 1920s. He worked with them, he respected them. Other people did not. They would rather have no team.

Tolmich: Coach Holmes was incredible. He accepted everyone, regardless. You know, though, I didn't see myself as the Jewish team member. I don't know that anyone saw themselves as a representative of some class of people. We were pretty much all poor. We had that in common.

Professor: And the track program was poor. So, everyone did what they could with what little they had.

Tolmich: Oh, boy, was the track program poor. No money, no facilities, no buses for meets, nothing. But I wouldn't have had it any other way.

Professor: There are two different stories about how you ended up on the Wayne track team. One story has you "discovered" by Coach Holmes as you were playing tennis. The other has you just showing up for practice. Which one is correct?

Tolmich: It's somewhere in between. I was on the tennis team and track team in high school.

Professor: Central High School?

Tolmich: Yes, Central. But the "new" Central, not the one at Old Main.

In fact, Tolmich was a product of the entire Detroit Public Schools system. He attended Custer Elementary School for grades 1–8, then Durfee Intermediate for grade 9, and Central High School for grades 10–12.

Allan was born on March 30, 1918, in Detroit to a family originally from New York. His parents, Morris and Dora Tolmich, immigrated to New York from Serbia, though his father was originally from Russia. They raised three children in New York and had Allan after they came to Detroit, attracted to the city because good-paying jobs were more plentiful there.

Tolmich: I did well academically, so I was promoted to senior status when I was sixteen years old. That wasn't good for me athletically, because I was competing against people a year or two older than me. That made a big difference. It hurt me in track especially. In order to get a varsity letter, you had to earn ten points in meets over the entire season. I earned my first track letter with the bare minimum: ten points. My senior year I earned a varsity letter with eleven points! So, I was not an overachiever in track in high school. Tennis was my sport. I loved tennis, and the age difference didn't make as big of a difference for me. I was fast and that helped me in both sports.

Professor: Were you a hurdler in high school?

Tolmich: Yes, oh yes. Very much so. Not a good one, but I was a hurdler. I ran the high hurdles in the Detroit City finals and finished last! [*laughs*]

Professor: Well, you made up for that at Wayne. So, back to how Coach Holmes found out about you.

Tolmich: Oh, right, right. Yes, well, so I was playing tennis and running track in high school, so that's what I did in college; simple as that. Coach Holmes didn't find me playing tennis and recruit me, but boy did he ever find me on the track team! He was very analytical. He watched films of the greatest track athletes and studied their form. He would then train his athletes to copy that winning form. Apparently, he saw something in the way I ran that made him think I could easily adapt to some of those championship forms. It worked, and we both had a lot of fun with it.

Professor: I want to hear more about your training and his coaching, but I'll come back to it later. First, let's explore your success a bit. You were so good at high hurdles that a newspaper article said you were destined for the 1940 Olympics. What happened?

Tolmich: Hitler happened. World War II happened. The 1940 Olympics were canceled because of the war. Originally, the games were scheduled to be held in Tokyo, Japan. Well, obviously, with Pearl Harbor, the United States wasn't going to stand for that. Same for other European countries. The location was changed to Helsinki, Finland. Ultimately though, due to the war, the entire Olympic games were canceled. And not just for 1940. They were canceled for 1944, too. That effectively wiped out any of my Olympic chances.

Professor: That's so unfortunate. I'm sure we'd be talking about your Olympic records and gold medals right now.

Tolmich: Ah, who knows? Hard to say. Lots can happen during competition. If you remember, at the 1936 Olympics it was over one hundred degrees. That changes people and their abilities.

Professor: Nineteen thirty-six: the Jesse Owens Olympics.

Tolmich: Four gold medals, exactly. In 1936 it was very controversial to have African Americans or Jews on your team. A large number of Jewish athletes boycotted the games. Those Olympics were held in Berlin, and under intense international pressure Hitler had to remove anti-Semitic propaganda posters and banners from the streets. It was an incredibly difficult time to be a Jew.

Professor: Terrible, terrible time in the history of the world.

Tolmich: There were only two Jewish athletes remaining on the US track team in 1936: Marty Glickman and Sam Stoller. The day of their 400-meter relay they were told they weren't running. They were replaced by Jesse Owens and Ralph Metcalf. Now, it's hard to argue with the qualifications of Owens and Metcalf, but why were the only two Jewish athletes pulled? Did Hitler exert some power over the US team management? No one knows.

Professor: I have read about that controversy. A terrible decision for both those young men. Speaking of Jesse Owens, did I read that you beat him in a race?

Tolmich: [*laughs*] You may have read it, but it wasn't true! Me beat Jesse Owens? No. But, I was in a race with him. In the 1936 Penn Relays I ran the 100-yard dash against him. Jesse came in first with a new Penn Relay record, Sam Stoller—the same Sam Stoller I just mentioned with the Olympic debacle—was second, and I was third.

Professor: Still very impressive.

Tolmich: Thanks. The two of them were a good yard ahead of me, which is a lot in a 100. But I had a real good view of Jesse setting a new Penn Relay record. [*laughs*]

Professor: Did you experience any anti-Semitism at the Penn Relays?

Tolmich: No. None that I can remember. You know, athletes are a self-centered bunch. Nothing is as self-centered as an athlete in an individual sport while competing. No one is thinking about, or talking about, religion or race. They're just thinking about winning.

Professor: During your time at Wayne, and also after your graduation, you had some incredible experiences as a member of the AAU All-American track team. Tell me about those experiences.

Tolmich: In the summer of 1937—I graduated in 1938—I went to Japan as part of the AAU team. I ran in Tokyo, Nagoya, Osaka, and Niigata.

I also competed in the Pan-American Games hosted by the Texas State Fair.

Professor: You were an AAU champion.

Tolmich: The AAU competition was good to me. I was AAU national champion in the 60-yard high hurdles in 1939, 1940, and 1941, and set a world record in that event in 1941.

Professor: Which, if I remember correctly, broke the old world record you set in 1940.

Tolmich: Correct. Those were difficult times in the world. In the summer of 1938, most of Europe was armed for war, yet I was competing with the AAU in England, Scotland, Germany, Switzerland, and Italy. In all the countries, our American team was running against the best team from the host nation. It was essentially Olympic competition one country at a time. I remember the Germans being on their best behavior toward American athletes. There was no denying us, as we were walking around in sweaters with huge USA letters on them. When I was in the States, I trained back at Wayne. The AAU paid for me to attend numerous events from 1939 to 1941. I traveled over six thousand miles to compete during those years. I competed from Boston to Toronto to Dallas to the West Coast.

Shortly after the bombing of Pearl Harbor, Tolmich enlisted in the Army Air Corps. In 1946, he was discharged as a captain. His subsequent career was in business, first in sporting goods and then in apparel. He retired as vice president and national sales manager of the Glazier Corporation in Chicago. After retirement, he and his wife moved to Indianapolis, Indiana.

During his track career, news columnists called Allan Tolmich "the Wayne whippet," a "track idol," "the greatest all-around athlete ever developed in Detroit," "the brilliant Wayne University hurdler and dash man," and, somewhat inaccurately, "the one-man track team from Wayne." One sportswriter termed him "the smallest hurdler ever to achieve greatness." Coach Holmes declared that "no man in sports ever reached the top against the odds that Tolmich has faced." Not only at dual meets but also at national meets, every athlete knew who Allan Tolmich was. One administrator at Wayne reported that no one at a national meeting he attended knew where Wayne University (which had only recently changed its name from City College of Detroit) was, but many of them knew that Allan Tolmich was on its track team.

Tolmich established ten and tied five national track and field records as an undergraduate and, following graduation, as an unattached amateur. Since he competed in short-distance events, the records he broke were already near the irreducible minimum. As a junior at Wayne, he entered twenty-seven events and achieved twenty-seven firsts in dual meets.

At another meet he broke the world record for the 220-meter hurdles twice, first in the trials and then again in the finals. In all, Tolmich won twenty-three firsts, two seconds, and one third in events in 1938. During one season he broke or tied hurdles records eleven times. One of Tolmich's greatest feats was winning both the NCAA and the AAU championships in the low hurdles in 1937.

The achievements of Allan Tolmich are even more remarkable when one realizes that sprints and hurdles come at roughly the same time at meets. Most athletes did one event or the other and rested after their event. Tolmich, however, competed almost simultaneously in both events. The races were so close together that he rarely had time to put on his sweat suit between races. At the Armour Relays in Chicago in 1936, Tolmich captured three first places in less than twenty-five minutes. At the 1937 Michigan Intercollegiate Championships, he did the same thing. While running at the Butler Relays in Indianapolis, he broke one world record and tied another. At every school where Wayne competed, he established new gymnasium, fieldhouse, or outdoor records.

Tolmich competed at a time when track was second in popularity only to football, and he did it extraordinarily well. What made his accomplishments even more incredible was the condition of the facilities in which he practiced.

> **Professor:** I have a quote from you about your track training facilities. It reads, "[Wayne had] a little gym with a tiny track—the worst track I ever ran on." Just how bad were the track facilities back them?
>
> **Tolmich:** [*laughs*] Well, you know, I had the advantage of running at other locations across the United States and the world. I always came back to Wayne to train. But the contrast in facilities was huge. It was very obvious Wayne had no budget at all for track or for track infrastructure. It took twenty-two laps to make a mile on the inside track. *Twenty-two laps!* That's just crazy. On the other hand, at least one of the facility problems helped propel me into the hurdler I became.
>
> **Professor:** What was that?

12

SPRINTING WITH OBSTACLES

Indoor Track Practice at Old Main

February 25, 1937

D.L. looked at his watch; 8:30 p.m. The last class at Wayne ended at 9:30 p.m., and more of his runners would arrive at any time. Others had jobs and were working and wouldn't arrive until later, or possibly not at all. Practice often went until 11:30 p.m. as various track men came and went throughout the evening. Tonight, they were lucky. They had the gym. That meant he could work with some of the athletes inside the gym before 9:30 if they didn't have a late class.

More often than not, D.L. used the college hallways for sprint and hurdle practice. He had no indoor athletic facility. The boy's gym was small, originally built as a high school facility. Its antiquated twenty-two-laps-per-mile elevated track was the only true indoor amenity dedicated to track and field. It would have to do. It was February, so there was no hope of consistent outside practice for two months to come.

Allan Tolmich would be there any minute. He was always one of the first to arrive. D.L. had a hurdle set up for him in the gym. He had several others against the wall in the hallways, waiting for the last class to be over and the hallways to be cleared. Due to the size of the gymnasium, Tolmich trained on hurdles during the indoor season by jumping one hurdle over and over. When the hallways cleared about 9:45 p.m., the sprinters and hurdlers could run the long corridors of Old Main. D.L. would set up five hurdles down the corridor. Tolmich would try and squeeze in some five-hurdle practice on a waxed maple floor in the hallway wearing tennis shoes instead of spikes. But he had to share the hallway with sprinters wanting the same available distance and pole-vaulters coming from the other direction into the gym.

D.L. paid special attention to Tolmich. This should be his best year yet. During his sophomore year, in eleven track meets Tolmich won fifteen first places, three seconds, and six thirds. Along with fellow sophomores Stan Mullins, Dwight Brooks, and Bruce Lawton, Tolmich surprised everyone at the Penn Relays by winning the mile relay with a 60-yard gap between them and second place. At the 1936 state championship meet in Michigan, Tolmich won not only the high and low hurdles but also the 100- and 220-yard dashes.

Everything was coming together for a spectacular junior year. If circumstances lined up correctly, Tolmich would be in a race with world record holder and 1936 Olympic gold medal winner Forrest "Spec" Towns. The nickname "Spec" was not a result of wearing spectacles, as one might expect, but for the freckles on his face. Towns and Tolmich would meet in July at the AAU Championship Track Meet in Milwaukee. That was four months away but seemed like tomorrow. Many things needed to happen between now and then.

First at hand, the Central Intercollegiate Conference Indoor Track Meet was taking place at Notre Dame in two weeks, and Tolmich was entered in three events. First things first. D.L. needed to get Tolmich and his other athletes ready for that track meet.

Preparation for indoor meets was especially difficult at Wayne. Even the five-hurdle hallway was half the number of hurdles Tolmich normally jumped in competition. Only the 65-yard high hurdles could truly be practiced inside Old Main. For sprinters, 100 yards down the hallway was the longest dash they'd ever practice before running over twice that length in a meet. Quarter-milers had to use the elevated track and put in 440 yards of circles when, depending on the track where they competed, the event might have only one turn.

The switch from the indoor track season to the outdoor track season often took place at the Penn Relays in April. Track men from other universities typically took weeks to adjust between running on an indoor surface and running on the cinder outdoor track surface. That was not a luxury afforded at Wayne. Athletes went directly from practicing in a hallway to competing on an outdoor track. The record spoke for itself, as Wayne almost always did well in Philadelphia.

D.L. had no time to concern himself with his minimal track facilities. Instead, he worked with Tolmich on speed. If he was ever going to beat Forrest Towns, he would have to be at least a 9.7-second 100-yard dash sprinter. That had been the goal the previous two years, and Tolmich was getting close.

D.L. knew that Tolmich was at a disadvantage being only 5'10" tall. Taller hurdlers, like Towns, who was 6'2" tall, simply slid right over the sticks. At

5'10" tall, Tolmich was jumping them. Sprinting to that first hurdle as fast as possible was D.L.'s objective for him. Hurdling was secondary.

It was 8:45 p.m. when D.L. saw Tolmich coming down the hallway. D.L. followed him into the locker room and went through everything he wanted to accomplish that night.

"We're going to work on getting you to that first hurdle faster than anyone else," said D.L. "Then, your three steps between hurdles are going to be faster than anyone else's."

"Right, and if I can get into the hallway maybe I can try the second hurdle for a change," said Tolmich, chuckling, with a lightness to his voice. He had heard all of this preparatory talk many times before. D.L. was nothing if not obsessively consistent. Tolmich was a sprinter, and those hurdles were just obstacles in the way of his run. He was sprinting with obstacles.

It wasn't easy getting to that first hurdle at full speed. Most other runners were concentrating on style, making sure they hit the sticks with the correct foot and stride. Going full speed into the first hurdle could throw off your stride for the entire race. The gym at Old Main was so small that getting to that first hurdle was about all Tolmich ever practiced. And as a result, he was good at it.

"Concentrate on balance in your landing," explained D.L., "in order to be able to get in those three fast steps after the first hurdle. All I want you to think about is that 'One! Two! Three!' Count them out as fast as you can count and try to make your legs work in rhythm with the count."

That first hurdle was repeated over and over and over. The result was that Tolmich began sprinting very fast to the first hurdle and stepping perfectly between hurdles. Some hurdlers saved their real speed for the last four hurdles so they could concentrate on stride length and creating the perfect rhythm leading up to them. For an athlete who didn't glide over the hurdles, the jump slowed down the process. To make up for it, Tolmich had to speed up every other part of the hurdling process.

D.L. and Tolmich practiced the first hurdle in the gym dozens of times before D.L. looked at his watch: 9:45 p.m. He could move the team out into the hallways of Old Main.

The conditions were not ideal, and D.L. knew it all too well. He had been promised better athletic facilities when he interviewed for the job with David Mackenzie over twenty years before. Unfortunately, Mackenzie had died in 1926, and it seemed the promise of better facilities died with him.

"Coach?" asked Tolmich. D.L. had been lost in his thoughts about the poor facilities and what his teams could have been like if he only had an indoor fieldhouse.

"Sorry. Just thinking about something. Let's get the rest of these hurdles set up and get to work," said D.L., shaking thoughts of what could have been from his head. "You've got South Bend in two weeks."

The same conversations, the same one-hurdle setup, the same "One, Two, Three, One, Two, Three," the same 9:45 p.m. move to the hallway occurred with ritualistic consistency night after night.

D.L. was convinced there was no other hurdler in the world getting to the first hurdle faster than Tolmich. He would find out if that was true in South Bend, Indiana.

No one anticipated what would happen on the journey there.

The drive from Wayne University to the University of Notre Dame took almost five hours. Tolmich had so much knee pain before they left that D.L. suggested he not attend the meet. Tolmich wouldn't hear of it. There was no way he wasn't going to compete in the Central Intercollegiate Conference Indoor Track Meet, even with all the pain. He was suffering from some sort of blood poisoning in his right knee. Quite a bit of fluid had built up under the skin, and it was putting painful pressure on his kneecap. D.L. pulled the car over and stopped at a gas station. Tolmich wanted the pressure relieved, so D.L. sterilized his pocket knife over the flame of a match and cut into the skin to release the fluid. The poison drained out.

They had no proper medical supplies and could only get a clean towel from the gas station attendant to stop the bleeding. Upon arrival at Notre Dame, D.L. asked for the medical staff to come examine Tolmich.

When they arrived, he was gone. Vanished.

Tolmich did not want a doctor looking at him, for fear the doctor would say he wasn't fit for competition. He went into hiding and only came out right before his first qualifying heat.

If his knee was bothering him during the two-day competition, no one knew it, and especially not his competitors. In the 65-yard low hurdles, Tolmich ran 7 seconds flat, setting a new American indoor record—and beating the previous record of 7.1 seconds he had set in the preliminaries the day before. He also won the 60-yard dash in 6.3 seconds and the 60-yard high hurdles in 7.5 seconds, tying the meet and field record. Wayne took third place out of sixteen teams, with Tolmich earning fifteen of Wayne's twenty-three points.

Back in Detroit, Tolmich had his knee examined by a doctor. It was healing nicely, and the doctor gave praise to D.L.'s roadside surgery. Tolmich didn't even miss a practice.

Overcoming his painful blood poisoning was one challenge, but an even greater challenge lay ahead of him. Looming a few months in the future, he would be meeting Forrest Towns in Milwaukee.

D.L. wasn't thinking about Towns right now. He had more pressing concerns.

There was the indoor season to complete and an outdoor season to begin. Many different dual meets and then track and field championship meets almost every weekend. It was a busy season, and with the success of Tolmich, it would be a fruitful one.

Prior to the fateful matchup with Towns in July, Tolmich racked up twenty-seven firsts his junior year for a total of 135 points in dual meets. He set state records and meet records wherever he went. He had a total of 205¼ points for the year.

A newspaper reporter asked D.L. about Tolmich and he said, "He is the most outstanding prospect ever to come under my wing."

The outdoor track season was over; over, except for the National AAU Track and Field Championship meet in Milwaukee, Wisconsin.

Wayne's track team almost always did well in invitational relays and in certain individual events at the National AAU championships. Wayne teams earned enough success to become a member of the Central Collegiate Conference, a sixteen-school conference of independent track powers. Started by Knute Rockne of Notre Dame and Ralph Young of Michigan State, the league allowed peer schools to compete in track and field. It also awarded the conference certification that would make winners eligible to compete in the annual NCAA outdoor championships. Despite Wayne University's lack of facilities, it had a national reputation in track.

Some of that reputation was earned through results. Wayne's track program had already produced two Olympians and several national champions. At the Penn Relays, Wayne's mile relay team finished first six years in a row from 1926 to 1931. The track program didn't go downhill in 1931. It was the Great Depression and the track program ran out of money and could not send a team to Philadelphia for several years. In both 1926 and 1927, the National Collegiate Athletic Association (NCAA) national champion in low hurdles, Ed Spence, was a Wayne track man. Wayne was respected in track circles across the United States.

Although he would deny it if given a chance, another piece of Wayne's national reputation was D.L. Holmes. In the first half of the twentieth century, the United States had a corps of noted track coaches. California coaches tended to head the list. The state's weather, facilities, money, and feeder high schools often produced track superiority. Dink Templeton at Stanford and Brutus Hamilton at Berkeley were noted, but the most recognized coach in American track was the politically and racially conservative Dean Cromwell of the University of Southern California, who was once called one of the top coaches of all time. In the Midwest, Earle Hayes of Indiana, Charles Hoyt of Michigan, and Lloyd Olds of Eastern Michigan had fieldhouses, money, boosters, and excellent track teams.

D.L. clearly belonged in this group. Viewed as gifted by other coaches and held in high esteem by his athletes, D.L. had been an outstanding track man himself. His study of the winning form of Olympic athletes was noted by track coaches across the country. His "Movies on Paper" book of the 1932 Olympic Games was flourishing right about the time Allan Tolmich came to Wayne. In 1936, D.L. patented his first starting block, the design of which was a large improvement over the rudimentary early blocks.

Although most of his contemporaries fielded teams composed almost entirely of White Anglo-Saxon Protestants (WASPs). D.L.'s track teams included Jewish, Catholic, Eastern European, and Black athletes. D.L. worked with the men he had, and he respected them deeply. Most other coaches of the time did not. D.L. was a motivator of young men. The devotion he felt toward his athletes was returned as intense devotion toward him.

There was no athlete more devoted than Allan Tolmich.

Although he was a gifted athlete on his own genetic ability, he knew he was better because of the coaching he received from D.L. He would have to be great today. The time they had been preparing for all season had now come.

Today was the day for which D.L. and Tolmich had spent countless hours in Old Main working on speed, step counts, and hurdles. Today Allan Tolmich would race Forrest Towns.

Towns was nothing short of a phenomenon. His best race, undoubtably, was the 110-meter high hurdles. In 1936 alone, he beat his previous world record of 14.2 seconds ten times. In Oslo, Norway, he blew through that world record with a time of 13.7 seconds. Towns had a winning streak of fifty-seven wins that included the NCAA Championships in 1937, where he became the event's first two-time winner.

Towns had not lost a race in two years.

Towns could not be taken lightly, and Tolmich knew it. However, when Tolmich set the new American indoor record for the 65-yard low hurdles, he took the title away from Forrest Towns.

Towns, a senior at the University of Georgia, was one year ahead of Tolmich. This year would be his last in intercollegiate competition. With fifty-seven consecutive wins under his belt, he had nothing to fear from Tolmich. He had an Olympic gold medal and a world record. He had heard about Tolmich breaking his 65-yard low hurdle record, but this was a kid from an unknown college in Detroit. In two years, no one had been able to beat Towns in any race he ran. He was looking forward to competing with Tolmich.

Having another fast hurdler to beat just might produce another world record for him.

It was eighty-nine degrees that day in Milwaukee. The humidity was high but the sky was mostly clouds and it was windy, helping to temper the heat. Even without the sun, ground level inside Marquette University's football stadium was very hot. Runners in some of the long-distance events were collapsing and vomiting on the sidelines. Twelve thousand spectators were on hand for the track meet.

One of the big matchups of the meet was the 1,500-meter run, also known as the metric mile. The competition between Glenn Cunningham and Archie San Romani was billed as the event of the day. Cunningham and San Romani were both from Kansas and had exchanged first and second places throughout the season's competition. This race was not only about bragging rights but an important back-to-back win precedent to set at the National AAU Championship Meet.

The Cunningham story drew at the heartstrings of track fans worldwide. He was the world record holder in the mile at 4:06.8, which he set in 1934. San Romani's best mile was 4:07.2 at Princeton earlier in 1937. At the 1936 Olympics in Berlin, Cunningham brought home the silver medal for America in the 1,500 meters, coming in second to Jack Lovelock of New Zealand by just 0.6 seconds. His time of 3:48.4 beat the Olympic record. But Lovelock beat the Olympic record by an additional 0.6 seconds in the same race.

He was interviewed by the press after the competition and asked about his disappointment coming in second. Cunningham said, "I ran a fast race and broke the Olympic record for the 1,500 meters, and only one person in the world ran faster."

Cunningham's story began in 1917, when he was a young boy, and his brother mistook gasoline for kerosene while getting a fire started in the fireplace of their school. It resulted in a large explosion and fire. The fire burned down the schoolhouse, and his brother, Floyd, died due to the burns he received in the accident. Glenn Cunningham was seven years old, and all the flesh on the front of his legs from the knees down was burned. Doctors were not optimistic. They told his parents that he would be an invalid and never be able to walk correctly, and possibly not be able to walk at all. If the burns became infected, his legs would have to be amputated.

Cunningham spent over a year recuperating inside his parents' home before he was able to go outside. It was more than six months before he could bear any weight on his legs. He had to learn to walk and run all over again.

Now here he was in Milwaukee, Wisconsin, competing in a national track championship as a world record holder and Olympic medal winner.

The story of Archie San Romani bore an uncanny similarity to that of Cunningham. San Romani was run over by a truck when he was eight years old, and his right leg was crushed. He wasn't expected to ever walk again. After he regained his ability to walk, he began running as rehabilitation for his leg.

His first significant win was the mile run at the 1935 NCAA Championships. A week later, he was beaten by Cunningham at the national championship meet at Princeton. When the time came for the 1936 Olympic Trials in the 1,500-meter race, San Romani was in front of Cunningham into the final 300 meters. Cunningham made his move, and the two of them battled for first place all the way to the finish line. Both hit the tape with a time of 3:49.9, but the finish line judges gave the win to Cunningham.

At the 1936 NCAA Championships, San Romani broke the collegiate record for the 1,500 meters, a record that had been held by Cunningham. At the 1936 Olympics, San Romani came in fourth, two places behind Cunningham and three spots behind Lovelock. Later that year, San Romani beat both Lovelock and Cunningham at the Princeton Invitational.

San Romani came to Milwaukee as the American indoor champion in the mile and the winner of the 1937 Princeton Invitational Mile. He had also set the world record for the 2,000-meter run in 1937 in Helsinki.

In twenty-eight races against each other leading up to today's AAU Championship, Cunningham had won fourteen and San Romani won fourteen. Today would be the tiebreaker.

There was little wonder why the Cunningham–San Romani matchup was getting so much attention. This was a grudge match, and twelve thousand people knew it was going to be an incredible race.

The loudspeaker announced the 1,500-meter final was about to begin. They introduced the runners.

"Ladies and gentlemen, please direct your attention to the track for the introduction of runners in the 1,500-meter race. The reigning AAU champion in this event, Glenn Cunningham." The crowd roared with appreciation. Cunningham waved to the crowd to thank them for the ovation. The announcer introduced Jim Smith from Indiana and Charles Fenske from Wisconsin.

"Ladies and gentlemen, the reigning indoor champion in the 1,500-meter race, Archie San Romani." Another huge round of applause thundered from the crowd. The anticipation of the race between San Romani and Cunningham added an additional level of excitement to the air. The crowd was so raucous it was difficult to hear the introduction of Gene Venzke from the University of Pennsylvania. Venzke did not get the attention given Cunningham and San Romani, yet he had also qualified for the 1,500-meter finals in the 1936 Olympic Trials, but pulled a muscle and did not make it to the

Olympics. Venzke had beaten Cunningham in the 1,500 meters in 1936 and simultaneously set a new world record in the event. He was just as much a serious contender to win this race as Cunningham and San Romani.

The starter's pistol went off, and the race began with a flash of speed from all of the runners. At the point where runners could leave their lane and go to the inside lane, it was San Romani in front with Cunningham immediately behind him. For the first two laps all five runners ran virtually together in one pack. By the third lap, three runners had dropped back a few meters while San Romani kept the pace and the lead. Cunningham was one step behind him, allowing San Romani to do the work of setting the pace.

With 300 meters remaining, Cunningham began his kick. San Romani knew this strategy well and matched his effort. With only 200 meters remaining, San Romani had the lead and did not look like he would relinquish it. The crowd of twelve thousand was on their feet. This was turning out to be the exact race everyone expected. Neck and neck to the end. Would Cunningham be able to find the energy and speed to catch San Romani? Would San Romani keep his one-step lead until the end? The anticipation was as high as the volume of the crowd.

At that moment, the unthinkable occurred. San Romani stepped on the inside curb that holds in the cinders, slipped, and tumbled onto the track. In the process, his feet flew up and the spikes of his track shoes caught Cunningham on his left leg, still scarred from the fire that had happened many years before. Cut and bleeding, Cunningham did not fall and finished out the remaining 200 meters strong. He won the 1,500 meters with a time of 3:51.8 seconds.

In the blink of an eye, San Romani watched the runners all pass him. He quickly stood up and became a short-distance sprinter for the remaining 200 meters. He caught Venzke and salvaged a fourth place out of a race it looked like he was going to win.

There was noticeable disappointment in the level of noise coming from the crowd. It wasn't because Cunningham had won. It was because what looked like a memorable finish had been taken away from them. An untimely and unfortunate accident had stolen an exciting finish away from the formerly raucous masses. Twelve thousand people sat in disbelief.

As the times were announced for each runner, track officials were setting up the hurdles for the matchup between Allan Tolmich and Forrest Towns. Given the finish in the 1,500 meters, this race now became the top match of the meet.

The hurdlers were warming up by the start of the 110-meter high hurdles. Fritz Pollard from the University of North Dakota would be in Lane Six.

Tom Moore from the Olympic Athletic Club would line up next to him in Lane Five. Next was Forrest Towns. Preparing for Lane Three was Roy Staley from the Southern California Athletic Association. Allan Tolmich would be in Lane Two. To his left was LeRoy Kirkpatrick from the Southern California Athletic Association. Only Pollard, Towns, and Tolmich were still college students. The other three had aged out and were now being sponsored by an athletic club.

Some of the runners were using starting blocks and some were not. They had been approved for use in 1936 and were being seen in sprint races more often than not in 1937. Because some athletes had been trained for many years with digging starting holes into the cinders, some still preferred that method. D.L. was always one for following the research—often researched by himself—and doing whatever made a runner faster. He liked starting blocks. D.L. had designed his own starting block, and Tolmich would be using one for this race.

In the gym at Old Main, D.L. bolted starting blocks to pieces of plywood and placed the plywood against a wall to offer the resistance necessary for a quick start. It was often more solid than driving the eight-inch spikes into a soft cinder track. Yet, a few months now separated Tolmich from plywood-mounted starts. He had had enough time to get used to starting blocks in cinders prior to coming to the AAU Championships.

The lane assignments had Tolmich and Towns separated by one other hurdler, although each would have sight of the other through their peripheral vision. It was Roy Staley between them. Staley had set the world record for the 120-yard high hurdles in 1935. If Tolmich and Towns couldn't be next to each other, Staley was a good person to have between them. He would definitely push the pace.

The formal introductions of the athletes had begun. Pollard, 1936 Olympic bronze medalist in the 110-meter high hurdles. Moore, tied the world record in the 120-yard high hurdles in 1935. Towns, current world record holder and unbeaten in two years. Staley, world record holder in 1935. Tolmich, unbeaten in twenty-seven starts this year. And Kirkpatrick, who qualified for the Olympic Trials in 1936.

This was the first year the AAU was using the new L-shaped hurdles. This new hurdle design allowed runners to hit the hurdles and not be knocked totally out of the race by the force of the blow. L-shaped hurdles could tilt and even fall over after being hit. The previous T-shaped design was immovable. The new design helped prevent injuries to athletes. From the athlete's perspective, they allowed for more risk to be taken with each hurdle.

Runners were called to the starting position.

"On your marks," said the starter. "Set."

The pistol went off, and the six hurdlers leaped out of the start. This was a race of champions. Tolmich's speed to the first hurdle put him over it first. The height difference in the other hurdlers allowed them to gain on Tolmich over the next few hurdles. It was neck and neck through hurdles six, seven, and eight. By hurdle nine, Tolmich had a slight lead. At hurdle ten, all six hurdlers leaped almost simultaneously. Tolmich had a lead of about one foot. The speed that he and D.L. had worked on over and over came to the forefront. "One, two, three, one, two, three," Tolmich quickly counted in his head.

The final tenths of a second seemed like they were in slow motion. Through his peripheral vision Tolmich could see runners to his right but slightly behind him. It was Staley that was running just behind, and he blocked the view of Towns. Tolmich concentrated on his fastest speed and lunged to the ribbon and felt it hit his chest. Victory!

Allan Tolmich of Wayne University had won the race! The crowd was on its feet. The cheers echoed miles from the stadium. Twelve thousand people had just witnessed history being made.

The AAU had a new national champion in the 110-meter high hurdles.

In a surprise that shocked the entire crowd, Forrest Towns not only had his two-year winning streak broken, he placed third behind Roy Staley. With a strong wind in the face of all the hurdlers, there were no world records set. Tolmich crossed the finish line in 14.5 seconds.

Dancing a modified version of an Irish jig on the grassy inside part of the track in a white shirt, tie, vested suit coat, dress shoes, and hat, with a stopwatch in his hand, was D.L. There was no bigger smile or louder cheer than his. He would wait until the athletes had shaken hands and spoken with each other before congratulating Tolmich. That too-small gym at Old Main had produced another champion.

As the other hurdlers in the race called it a day, Tolmich prepared for the 200-meter low hurdle event, which was coming up in about twenty minutes. The events were so close together that most hurdlers chose one or the other. Not Tolmich. He went on to win that event also, setting a new meet record and becoming AAU national champion in the 200-meter low hurdles.

Allan Tolmich was inducted into the Wayne State Sports Hall of Fame in 1976, the Michigan Jewish Sports Hall of Fame in 1999, and the International Jewish Sports Hall of Fame in 2002.

13

THEY'RE HERE AGAIN

Interview with Irving "Pete" Petross, Class of 1950, and Robert
"Bob" Wingo, Class of 1947
Interviewed by Professor David L. Holmes Jr.

June 7, 1997

Bob Wingo: Here's a letter your dad wrote me. This is in 1945. I wasn't back
in school. I had dropped out and he was on my case. I had to, well, I owe
it to him because he stayed on me until I went back. When I got out of the
service I went back to work at Ford. He got me to come back to Wayne.
[*Wingo reads the letter aloud*]

Dear Bob,

I haven't seen you for a week, don't know whether this is your correct address,
but if not it will reach you anyhow. The veterans are enrolling tomorrow.
I think some have already finished registration. I am hoping you have not
given up coming back. And don't forget that the double meet with State
College is February 16 and the Nationals are February 22 and 23. If you
get into training now, there is no doubt in my mind but that we will have a
pretty good sprint relay team; yourself, Watkins, Berkley and Ford. Also
a new return entry who was on the spring relay team. I have Jackson putting
the shot forty-five feet now and a couple high jumpers going well over six
feet. Let me hear from you. Dick, Harold, etc. are asking about you.

Sincerely,

Coach D.L. Holmes

Robert "Bob" Wingo's tenure at Wayne University was a long one, 1939 to
1947. However, he served in World War II in the middle of it. Prior to his

military service, Wingo was part of the national championship 1,600-meter relay team in 1942. That same year he placed fourth in the national AAU 440-yard dash finals with a blazing time of 47.3. In that same race he defeated the then world record holder in the event, Bob Ufer.

Wingo loved the thought of flying and applied to the Tuskegee pilot training program. While his admission was pending, he drove a truck for the program. His gruesome job was to load and carry away airplanes that had crashed during training. After two such experiences when all those on board the aircraft had been killed, Wingo had second thoughts about becoming a pilot. Instead, he was accepted into a diesel mechanics training program.

After the war, Wingo returned to the track and won four state intercollegiate AAU championships. His younger brother, Leon, would follow in his footsteps and become a member of the Wayne track team. Bob Wingo stayed in sports, working at Mumford High School in Detroit and serving as its track coach.

> **Pete Petross:** See that picture right here?
>
> **Professor David L. Holmes Jr.:** Yes, the Pace-Setter machine! And there you are with Bob Grant.
>
> **Wingo:** Your dad had rigged up this contraption that timed laps. You had to cross the line when the bell rang to know you were on pace. I remember, oh yes! Ohhh, that thing! [*laughs*] Almost killed me.
>
> **Petross:** Especially for a sprinter, because that thing went off so fast.
>
> **Professor:** Well, you were so fast.
>
> **Wingo:** That thing was a killer.
>
> **Petross:** We had some fast guys, but Lorenzo [Wright] was the big show. We were his supporting group. We trained with him. As anyone on a relay team knows, you have to have people running with you. Trained with him. But Lorenzo was probably our most phenomenal guy that I ever ran with.

That was quite a statement coming from Irving (Pete/Irv) Petross. Petross was a sensation himself. He ran on the 1949 Penn 440 relay team from Wayne that took first place with a 41.7. At the same relays, his Wayne relay team took first in the 880 relay with a 1.26.0. Incredible times! He was a state champion in sprints seven times. At thirty-two years old, Petross ran for the Detroit Track Club and recorded a 100-yard dash time of 9.6—eighteen times! His 20.8 in the 220 was a Detroit Track Club record. Petross was principal of Mumford High School in Detroit.

Wingo: And listen to this: my last race, I ran a mile relay up in western Ontario with Leon, my brother, and Lorenzo. That's the only time I ever ran with my brother—we were eight years apart, you know.

Professor: Was it a fast relay team?

Wingo: Oh, yeah! The relay, when I ran with them, it was the only time I ever ran on a half-mile relay. It wasn't 880 yards or 800 meters, it was the half-mile relay. We ran under 1.30. The only time in my life I ran on a half-mile relay team that ran under 1.30. Incredible!

Professor: Indeed, incredible! And on a cinder track, too. What position did you run?

Wingo: Oh, probably second. Lorenzo was usually the anchor.

Professor: Save your fastest guy for the last leg?

Wingo: Yes, right! Hey, Pete. You remember that national meet in '47? It was an AAU meet somewhere in Nebraska. Wayne came in fifth place out of over forty universities, and Lorenzo was the only one there! [*laughs*]

Petross: [*laughing*] Yeah! Wayne sends one guy and he places fifth overall in points! I don't remember everything about that. But I know he beat Ohio State, Penn State, the Naval Academy, Wisconsin, and a bunch of other big schools all on his own!

Wingo: He won the broad jump, came in second in the 100, and second in the 200-yard hurdles and I'm not sure what else. Amazing!

Professor: Wow! Yes, amazing! So, Lorenzo didn't seem to be hurt by the athletic facilities at Wayne. What was the track like when both of you ran?

Wingo: Well, first you had to leave the main building and walk over to Kelsey Field.

Petross: And it wasn't a 440 track. It was a 380.

Wingo: Something like that.

Petross: You get some times . . . like once I remember I think I ran a 39.4. I thought it was a new world record. Forgot it wasn't 440! Well, I thought I'd set a record of some kind until I ran into the coach. Your dad, rest his soul, was always very good at giving you a little extra on times, which is good. It's a good motivator.

Wingo: He was a motivator, all right!

Petross: Yeah, he'd give you a little extra on times. Say you'd run a 49.0, he'd give you a 48.0. And this particular day, the only reason I ran this race was they wanted to take a mile relay team to Penn. Lorenzo was the whole show in the long jump. He won it that year and he won it the next year, too. But, the year prior to that coach says, "Well, I don't want Lorenzo to go there by himself because it's a big town" and etc., etc. So, we somehow made up this mile relay team and we went along with him, by car.

Wingo: Right, by car. Your dad was some driver!

Professor: Well, please tell. The man taught me how to drive and I'm not a very good driver.

Petross: [*laughs*] I remember you well! But, anyway, we got into his car for a long drive to the meet. Your father would stop at a place to eat. He always went in first to see if they were going to accept us, because we were Black; "Negro" at the time. We could tell by the way he came out if the answer was yes or no. If he came out walking briskly, like he used to walk, then he would say, "Fellas, let's get fed" and "we're going in." But if he came out and he'd kind of look, but didn't say anything, he'd just kind of look. He'd get in the car, start up the car, and drive off. And all of us would say, well, I guess we're not eating there!

Wingo: And listen, we're not talking about the middle of Tennessee. We're talking about Ohio or Indiana. Indianapolis! We went to the YMCA in Indianapolis.

Professor: These places turned you away?

Petross: That's right. The Y would take us, or we ended up down in the neighborhoods. The Black neighborhoods.

Professor: Probably in small hotels?

Petross: Yeah, small.

Professor: When you were in Indianapolis, who were you competing against?

Petross: University of Indiana, Butler, Michigan, Pittsburgh. All those schools there.

Professor: I've heard that most schools divided their Black and white athletes and ate or slept different places when they ran into that situation.

Petross: No, no. Coach never did that. We were all together.

Wingo: No, he never did.

Petross: As I was saying earlier, he would walk out briskly wearing his little black suit and you'd say "we're eating today!"

Wingo: And right away and right there! If not, another sixty miles down the road at a truck stop before we could finally eat. We had that experience, too.

Petross: After I came back from the service, Coach made me come back to school. I was running AAU, but couldn't nearly do what I had done. But we went some places and I remember staying in a trailer park once.

One fellow slipped out and tried to get back before Coach found out about it. Every once in a while we'd have a guy on the team who didn't abide by the rules, and we'd have to go out and get him.

Professor: When you went to out-of-state meets, was Wayne recognized? Or was it small potatoes?

Petross: I met Coach Alonzo Stagg once. I went to a track meet in California while I was in the Army. This was 1943, I guess. Coach Holmes sent me stuff to wear. I had Wayne sweatshirts, Wayne shoes, Wayne shorts. He sent it all to me. So, I went out onto the track and I jogged around the track with all this stuff on. Coach Stagg comes up to me and says, "You must be one of Dave Holmes' boys." They were honoring Stagg on that day for some reason. I said, "Yes," and we talked for a few minutes. Stagg said, "When you see your coach, when you see Dave, tell him I said hi." Well, I was inspired that day. I ran pretty good even though I wasn't in good shape. He and Coach almost looked alike. I think he was a little shorter than him, Coach. He had a little stoop.

Wingo: Coach Stagg knew Coach Holmes?

Petross: Well enough to recognize the uniform right away.

Professor: Stagg was a football player at Yale, but he was most famous for making basketball a five-man sport. He was never a track man, yet he coached the 1924 Olympic track and field team.

Petross: Your dad was a track man, though, right? Long jump, right? Twenty-five feet or something. Whoa! And on those runways they had back in those days! You have to know the difference if you're a runner. I wish I'd had the chance to run on an all-weather track. I never had the chance. Even at Penn, if you see it, they never had an all-weather track. All dirt, ground up, packed. After you run it once, it's all uneven.

Professor: Right, my dad was long jump and triple jump. Those all-weather tracks were 1960s, I think.

Wingo: [*handing an old newspaper article to the professor*] Here's the article I like about my brother Leon and Pete, here.

[*Professor Holmes reads the article aloud*]

WAYNE THINCLADS SWEEP PENN RELAYS
Wright, Coleman, Wingo, Petross star in races.
Philadelphia.

Four Wayne runners grab the Penn relays by the throat and shook it almost to death. Before an excited, intense crowd of 30,000 in Franklin Stadium here, Tartars Lorenzo Wright, Leon Wingo, Buddy Coleman, and Irv Petross staged a remarkable performance of team feats and individual stamina by taking three firsts, a second and a third. It all started at 1:30 p.m. last Friday when Wayne won its heat in the quarter-mile relays prelims in 42 seconds. Indiana and Penn State had equal chalkings. In the final heat an hour later, Wingo went all out, handing the baton to Petross. Petross turned the stick over to Wright and from there it went to Coleman who snapped the tape in what proved to be a blinding finish. Indiana was second, Army third, Penn State fourth. Winning time 41:07. The next day the Tartars began class with Indiana in the prelims and tallied a first in the 880 relay.

Wingo: One relay, they didn't have a photo finish in those days, it took them better than two hours to determine who won the race. So, we waited and waited in the middle of the field and when they announced that Wayne won, we were jubilated. We had it on film. I tried to find the film, but somehow it got stored down at Wayne. I wanted to keep it, but I went down there and couldn't find it. But Wayne won at Seton Hall, too, that same year. We won at Central Collegiate that year, too. In fact, the only place we lost was the national championship. But other than that we were successful in winning just about everywhere we went.

Professor: 1949?

Wingo: Yes, 1949. Indoors and outdoors. In fact, you'd hear the guys say, "Oh, they're here again." They would wonder if we were there. They'd look around and they'd see my brother, and Buddy, maybe Buddy Coleman. Lorenzo might be someplace else. Then, all of a sudden, oh, they're here. "Oh, no!" Michigan State and Michigan, they wouldn't run us. They avoided us as much as they could. For obvious reasons. For obvious reasons. They didn't want little Wayne University beating a big power-house. Every now and then we thought we were cheated by the time-keepers. Back in those days it was all hand timed; stopwatches. A guy would come up to you and say, "Look what I got," and you'd look and say, "My god, it's 39," when in reality it was something else.

Petross: And another thing, they were those big schools. If it was close between you and them, they usually got it. Because we ran into that up at Michigan State. We ran a relay there and they beat the hell out of us for three legs. Not speed, I mean they kicked us and everything else. One of our guys got a cut on him from the spikes. And we won, but the officials said we didn't win, because they didn't want to embarrass the host school. You want to talk about someone who was mad? Coach David L. Holmes! He was madder than I ever saw him. He just walked up and down and he fumed at the officials and everything else. All we could do was stand back because there was nothing else we could say. He was the man and he was doing everything he could do. He told them, "I may never come back to this meet again."

Professor: Sounds like Lorenzo Wright and the Olympics.

Petross: Exactly.

14

THIRD MAN UP

The 1948 Olympics, London, England

August 7, 1948

He was there to compete for the United States in the long jump, yet Lorenzo Wright found himself assigned to the 400-meter relay team. Although Wright was extremely capable, this assignment was unexpected. Ed Conwell, a dynamic sprinter from Palmyra, New Jersey, was scheduled to run. Conwell was the co-holder of world records for the 50-yard and 60-yard dashes, and in 1947 he set the European record for the 100-meter dash. At race time for the preliminary heats he was suffering from an asthma attack and could not participate. Wright was inserted in his spot.

Wright was surprised and had not practiced baton exchanges with his new relay team members. It was something he knew D.L. would have worked on for endless hours, especially for Olympic competition. Conwell's unfortunate illness was a chance for Wright to redeem himself at the London Games.

The long jump had not gone well. Wright should have already had a silver medal minimally, possibly a gold, around his neck. Nerves? Form? London smog? Or possibly having his long-time track coach on the wrong side of the ocean, replaced by an Olympic coach he didn't know? Whatever the cause, Wright placed fourth in the long jump. His best jump of 24′5″ was nowhere close to the 25′11″ he had jumped earlier in 1948. Wright had gone into Olympic competition ranked second among those who qualified. He fouled on his best jump, which likely would have placed him second in the competition.

First in the Olympic Trials was Willie Steele, who was ranked the number-one long jumper in the world by *Track and Field News* in 1947 and 1948. Steele was from San Diego State College and had a personal best jump of 26′6″ in 1947. He was a two-time NCAA long jump champion. However,

Steele had suffered an ankle injury prior to the London Games. He was not at the top of his ability. It left a door open for Wright to capture the gold.

The third overall qualifier in the Olympic long jump trials, after Wright's ranking of second, was Herb Douglas, another American. Douglas hailed from the University of Pittsburgh. Surprisingly, the Douglas resume did not include college, state, or national wins in the long jump. More likely, he was standing on the podium next to the guy who collected those accolades. Prior to the Olympic Trials, his most notable accomplishment was being on the 440-yard relay team that won the Penn Relays in 1942 with a time of 41.7 seconds. At the time, he ran for Xavier University in New Orleans, Louisiana. It was the first time a historically Black college and university won a relay at Penn. Douglas' Olympic qualifying jump was 25'3".

Wright had qualified for three events leading into the Olympic Trials in Evanston, Illinois. Because of his performance at the national AAU meet in Milwaukee, Wisconsin, he would also go to the trials for the 100-meter dash and the 200-meter dash. Only the top three competitors would move on to the Olympics in each of those events.

Wright had a disappointing showing in both dashes, not even approaching his best times. He came in sixth in his 100-meter dash heat, with a slow 10.8 seconds. In the 200-meter dash he ran a 21.7-second race, but tenths of a second are everything in track and he was fifth in his heat—a full second behind Barney Ewell, who ran a blistering 20.7 seconds.

Only his long jump distance at the trials kept him in the Olympics. Then that had turned to disaster with a foul and an unexpected fourth-place finish. Now, he had a new opportunity. The 400-meter relay was his final chance; his only chance to take home a medal to his proud fans in Detroit. Wright had uncountable wins throughout high school and college. He had been called Wayne's "one-man track team" and had contributed hundreds of points toward the win of dual meets and relays. None of that mattered. This was different. This was the Olympics. Now he would find out if he was good enough to compete against the best in the world.

Dean Cromwell was coach of the US Olympic track and field team. He saw Wright as a long jumper, not a sprinter. Originally, he selected Cliff Bourland of Los Angeles to replace Conwell on the relay team. Bourland had come in third in the 200-meter dash, but developed some leg pain and was scratched in favor of Wright. The relay team was now Barney Ewell, who had tied the world record in the 100-meter dash at the trials; Harrison Dillard, who came to the games with world records in both the 120 and 220 hurdles; Mel Patton, who held the world record in the 100-meter dash—a record he now shared with Ewell; and Lorenzo Wright.

Wright was the only member who was not a world record holder. He did poorly in the trials in both dashes, and his performance in his best event, the long jump, resulted in fourth in Olympic competition. He was rushed onto the relay team at the last minute. If the events for which he was fully prepared went badly, how would this relay transpire when he had no preparation at all?

Adding to the complications was the weather; it was terrible. It had been raining consistently for a couple of days. The track was wet, the batons were wet, their hands were wet, and rain and mud flung up by track shoes was flying into the faces of the runners. Conditions were not good for a relay team bandaged together with no time to get in much practice.

It was Friday, August 6, 1948, the day of their qualifying heat. Ewell was lead-off man, handing off to Wright. Dillard was third, with Patton completing the final leg. Three world record holders . . . and a kid from a little-known university in Detroit.

Fifty thousand people were in the stands watching track and field competition that day. All of them soaked from the rain. Yet, the crowd had been mesmerized and was cheering wildly. Fannie Blankers-Koen, a thirty-year-old housewife and mother of two from the Netherlands, had won the women's 220-meter dash, her third gold medal of the Olympics. (She had not yet earned her fourth.) The attention was all on her. Wright felt a sense of relief. Qualifying heats of a relay would not be the focus of the fifty thousand sets of eyes when all they were thinking and talking about was the first triple Olympic gold by any female athlete. They had just watched history being made.

The rain became an afterthought, as did the inexperience he had within the relay team. They needed to place first or second in their heat to move on to the final Olympic competition. Wright now felt confident he could help this team pull it off.

Ewell practiced his baton exchange with Wright. Wright practiced his baton exchange with Dillard. It felt good; wet, but good. Fifteen countries were entered in the event. There would be three heats, with five teams in each heat. The top two teams in each heat would move on to the finals. The first five teams, which included the Americans, split up across the track, taking their spots within their respective baton exchange areas. It was time.

Wright looked at the track in front of him. The footprints of previous runners were pressed into the cinders and filled with water. Raindrops danced in the puddles and brought a smile of familiarity to his face. This was a mess just like Wayne's track at Kelsey Field. He felt like he had run here many times before.

Then Wright became grimmer as a myriad of thoughts went through his mind. Two other people had had to be eliminated from this relay team in order for him to be there that day. He had qualified to be in only one of the three events in which he had hoped to compete in London. How had he ended up here? He knew Coach Holmes would find a way to listen in on the results of the heat on the radio in Detroit. He wanted his family to be proud, his coach to be proud, his university to be proud, his city to be proud. But most of all, he wanted to perform in a way that he could be proud.

He shook his head hard, as if to throw out any lingering doubt. Then, he looked behind him at the footprints and puddles covering the track between himself and Barney Ewell. The preliminary race was about to begin. Wright focused and readied himself.

The runners took their marks. Set. *Bang!* went the starter's pistol.

Ewell ran like lightning. His world-record status showed as he covered his 100 meters in the blink of an eye. The handoff to Wright went perfectly, even with the rain and slippery baton. Wright flashed through his 100 meters and made a beautiful pass of the baton to Dillard. Dillard was fast. So fast he surprised Patton a bit and ran into him in the exchange zone, slowing both of them to a stop. Their baton pass did not go smoothly. Yet, they held onto their first-place margin by a yard with a time of 41.1, with the Italian team not far behind at 41.3.

The US 400-meter relay team was going to the finals!

Shoes soaked, uniforms soaked, the relay team embraced the victory. The three world record holders were now confident that Wright was the person they needed, and wanted, on their team. A newfound respect toward him was provided by the win.

It had been accomplished. A relay team with a third-choice member had qualified for the Olympic finals! Lorenzo Wright, from Wayne University, had a second chance at Olympic glory.

But tomorrow was another day.

The entire aura of the 1948 Olympics was strange, and Wright could smell it and feel it. London had not yet begun the rebuilding process after World War II. Much of the city was filled with piles of bricks and rubble from the devastating bombings of the Blitz. Food shortages were still very real, and the rationing of the war was enforced fully, with each resident allowed only 2,600 calories per day. Olympic athletes were afforded more, although many brought their own food to the games. No buildings or stadiums were built for the Olympics. London used whatever facilities they already had. Athletes were housed in college dormitories, in school gymnasiums, and in military camps. All contestants were asked to bring their own towels. The track and field competitions were held on a greyhound dog-racing track. London residents brought ashes from their fireplaces to assist in building the cinder track there.

Piles of building rubble were ground more finely and added to the track. The track smelled like a firepit, and its hue was slightly red from the bricks of once-great English structures.

The games had been nicknamed the "Austerity Olympics" for their lack of funding and absence of the usual preparation of the infrastructure. There had not been an Olympic competition since the 1936 games in Berlin. Many participating countries pitched in to help the effort. The Netherlands sent fruit and vegetables, Denmark donated 160,000 eggs, Switzerland donated gymnastic equipment, Canada supplied the wood to make diving boards, and Finland provided lumber for a new basketball court. So dire were the circumstances that many of the athletes made their own uniforms. Blankers-Koen won her four gold medals in homemade orange shorts.

Many critics thought holding the Olympics in London was a vast waste of money when the British people were suffering. However, the government saw the benefit of tourists coming to the Olympics and spending cash in London. Even on an austerity budget, the games cost £734,268 in 1948, or £28,369,488.22 (over 36 million US dollars) adjusted for 2024. For comparison, the 2020 Tokyo Olympics cost over $35 *billion*. The 1948 Olympics made a profit from ticket sales, which did not include the money attendees spent on hotels, meals, transportation, and souvenirs. Yet, it was not only a success financially. It also gave the world a chance to reunite for a different cause after a ravaging world war.

Lorenzo Wright had none of that perspective. He attended Wayne University and was used to austerity. Athletic facilities built in 1908 were the ones in which he still practiced in 1948. The makeshift dog track was a step up from what he found at Kelsey Field in Detroit, even with the firepit smell and puddles. What shocked him was the city. In 1948, Detroit was a bustling metropolis booming after the switch back from war production. There was a demand for everything Detroit made, and jobs were high paid. It was also a time when Blacks were beginning to break some color barriers they had not previously. Bob Mann became the first Black player on the Detroit Lions that year. Detroit was a city rising up, and clearly London was a city falling down.

Detroiters had their eyes on Wright. A group from Wolverine Barber College and the Urban League raised funds to send Detroiter LeRoy Dues to the Olympics in a quasi-official capacity with the track team. Dues had been Wright's high school track coach and was another of Coach Holmes' former track stars. While Dues was not allowed to coach, what he brought with him was even more valuable. He brought something from Coach Holmes.

Dues caught up with Wright the morning after the preliminary victory; the morning of the Olympic finals in the 400-meter relay. After a time of reminiscing and discussion of improvements Dues thought could be made with the baton exchanges, Dues said, "I have something Coach Holmes wanted me to give you." Wright expected a pair of Wayne track shoes or a Wayne sweatshirt, but there was no box of shoes or bag of outerwear. Instead, Dues wrapped his arms around Wright and hugged him. Taken aback and surprised, Wright's instinct was to pull away. Dues didn't allow it. It was then that he felt Coach Holmes' embrace. It felt like home. Dues then put a hand on each of Wright's shoulders, looked him intently in the eyes, and said, "You are only the third Wayne track man to go to the Olympics. In that, you are already a champion. You are here so that others may stand on your shoulders. Congratulations on what you have already accomplished."

Then Dues placed his palm gently on Wright's heart. "Coach Holmes is right here, Lorenzo. He'll be with you today."

Wright heard those words and it was as if Coach Holmes was standing there saying them himself. He shook Dues' hand and thanked him, turning quickly, hoping Dues would not notice the tears welling in his eyes. He walked back to the track stadium where the race would take place that afternoon.

The finals in the men's 400-meter relay were scheduled for 3:30 p.m. that day, Saturday, August 7, 1948. The weather had cleared; no rain, and temperatures in the mid-70s. Perfect weather. At 1:00, Ewell, Dillard, Patton, and Wright all met to practice baton exchanges. Dillard and Patton especially wanted to work on theirs to not repeat the mistake of the preliminaries. At 2:00, the four relay men made their way to the track.

In the race today, in addition to the Americans, were teams from Britain, Italy, Hungary, Canada, and the Netherlands. The British team would be a challenge due to Jack Archer, who won the 1946 European Championships in the 100-meter dash. The American team, however, had three world record holders. They were not feeling the intimidation.

The wait seemed like an eternity, but at slightly after 3:00, the relay team was called to the inner track to stretch and prep for the event. A few last baton exchanges on the grass and the Americans felt ready to go. They had drawn the fourth lane. The inner lane was not being used, so the American team was positioned at the third stagger, allowing them to see the English team next to them in the fifth lane, as well as the teams in Lanes Six and Seven. It was a good position strategically.

A capacity crowd of eighty-four thousand was on hand to watch the event. It was electric. The crowd leaned heavily British, and there were wild cheers as the British team was introduced. Archer was definitely a hometown favorite.

The Americans also earned their share of respect and cheers, as Dillard's gold medal in the 100-meter dash and Ewell's silver medal in the same were noted once again. And there was no forgetting the Italian team, whom the Americans had narrowly beaten in the preliminary race.

Wright was hoping the pomp and circumstance of the event introduction would be over quickly, as he wanted to fly around his quarter of the track. The introduction of the six teams ended and the runners were told to take their marks. The first-position runners all used starting blocks, which were now being used almost universally in the Olympics. They had not been used in the 1936 Olympics. After the start, the blocks would be removed from the track so as not to interfere with the fourth-position runners.

The noise of the crowd heightened. The adrenalin pumped. The wet hands from the previous day's rain were replaced by the wet hands of nervous perspiration. Wright wiped his hands on his shorts in anticipation of Ewell's handoff.

The leadoff men were in their starting blocks. Set. *Bang!*

Ewell flew off the blocks and pumped his arms aggressively as ash from the track flew up behind him. He had already closed the gap on the English runner before his handoff to Wright. The handoff went perfectly, and Wright dug into the track as he flew through his leg of the race.

Wright could feel the crushed bricks of English buildings beneath his feet. The noise of the crowd became a faint sound in the distance as he had his focus on Harrison Dillard's eager anticipation ahead. Wright had extended the lead by the time he entered the exchange zone. Dillard matched Wright's speed perfectly and the handoff was flawless.

Dillard's speed was incredible, and he left the rest of the runners far behind him. He was at least 10 meters ahead of everyone else as he neared the exchange zone. Once again, Dillard ran up on Patton, who hadn't left his mark on time, but the exchange went well. Patton tore through the final leg of the race and broke the tape with his arms in the air triumphantly. The American 400-meter relay team won with a gap of 10 meters between them and the second-place English team. It was a decisive victory! They had won gold!

Lorenzo Wright had won a gold medal! And he heard Coach Holmes saying, "others will stand on your shoulders." He looked for Coach Dues but couldn't find him in the mayhem.

Coordinated shouts of "U.S.A." could be heard throughout the boisterous crowd. By now, Ewell, Wright, Dillard, and Patton had found each other and were celebrating on the track. It was exhilarating. Wright looked at his teammates; he looked at the stadium full of cheering spectators. It was truly the crowning moment of his entire track career.

The four Americans made their way over to the medal podium to accept their gold medals. They excitedly talked to each other, reviewing every second of the race. The joy was overwhelming as they shook hands and slapped each other's backs frequently. Each of them looked at the crowd and pointed to Americans standing and cheering. Their smiles were unstoppable.

Then, an announcer came over the loudspeaker. Met with a chorus of cheers and boos, the announcer said "The United States team has been disqualified. The disqualification was due to the first exchange going out of the change-over zone."

That was one of Wright's exchanges. Disqualified because of one of Wright's exchanges? Shock. Dismay. Anger. Bitterness. Sadness. Ewell came up to Wright and said, "I wasn't out of the zone. They're wrong! It was a perfect exchange." Wright didn't think it was a bad exchange either. They told Coach Cromwell. Cromwell told an official with the US Olympic Committee, but the official said there would be no formal protest. "It was a clear foul. I saw it."

Cromwell believed his runners. They were on the track. Cromwell had also seen no issues with the exchange. He lodged a formal protest. The exchange zone judge in this case was British. The team in second behind the Americans was British. The gold medal now went to the British—their only gold medal in track and field events at the 1948 Olympic Games. Was this politics? Was it simply a mistake in judgment? Or did an exchange zone foul actually occur? Film of the event would have to be studied.

At this point, all the American team could do was stand back and watch the British relay team accept their gold medals. It was gut-wrenching.

The British press disagreed with the United States, saying it should not protest. The *Daily Herald* stated that the United States "might have accepted the official decision with better grace. After all, rules are rules and a faulty changeover is just as much a track offense as beating the gun at the start."

The 1948 Olympics were the first to use photo finishes. They also were the first to sell TV rights for broadcasting. These games had film when others did not. However, film needed to be developed and then studied. The protest would run a few days before anything could be determined.

So, they waited. They waited until the film could be studied. They waited to find out what information, if any, the films might reveal about the baton exchange.

They waited, but not in London.

Their events were over and their time overseas was done. It was time to return home. Ewell was coming home with two silver medals. Dillard and Patton were both coming home with a gold. Wright was just coming home.

On August 11, 1948, a special ceremony was held in London. The Olympic Committee had examined the relay event film and determined there was no exchange zone violation. The Ewell-to-Wright baton exchange had gone perfectly and, more importantly, met all the requirements of the rules.

The American team was declared the winner of the 400-meter relay race. Lorenzo Wright had won a gold medal!

But there was no cheering crowd, and there were no athletes to accept their medals, no reporters covering the event, and no photos on the winner's podium to grace the front page of hometown newspapers. The only spectators were a few that had come to watch an English soccer game taking place in the stadium soon after the announcement.

The thunderous ovation that should have been received by the American 400-meter relay team was, instead, a footnote in newspapers and a footnote in history. The athletes were all back home, welcomed back under the pallor of disqualification. Ewell, Dillard, and Patton all had medals to hold high. Wright just tried to hold his head high.

Several weeks later, a package arrived in Coach Holmes' office. It was from the Olympic Committee and contained the gold medal for Lorenzo Wright. D.L. contacted the Wayne University president, and they set a plan in motion.

The mayor of Detroit proclaimed Saturday, November 13, as "Lorenzo Wright Day." In front of a packed University of Detroit football stadium during halftime of the Wayne vs. University of Detroit football game, Lorenzo Wright received his gold medal from Coach Holmes. Wayne's President Henry and Detroit Mayor Van Antwerp were also there to help in the proceedings. The jubilant crowd Wright was cheated from receiving in London was there to vigorously cheer him in Detroit. Chants of "U.S.A." took over the crowd. Detroit had a hero that day.

Wright looked at the huge crowd in the bleachers and at the others standing around the field. He slowly turned all around the stadium with his right hand up, waving "thank you" to the gathered masses. Then he turned to Coach Holmes. D.L. had some words prepared, but there was no way the crowd was going to stop cheering. Instead, he held the medal high for all to see. He placed the ribbon around Wright's neck. And as Wright leaned close to accept the medal, D.L. whispered in his ear, "With or without this gold medal, you have always been the best example of what a man should be."

D.L. then picked up the microphone and yelled into it, trying to out-yell the crowd, "Ladies and gentlemen, gold medal winner Lorenzo Wright!"

Cheering that one would think could not get louder doubled in volume. Everyone was on their feet. Several of Wright's Wayne track teammates picked him up and carried him around the stadium. Even the University of Detroit football team was on its feet applauding.

Lorenzo Wright, gold medal winner, 1948 Olympics in London.

Lorenzo Wright went on to be a track coach in Detroit. For a time, he worked as an assistant to Leroy Dues at Miller High School.

Wright was inducted into the Michigan Sports Hall of Fame in 1973 and the Wayne State Sports Hall of Fame in 1976, both posthumously.

In 1972, at age forty-five, Wright was stabbed to death by his wife during a dispute at their home.

1922 ?

D.L. moved from coaching at Cass Tech to athletic director and coach at the newly formed Detroit Junior College in 1917. This photo was taken around 1922. Photo credit: Gainsboro Studios, Detroit. From the estate of Jean Holmes Wunderlich.

Ken Doherty competing for the College of the City of Detroit in the high jump at the Penn Relays in 1927. Photo credit: ACME Newspictures, New York, NY.

Old Main, the original building of the school that became Wayne State University. Pictured here in 1930. Photo credit: Walter P. Reuther Library, Archives of Labor and Urban Affairs, Wayne State University.

In a suit, tie, and hat, D.L. strikes a familiar pose with a stopwatch in hand. Photo credit: Jean Holmes Wunderlich Estate.

Leroy Dues puts the shot to win first place at the Penn Relays in 1933. Photo credit: Getty Images.

1935

By the 1930s, D.L. was well known for his analysis of precise movements of championship athletes. He produced his book "Movies on Paper" in 1933, 1934, and 1935. This 1935 photo shows D.L. examining pole-vault photos that he would later turn into illustrations. Photo credit: Jean Holmes Wunderlich Estate.

Advertising brochure for the 1935 edition of "Movies on Paper" and Holmes Starting Blocks. Photo credit: Jean Holmes Wunderlich Estate.

Allan Tolmich practices his championship hurdle form on the roof of the *Detroit News* building in 1937. Photo credit: *Detroit News*.

The elevated running track in the gymnasium at Old Main was one of the worst tracks on which most athletes had ever competed. It took twenty-two laps to cover the distance of one mile. Photo credit: Walter P. Reuther Library, Archives of Labor and Urban Affairs, Wayne State University.

D.L. in his Old Main office, 1940. He is holding a memento of a game between Detroit Junior College and the University of Detroit that took place in 1918. The Junior College won! Photo credit: Jean Holmes Wunderlich Estate.

National Senior AAU Championship at Randall's Island, June 20, 1942

Qualifying heat—Bob Wingo qualifying for finals. Cliff Bourland first, Jimmy Herbert, second

Wayne sprinter Bob Wingo (*second from right*) qualifies at 1942 National AAU meet. Photo credit: Walter P. Reuther Library, Archives of Labor and Urban Affairs, Wayne State University.

An undated photo with D.L. standing at the finish line with a stopwatch in hand. Photo credit: Jean Holmes Wunderlich Estate.

D.L. having a fun conversation with his 1942 national AAU 1,600-meter relay championship team. Time: 3:18.7. From left to right are Robert Grant, Wayne Hatfield, Bob Wingo, Linwood Wright, and D.L. Holmes. Photo credit: Jean Holmes Wunderlich Estate.

D.L. sets his lap-timing device, the Pace-Setter, for runners at Old Main in 1949. Photo credit: *Detroit Free Press*, USA TODAY NETWORK.

Left to right: Distance man Owen Clinton, quarter-miler Cliff Hatcher, D.L. Holmes, sprinter and broad jumper Vic Zucco, and distance man Joe Babb discuss the details of an upcoming track meet in 1954. Photo credit: Walter P. Reuther Library, Archives of Labor and Urban Affairs, Wayne State University.

The 1956 Wayne Track team was one of D.L.'s last prior to his retirement in 1958. This team would go on to be the President's Athletic Conference champion. Photo credit: Jean Holmes Wunderlich Estate.

Two sprinters take off on a practice run in the halls of Old Main, 1958. Note that D.L. is using a starter's pistol inside of Old Main! Photo credit: Walter P. Reuther Library, Archives of Labor and Urban Affairs, Wayne State University, and Detroit News Staff.

Lorenzo Wright, 1948 Olympic gold medalist, and D.L. look over some new track shoes in 1958. Photo credit: Jean Holmes Wunderlich Estate.

D.L. setting up his Holmes Folding Hurdles at an unknown location in 1958. Photo credit: Jean Holmes Wunderlich Estate.

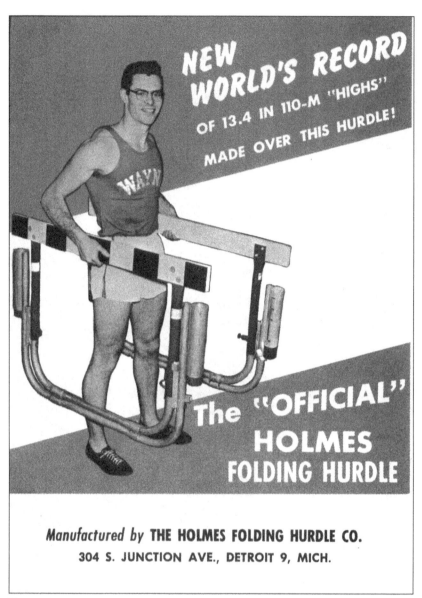

The new Holmes Folding Hurdle brochure for 1958. The runner holding the hurdles is John Telford. Photo credit: Jean Holmes Wunderlich Estate.

John Telford breaks the tape on a muddy Redford High School track in 1957. Wayne often held track meets at Redford High School. Photo credit: Walter P. Reuther Library, Archives of Labor and Urban Affairs, Wayne State University.

The last official portrait of Coach David L. Holmes was taken on May 3, 1957. It is this photo of him that is seen by visitors to the Michigan Sports Hall of Fame. D.L. died in 1960 at the age of seventy-two. Photo credit: Jean Holmes Wunderlich Estate.

15

D.L.'S LAST ALL-AMERICAN

Interview with John Telford, Class of 1957
Interviewed by Keith D. Wunderlich

January 10, 2023

The crisp January air in Detroit made for a beautiful day to visit Dr. John Telford in his apartment overlooking the Detroit River. I made sure to acknowledge John first but was immediately drawn to the windows. What an incredible view. The blue roof of the Roostertail could be seen to the left. The Berry Subdivision where the mayoral Manoogian Mansion is located was directly adjacent to his apartment building. Belle Isle and the area of the river where the hydroplane races take place every August was right out his window. To the right, past several marinas, stood the towering buildings of downtown Detroit.

It was hard to remember I was there to interview John Telford! My initial inclination was to enjoy the view out the windows for a while. I was not sure how he had landed here in this amazing spot, but I was happy to be sharing it with him for a short period of time.

It was slightly before ten o'clock in the morning, and John asked me if I wanted a beer. I declined, saying it was a bit too early for me, which was most likely a profound disappointment to Jimmy Buffett, who would have found five o'clock somewhere. I sensed John was a little disappointed, too. Maybe later.

There was no doubt that my uncle had already done this interview with him back in the late 1990s. Yet, neither a tape nor a transcript could be found. So, here I was in the presence of one of Wayne State's greatest runners, who still holds the Wayne 440-yard dash record at 46.8 seconds. For this interview there was no compact cassette recorder and no flipping of mini-cassettes. Technology had changed quite a bit since my uncle's last interviews over twenty years prior. Instead, I set my iPad to "record" and opened my notebook to get my list of questions.

Telford was Coach Holmes' last All-American runner. Now eighty-seven years old, he was as sharp as a tack and could remember every competition and every event time for not only himself but much of Wayne track history. Telford still hosted a radio show on Detroit's WCHB and an internet television show. He was "Poet in Residence" for the Detroit Community School District and an author of seven books, with book number eight at the publisher.

He sat in his easy chair surrounded by memories of family, friends, and track. Photos of his late wife and several dear friends adorned the top of a nearby television cabinet. One wall had framed cases of some of his medals and another wall had a large photo of him breaking the tape in a race.

His apartment was a testament to a life well lived.

One would never guess that Telford was eighty-seven years old. Sure, he had gray hair and a gray beard, but his backward baseball-style track cap covering his long gray locks and his spirited conversation took at least twenty years off his real age. I didn't even look at my list of questions for about ninety minutes. I think I was the first person in a while who wanted to hear all of his track stories. And he told them.

> **John Telford:** I was sent to Denby High School. Well, I was in an altercation with an assistant principal at Northwestern High School and got sent to Denby in 1951. I got sent to live with my father. He was an old fighter, a Scotland-born guy. I never would have gone back to school if I hadn't gone back to live with my father. His fight manager had connections with the superintendent and he got me into Denby High School. That's where I started setting track records. Pete Petross, who ran on a great relay team for Coach Holmes, saw me running one time against Miller High School. They had won forty-five straight meets. I had just transferred from Northwestern to Denby, and I decimated that team. I won the 100, the low hurdles, and the long jump and anchored a relay, and we won by about two points. We snapped their forty-five-meet winning streak. I was a junior then.
>
> **Keith Wunderlich:** Amazing!
>
> **Telford:** Petross was another mentor of mine, wonderful man. He's passed now, too. He told me he wanted me to come down and run at Wayne State. And I said, "Well, talk to me next year because I'm a junior." And he did! He came and talked to me the next year. I owe my whole life to the sport of track and field and the Detroit Public School District. And I owe the success of my running career in college to Coach David L.

Holmes. When I went down there, Coach Holmes said to me—and I had never lost a high school 100-yard dash—Coach Holmes said to me, "Do you want to be the conference 100-yard dash champion or national quarter-mile champion?" I told him I wanted to be the conference 100-yard champion! I didn't want any part of that quarter-mile. I had run it a few times at Denby and it was not my favorite race!

Wunderlich: [*laughing*] Right! A quarter mile is a long race for a 100-yard dash guy!

Telford: Wide open around an outdoor track the whole way with about two steps of coast in the back stretch. Coach Holmes said, "Well, son, I have news for you. You're going to be a quarter-miler at Wayne State." Turns out he was right.

Wunderlich: I couldn't believe it. I looked up some of your times. Your best 440 at Denby was a 51.3—which is darn good—my best was a 52. You would have been beating me.

Telford: Well a 52 in high school, back in the old days, that's the mark of a quarter-miler. I had a 50 point something on a relay team split. Interesting story. This guy, Sandy Wittington, was the only guy who ever beat me in high school, and he beat me in the quarter mile. I was so mad! My father saw that race. The next week, I was anchoring this sprint relay at the Wayne Relays at Redford High School. Sandy Wittington was anchoring for Cass Tech. I got the baton a few steps back from this guy who had beaten me the week before, and I chewed him up and spit him out! I went home and said to my dad—because I'd heard nothing but that guy's name for an entire week—"guess who I got today?" And Sandy was at my retirement party. He's passed now, too. He was Detroit city quarter mile champion.

Wunderlich: At Wayne, you had a 46.8 in the 440. Unbelievable! That is lightning. And you were running on cinders in crappy shoes.

Telford: [*laughs*] Right, with spikes that long [*raising his hand and showing his fingers about an inch and a half apart*]. The world record then was 46.2, by the Jamaican, Herb McKinley. So, I was only six-tenths of a second from that record.

Wunderlich: That's amazing. What about the Olympics? Was that a possibility for you?

Telford: When I ran the race where I got the 46.8, the current Olympic champion was third. But the whole thing is the Olympic Trials. If you don't get on the Olympic team there's no way you're going to get that gold. I got so many golds over my running career, but none of them were the gold that I wanted. You know.

Wunderlich: Yes, sorry.

Telford: But I can't complain. I mean, I owe my whole life to the sport of track and to Coach Holmes.

Wunderlich: You were his last All-American, right?

Telford: Yes. Hal Schram of the *Detroit Free Press* said I was the last great sprinter of Coach Holmes'. The coach had a lot of them, you know.

Wunderlich: Yes, I know.

Telford: He had Lorenzo Wright, John Lewis, and Buddy Coleman. I'm trying to think of some of the other ones he had.

Wunderlich: Well, Petross was one of them.

Telford: You bet he was! Petross was five-time Michigan AAU sprint champion. I remember one time I won the quarter mile in an AAU meet and I wanted to run the 100. Guess who beat me in the 100? Petross! He was running 9.6 seconds when he was thirty-two years old.

Wunderlich: I read somewhere that when he was with the Detroit Track Club he ran 9.7 multiple times in his thirties.

Telford: He was actually running 9.6's! Consistently 9.6!

Wunderlich: Just unbelievable.

Telford: You couldn't beat him. You had to be a world record contender to beat Petross. Petross was a great Detroit runner. There's only four people that have had high school tracks named after them in Detroit. Petross is one of them. I'm one of them. Lorenzo Wright is one of them. And then there's Henry Carr. Do you know who he is?

Wunderlich: No. I don't know the name. Was he a Wayne runner?

Telford: No, he never ran for Wayne. He ran at my old high school, Northwestern, about ten years after me. He is probably the fastest human being who ever stepped foot on a track. In his junior year they brought him over to me at Southeastern—I was track coach over there at the time. I was a volunteer coach, twenty-four years old, trying to make my comeback in track. Carr was seventeen. We were taking 220-yard straightaways on the track at Southeastern when his coach brought him over to me and wanted me to work on his finish. I had some good runners—some of the best in the city. We're taking these 220 straightaways and I was still running. So, I'm running with them. This kid comes over wearing his sweat clothes and runs with us. He's running loop, loop, loop and I'm running my ass off. I can't keep up with this kid. I've never seen anything like it. That year, his junior year, at Northwestern High School, he took a tenth of a second off of Jesse Owens' national high school record. He ran a 220 in 20.6 seconds. I went down to my old coach from Denby, Jim Stout, who was now the athletic director for the district, and I said to him "Coach, I've qualified for the Olympic Trials and I want to take Henry Carr with me." Stout said he couldn't go due to a rule about competing more than twenty-five miles outside of Detroit. If he competes outside of that radius he won't be eligible his senior year of high school. I told Stout he might want to make an exception to that rule because this kid is going to win the 1960 Olympics in the 200 meters. Stout said to me, "What have you been smoking? This kid's not going to do that." And I said, "Oh yes he is! He's going to win the Olympics, there's no doubt in my mind."

Wunderlich: So, did he let him go?

Telford: Well, I went to Henry's dad and told him my thoughts. He asked what Stout said, and I had to tell him. So, no, he didn't go to the 1960 Olympic Trials. Henry did not go to the Olympic Trials, but you know what he did the following year?

Wunderlich: What?

Telford: He tied the world record for the 220-yard dash in 20 seconds flat. There's only one other runner in high school history who did that, and he did it in 1933 at Cleveland's East Tech High School: Jesse Owens.

Wunderlich: Amazing! Jesse Owens and Detroit's Henry Carr.

Telford: Three years later he went to the Tokyo Olympics and broke the world record in the 200 meter and ran on the 4x400 meter relay that won the gold with a faster carry than the Olympic 400-meter champion, Mike Laraby, who ran on that same relay team. He ran a 44.3 split in Tokyo—the last Olympics run on a cinder track.

Wunderlich: Wow!

Telford: Put him up against Usain Bolt on a synthetic track today and my money would be on Carr.

Wunderlich: That's saying something!

Telford: They've done some math on old race times with dirt tracks compared to synthetic surfaces and 220-yard dashes compared to 200-meter runs, and the calculations put Carr right there with Bolt. It's all speculative, of course. But fun to think about.

Wunderlich: Absolutely. The conditions and equipment were so different then than now. You just wonder what Jesse Owens would have done with starting blocks and good shoes. He earned three gold medals without them.

Telford: Exactly.

Wunderlich: So, you went to the Olympic Trials without Henry Carr.

Telford: Yes, right. I wanted to take him with me, but I ended up going out there by myself. I needed a 46.6-second 440 to qualify for the semifinals and I got a 46.7. I missed it by a tenth of a second. That, basically, was the end of my serious running career. I ran a couple more years for fun, but I was coaching and getting my doctorate and doing so many other things I didn't have the time to dedicate to running anymore. Nineteen fifty-six should have been my year. That was my best year. In '56 I was running 100 yards in 9.7 seconds, 220 in 21.0 seconds, the quarter-mile in the 46's. On relays, I had a 45.8 on an anchor leg at Penn.

Wunderlich: What happened?

Telford: I pulled a muscle. In the semifinals of the Olympic Trials I pulled a muscle. I ran a 47.8 in my first heat. Then, in the semifinal heat, at the 300-meter point I started my gather and—I think I could hear it—*czzzittt*—I tore it so bad. It was right behind my knee. They said I needed surgery, but I couldn't afford surgery. So, the Olympics were over for me. One moment of one preliminary race, gone.

Wunderlich: Oh, wow. That's horrible.

Telford: The next spring, indoors, I taped it up. I started competing again, gently. I didn't run any 60-yard dashes. I ran 600 yards, quarter miles. I didn't start fast. I'd just gradually pick it up and try to catch them at the tape. Outdoors, well, Coach Holmes said there has to be a time when you can do it or not do it. You have to take the tape off and see. So he put me in a 220. Tape gone, I won it. Coach said he thought I was ready. He took me to the state meet to see what happens. I won the state meet. Then, it was off to the NCAA meet. That was 1957. I came in second to Bob McMurray of Morgan State in the 440. In 1956, that year I could have beaten the world.

Sixty-seven years later, Telford's voice trailed off, wistfully wishing he could have it all back and do 1956 all over again. His eyes betrayed the pain that still stung from what he had not accomplished. So many medals, so many wins, so many championships—yet it was the one thing he hadn't accomplished that was clearly just below the surface.

I stumbled a bit trying to change the topic and ask a question to bring him back to 2023.

Wunderlich: Ahhh, so what other Wayne track names stick out in your mind that I should make sure are included in this book?

Telford: I ran with some absolute stars. Unfortunately, I could name some names but they're all dead.

Wunderlich: Right, of course. But I can look up accounts of what they did in old newspapers and Wayne records.

Telford: Ok. Well, there was Petross.

Wunderlich: He's included.

Telford: There was Buddy Coleman.

Wunderlich: I know he's mentioned, but not to a great extent.

Telford: Elmer "Buddy" Coleman. He broke the world record in the 70-yard dash at the Washington Evening Star Games in Washington, DC, in 1949 representing Wayne State University. He later became a policeman.

Wunderlich: I'll see what else I can find on him.

Telford: Then, of course, Lorenzo Wright.

Wunderlich: Yes. I have an entire chapter on him.

Telford: Did you know that he was the national indoor long jump champion in 1952?

Wunderlich: I have his Olympic story.

Telford: This was four years after he was in the Olympics. In an early comeback, he won the national AAU long jump title at the old Madison Square Garden. That's also where we ran—the Detroit Track Club, Petross, Bullet Billy Smith, Jim Bibbs, and me—we won our afternoon heat in the 880-yard relay. In the finals—this was 1958—I gave Jim Bibbs the baton and the lead and we bobbled the baton. It fell to the track. Bibbs leaned down and snatched it up. We went from first place to sixth place in about two seconds. Bibbs chased the pack and gave the baton to Bullet Billy. Billy caught the pack and moved us from sixth place to fifth place. He handed off to Petross in fifth place. Petross ran the anchor leg and went from fifth to fourth to third to second and leaned into the tape and almost took the gold—after dropping the baton. We could have shattered a record that day. Oh, I have some stories!

Wunderlich: That's why I'm here!

Telford: The stories are all in my head! I can remember all this stuff very, very well. Right down to the tenth of a second. But I can't remember where I put my glasses! [*laughs*]

Wunderlich: [*laughing*] Any other runners I'm missing?

Telford: Do you have John Lewis?

Wunderlich: Yes. A whole chapter on him and what happened to him.

Telford: I knew Lewis. Holmes went to Lewis to have him get me a summer job working for the Detroit Recreation Department. I worked for the Rec Department every summer. I started working at the bathhouse on Belle Isle. Then, later, I got moved up to be the supervisor of a work crew on Belle Isle. All thanks to Coach Holmes and John Lewis.

Wunderlich: Coach Holmes always seemed to find jobs for his guys so they could afford to be in college.

Telford: Right. We all paid our own way through. Almost no one came from a family that could afford it.

Wunderlich: Tell me about Cliff Hatcher.

Telford: Ahhh, Cliff Hatcher. He's passed now. He was my best friend for fifty-two years. We spent every weekend at each other's houses. He was on that 880-yard relay team of mine. Hatcher, in 1951, at Detroit Central High School, ran the quarter mile in 48.8 seconds. He was High School All-American. When I came out of Denby, he was just coming off a bad muscle injury. He hooked up with me, Bullet Billy, Ralph Carter from Detroit Northern—who was the Marine Corps quarter-mile champion, and a guy named Ralph Williams from the island of Saint Kitts in the West Indies. There were five of us and only four places on the relay team, so those workouts were wars!

Wunderlich: I bet! No one wanted to be the fifth man.

Telford: Exactly! My freshman year at Wayne, I had just come out of Denby—I was living at Forest Arms Apartments over on Second Avenue and West Forest—and our relay team was smoking! We were running so fast. We were beating Michigan and Michigan State in the 880 relay and the mile relay. Little Wayne!

Wunderlich: Wayne always did well in the relays. Coach Holmes didn't have enough of a team for a whole meet, but he'd go to those relays and place.

Telford: And he loved quarter-milers, too. That's why he saw something in me that I didn't. I hated the quarter mile. I only ran it about three times in high school. I lost the one against Cass Tech. He loved quarter-milers. Cliff Hatcher, he was a great quarter-miler. We won the Ohio Relays in both the 880 relay and mile relay. The next week we went to the Penn Relays. We won our heat of the 880 relay and won the mile relay. When we won our heat of the 880 relay, I anchored the relay, and anchoring against me was Jim Brown of Syracuse. Jim Brown the football player. I'll never forget, they put me in Lane One and Brown in Lane Two. Wayne was coming in hot with a nice lead. The only interaction I ever had in my life with Jim Brown. He said to me, "You're going to need that lead, my man." I've never forgotten that! But I didn't need it. We won the heat, but it didn't qualify us for the final.

Wunderlich: Really? Must have been some amazing other heats.

Telford: Penn Relays always brought out the best relay teams.

Wunderlich: Yes. And seems like it was close enough that Wayne could get there easily and they always did well.

Telford: It reminds me of an interesting story about the 1924 Olympics. Have you ever seen the movie *Chariots of Fire*?

Wunderlich: I have, but not in a while.

Telford: Remember the guy who wouldn't run on Sundays? He was the British Empire's 100-meter champion. But he was a preacher. His name was Eric Liddell. Well, he wouldn't run the 100-meter heats on Sunday. The Prince of Wales tried to talk him into it, but no, can't run on Sundays. They arranged to get him a vacant lane in the 400-meter. That wasn't his race, but it wasn't on Sunday. So, he took the lane. He ran a 47.6 and broke the world record.

Wunderlich: That's an amazing time. 47.6 seconds on a dirt track with no starting blocks and, I'm sure, lousy shoes. Incredible!

Telford: Absolutely! The sad end is he became a missionary in China and ended up in an internment camp, like a prison camp. He was malnourished and suffering from a brain tumor and died in 1945, five months before World War II ended and the camp was liberated.

Wunderlich: Oh, that is a sad ending. Other than Wayne, who was recruiting you from high school?

Telford: You know, Michigan never tried to recruit me out of Denby. I don't know why. I went from Northwestern, which was a predominantly Black school, to Denby, which was predominantly white. They should have known I was white. Maybe they thought I was the only Black man there, I don't know. They were drawing the color line.

Wunderlich: That's why I think Wayne ended up with some of these great track stars. The other big schools wouldn't take them because they were Black or Jewish or something else that didn't fit.

Telford: This was 1953, and Michigan had Aaron Gordon out of Detroit Miller as well as Charles Fonville, also out of Miller, who had the shot put world record. But, they had an unspoken quota. They may have had a fifty- or sixty-member track team and only two Blacks. Aaron Gordon ran on a world record distance medley relay team for them. In fact, he and I founded the Detroit Track and Field Old Timers group. But back to the University of Michigan. I was insulted that they didn't recruit me. A lot of other schools were trying to recruit me. I had a letter from the University of Southern California, who wanted me for long jump. But Michigan never recruited me. So, I spent the next four years kicking their butts. [*laughs*]

Wunderlich: [*laughing*] That's great.

Telford: So, that's not the end of the story! I'm at Wayne a couple of years and Michigan sends down an assistant track coach to talk to me. He wanted to steal me away from Wayne and David L. Holmes and my teammates. It was too late, I had already bonded. Even though we were running on that twenty-two-laps-to-a-mile fish dish up there. And Tartar Field, which half the time we had stacks of cinders and they were always repairing the track. We'd run inside the curb to avoid them. I could have gone to Michigan with Yost Fieldhouse and a nice outdoor track and all their facilities, and I wouldn't go. I was a junior and I'd been beating them. I did that with special relish every time there was a maize-and-blue runner in a race with me. And Michigan wouldn't put our records up. He'd just ignore them. We had the track record for the 600, the 300, a piece of the 60, and he didn't put any of our records up. Ah, you're bringing back a lot of memories, Keith.

Wunderlich: Not all of them good, unfortunately! [*laughs*]

Telford: [*laughs*] No, they're all good. Just miss these guys. Lorenzo Wright. I loved Lorenzo Wright. He and I were on the executive board of the old Detroit Varsity Club. We used to sponsor runners and buy track shoes for them. We'd raise scholarship money for second stringers who couldn't get a full ride based on their merit. We sponsored Hayes Jones. He ran for the Detroit Varsity Club and broke some world records indoors. The Detroit Track and Field Old Timers kind of morphed from that old Varsity Club when it phased out. We phased right back in, in 1992. We honored Hayes. We honored Henry Carr before he died with a lifetime achievement award. Some of the great sprinters came out of Detroit. Petross was in that club. Cliff Hatcher was in that club. Keith McClennan was in that club and he wrote a book on track and field.

Wunderlich: Yes, I have that book. It's an incredible resource.

Telford: See that photo over there? That's Will Robinson. He was a magnificent coach and a great man. He was a mentor of mine. He, Petross, and Holmes were my three major mentors.

Wunderlich: Did you know Mark Smith?

Telford: Oh, yes. Mark Smith. Great man. Wonderful educator. All-American high jumper. In 1953 at the NCAA outdoor championships, he tied for first with Papa Hall from University of Florida and Milt Meade from Michigan. Three-way tie for first place at 6'8". The old belly roll, before the Fosbury flop.

Wunderlich: And before a mat.

Telford: Oh yeah, he was always hurting his back coming down. Those sand pits could be like landing on cement. After graduating from Wayne, Mark Smith was a principal in Highland Park for a while and eventually became an assistant dean of education at Wayne State. He died last year. Wonderful man. Oh, when Mark went into the Navy and jumped a 6'10" using that same belly roll.

Wunderlich: He was one of Coach Holmes' "discoveries." Pulled out of a gym class.

Telford: Right. That's right. He came out of Detroit Northwestern High School. Allan Tolmich came out of Detroit Central High School. He was a great hurdler. He would have been an Olympic champion in 1940, but they canceled those Olympics. Coach Holmes developed him, too.

Wunderlich: Yes, Tolmich was spectacular. One of the things I haven't heard much through the interviews my uncle did was Coach Holmes' funeral. I assume I was there, but I was three years old and have no memory at all about it. What can you tell me about it?

Telford didn't answer immediately. He lowered his head and put a hand up to his face. When he looked up, the tears in his eyes glistened in the sunlight streaming through his apartment windows. He looked off in the distance and took himself backward in time to 1960. You could tell from the look in his eyes and the pain on his face that the event sixty-three years before was still fresh in his mind. After some time in thought, he looked at me and began to answer.

Telford: It was a terrible, terrible . . . he was like my father. It was like my father had died.

John Telford was inducted into the Wayne State Sports Hall of Fame in 1978.

16

THE FINAL LAP

The Funeral of Coach David L. Holmes

June 22, 1960

Track, contrary to the popular belief of the uninitiated, is not an unscientific natural sport. It requires extensive study, training and just plain hard work if it is to meet with any form of success. It would be found in a study of great runners and trackmen of the past and present that they achieved their stellar performances not through "blind luck," but through carefully planned practice and objective research in their own particular specialties.

All great trackmen share the attribute of fierce determination and the desire to be the best. This ferocity of determination is exhibited in the "greats" of track in the form of explosive hard-rock desire to run a little faster, jump a little higher and throw a little farther than the next man. These "greats," mild in normal life, are savage in performance. It is this savage attitude that coaches look for in their trackmen and it is this attitude that separates the also runs from the stars.

—WSU freshman, 1958

D.L. had always been particularly proud of that two-paragraph explanation of track, which was written by a student as part of an assignment in 1958. D.L. taught a "Fundamentals of Track and Field" class at Wayne and took it quite seriously, with written assignments and physical requirements. He copied those two paragraphs and sent them around to other coaches and to some of his former Wayne athletes. He thought it was the best description of track excellence he had ever read.

"Mild in normal life, savage in performance."

It also described D.L. perfectly. He was the most kind and gentle person, yet he wanted nothing more than to win.

The funeral home was packed full of people who knew D.L. as both the gentleman and the competitive athlete. None of them could believe that he had run his last race.

The most bewildered person in the room was Hazel Holmes. Just days before, D.L. was perfectly fine. Today she would bury him.

Everything was a blur. There were hundreds of handshakes and hundreds more hugs. Each person said something to the effect of "I'm so sorry," but their exact words were lost in the shock she still felt vividly. At times she had the strength to stand. Other times she sat in a chair, hankie in her left hand and daughter, Jean, on her right side, and son, David. Jr., to her left. She was overwhelmed by the number of people who came by the funeral home.

The McCabe Funeral Home on Grand River was packed with people of all ages, colors, and ethnicities. Black and white, Jewish and Christian, old and young; grown men in tears hugging each other in the shock and disbelief that their coach, their surrogate father, was dead.

Huge men who had been football players for D.L. sobbed in her arms. Many could not offer any words of condolence, as they were too broken up to speak.

Hazel was able to manage a well-meaning smile for most. The faces were all familiar, as they had all been to her home on Faust many times. A few of them seemed as though they were over at the house more than her own daughter and son. There were many stories told about various track events or some impromptu demonstration D.L. did in full dress clothes. There were other stories about his driving, but she knew those all too well from her own experience as a passenger. All of the stories were of love for a man she had to share with thousands of athletes.

The time for the formal funeral service was drawing near.

Just a week earlier they had been on vacation—and sold some hurdles—in California. When they returned to Detroit, D.L. had gone golfing. He was about to tee off and remembered he had left a club in the car. He sprinted about a hundred yards back to the car to retrieve it and sprinted back to his group. By the third hole, he wasn't feeling well. He played through the fifth hole, and they brought him back home.

He went to the hospital the following day and had all sorts of tests. His heart checked out fine, and the diagnosis was indigestion. He was sent home. At 5:00 a.m. the following morning, Hazel took him back to the hospital and he was placed on the critical list. By 8:00 that evening he was gone. Heart attack.

Coach David L. (D.L.) Holmes was dead at the age of seventy-two.

Hazel had already spent time being mad at the doctor for his misdiagnosis. But anger would do her no good now. Her beloved husband of forty-three years had passed. She told some at the funeral home that D.L. had said he never wanted to grow old, and he never had to. His suffering was limited, and she was at his side when he breathed his last breath. If D.L. could have written the script, this is exactly the way he would have wanted it.

If Hazel could have written the script, they would have had many more happy years together.

It was June, and she should have been preparing for their annual trip up north to Georgian Bay. She grew up in Marquette, Michigan, and loved the uncluttered and unpopulated North. She presented herself as a lady of dignity and grace. But as D.L.'s fishing partner she was not apprehensive about picking up a .22 caliber rifle and shooting some mullet from their boat. Filleting a fish was as natural to her as making a fancy dessert for a party. She could pitch a tent, row a fishing boat, cook over a bonfire, and shoo off a bear with a flawless level of success.

During the World War II years, Hazel was a "Rosie the Riveter" of sorts, driving ambulances and military vehicles made in Detroit to the port in New York for delivery overseas.

When D.L. was gone on trips to track meets, her spare time was filled with crossword puzzles, reading, piano playing, and coin collecting. This time his absence was entirely different. This time he wouldn't be coming home.

The funeral director whispered in Hazel's ear that the service was about to begin.

Everyone was asked to take a seat. But there were not enough seats for the hundreds of people who were there. People lined up against the walls of the entire room, two and three deep, with others out in the hallway trying to hear the proceedings. Some were unable to get inside the funeral home and waited outside, unable to see or hear anything, but knowing they had to be there to honor this great man.

An organ began to play as Hazel, Jean, and David Jr. embraced each other on a couch in the first row of the crowd.

Reverend Forsyth from Bushnell Congregational Church did the proceedings. There were the usual readings, prayers, and favorite hymns. Tom Adams represented all Holmes' athletes when he got up and said a few words about the Coach.

> It is my privilege and honor to be at this podium today to speak about Coach Holmes. I was one of his "boys." There are so many others that could be here in my place to tell their story about the Coach.
>
> None of us can tell the entire story about Coach Holmes. For one thing, there is not enough time allocated here today to tell his story.

More importantly, each one of us has a very personal story to tell about him. He impacted each of us deeply, and we would have to tell the stories of each of our lives in order to fully gauge the impact this great man had on us.

The story of David L. Holmes is not in the record books, the athletic archives or any other written sources. It is in the hearts and minds of every man he touched during his long and productive career. As I searched my memory to find a way of reminding you who knew him, and to give you who did not know him, the real sense of this man, these ingredients of his character came back to me.

I cannot recall ever hearing a profane or obscene word come out of his mouth, and yet he was certainly all man. I also recall that his presence minimized the obscenity or profanity falling from the red-blooded American boys on his team. And yet it was not from a sense of fear, but a result of genuine respect.

As I ruminated over my years with him, from 1938 through 1941, it suddenly occurred to me that I never completely lost a race when I was running for Coach Holmes. I certainly did not win them all, but his sense of explanation of what happened to me made me feel a sense of reward for my effort. It was his wont to concentrate on the next opportunity.

Perhaps his greatest virtue was to treat his boys as friends and not as a group of passing athletes. I always felt he was sincerely interested in my past, present and future.

There is no doubt in my mind that the most important lesson he taught all of us, by his example, was that a man should be measured by his performance and not his race, color or creed. David L. Holmes was very much ahead of his time.

And so you will not be misled to the point of thinking of the Coach as an absolute paragon of virtue and not a mortal with some human frailties, let me remind some of you about the terrifying experiences of being a passenger in his car. The Coach was obviously a frustrated Indianapolis 500 driver. It was not unusual for him to set a world record speed mark just pulling out of his driveway. Among my most vivid memories are those of arriving at a track meet, having been a passenger in his car, and being so frightened that I ran beyond my capabilities. This may have been one of his better coaching techniques.

There are so many memories of him that bring a smile to my face; his three-piece suit, tie and hat no matter how hot it was, his pockets full of stopwatches, his flawless demonstration of technique, and the love he had for track and field—and for each one of us.

There isn't a man in this room that thought of him only as their Coach. He was a second father to many, and a first father to even more.

I cannot picture this world without Coach Holmes. He was the greatest man I have ever had the pleasure to know. I'm absolutely sure many of you feel the same way. There is not a day that goes by when I don't put into practice something the Coach taught me—and I'm no longer a runner. But I deal with people every day. His example taught me skills of interaction I use in my job and in my personal life. I am a better man because of our dear Coach.

I am positive he is already in heaven coaching the angels to get a faster start.

May God bless David L. Holmes.

The casket had been closed prior to the start of the service and was now wheeled so it could go down the aisle to the hearse waiting outside. Two of D.L.'s track men, one Black and one white, rose to fold the Wayne State athletic blanket that covered his casket. In a ceremony similar to the folding of an American flag at a veteran's funeral, the Wayne blanket was slowly and carefully folded and presented to Hazel. The room was silent except for the soft sounds of crying almost everywhere.

Reverend Forsyth asked for anyone in the room who had been coached by Coach Holmes to come forward. He was not expecting so many to rise. They formed two rows of track, cross-country, football, and basketball athletes from the front of the church, down the aisle, all the way to the hearse.

He laid his hand on the casket, gave a final blessing, and ended the service with these words:

> There is no greater testament to a life everlasting than the hundreds of people here today. Coach Holmes has not died. He will live forever within each one of you.

The pallbearers came forward: John Telford, Lorenzo Wright, John Lewis, Leroy Dues, Al Langtry, and Dick Waskin. Tears were streaming down their faces as they prepared to take their beloved Coach on his final journey through the long line of shoulder-to-shoulder athletes representing every decade of his Wayne career.

In his own life, D.L. had never achieved some of his biggest dreams. He himself did not make the Olympic team. He did not personally set any world records. The athletic facilities he so dearly wanted at Wayne were never built.

As the casket made its way down the aisle of Bushnell Church, carrying it were two Olympians and the holders of multiple records. What D.L. was unable to do personally, he did for others. He taught young men that they could be more than they thought they could be, on and off the athletic field.

An endless procession of cars followed the hearse to Grandlawn Cemetery in Detroit. There was a short ceremony as D.L.'s body was interred. Those in attendance were not quick to leave. Many stayed to pray and pay their last respects. Over the course of the next hour, mourners slowly made their way back to their cars, leaving Hazel and her immediate family by D.L.'s graveside. One additional mourner stayed: Lorenzo Wright.

Wright had been the first one at the funeral home both days of visitation and the last one to leave. So impacted was he by Coach Holmes that he would not give up these final minutes with him. D.L. and Wright had always had a special bond. He had been a regular houseguest at Faust, and Hazel knew him well.

Wright hugged each member of the Holmes family and retreated a distance away to give them their privacy during this most difficult day.

Another thirty or forty minutes later, Hazel said her final goodbye. She found the strength to rise from her chair by the graveside. Her solemn face betrayed her feelings of shock and loss. Jean and David Jr. helped her to the car.

Lorenzo Wright slowly walked up to D.L.'s headstone. He reached into his pocket and pulled out his Olympic gold medal and placed it gently on the headstone.

"You never got to wear one of these, Coach. I wanted you to have that chance. You deserve it," said Wright.

He then kneeled at the headstone with tears running down his cheeks.

David L. Holmes was inducted into the Michigan Sports Hall of Fame in 1975. He was a charter inductee in the Wayne State Sports Hall of Fame in 1976.

APPENDIX

My grandfather had a scrapbook full of hundreds of clipped newspaper articles about the success, and often the lack of success, of his track teams. Unfortunately, in almost every case, none of the articles had the newspaper name listed and many didn't have a date. If the article happened to be at the top of the newspaper page it was sometimes possible to get the name of the paper. Many of the newspapers I was able to identify through online searches. Others I could not. While the unknown articles provided invaluable information for writing the book, they were difficult to document in this reference section.

When my uncle did his research he quite often did the same thing and copied only the article. He may have written the date of the article but usually did not include the name of the publication. I have two legal boxes full of articles from my uncle's research.

I have included only those articles for which I know both the publication's name and the date of publication. What has been included will still paint a full picture of each of the chapters. Any researchers will be able to find more than adequate references to back up the facts.

You will also find a discussion section that reveals what information creatively filled in the blanks where no source was found.

Chapter 1
References

Associated Press. "Wayne Marches to Last-Period Touchdown." *Detroit Free Press*, November 17, 1940, 27.

Detroit Free Press. "Business Briefs." June 22, 1955, 11.

Detroit Free Press. "Shenanigans against Japs Brings Award." February 11, 1945, 15.

Dowdy, John. Navy Cross accommodation (February 27, 1944). Find a Grave, September 4, 2014. www.findagrave.com/memorial/135430364/thomas-brooks-adams.

Holmes, David L., Jr. Interview transcript of Tom Adams, June 6, 1997. From the written records of David L. Holmes Jr.

Kritzer, Cy. "Wayne Touchdown in Final Quarter Beats U.B. 6–0." *Buffalo News*, November 16, 1940.

McClellan, Keith. *The Hero within Us: A History of Track and Field in the Twentieth Century from a Michigan Perspective.* Oak Park: Eastern Michigan Press, 2001, 297–98.

Ryan, Ray. "Wayne Downs U-B, 6–0, on Frozen Field." *Buffalo Courier Express*, November 17, 1940.

Schmitt, Ben. "Tom Adams; Excelled in Football and Advertising." *Detroit Free Press*, February 2, 2005.

Sports Illustrated. "1965 Silver Anniversary All American Awards." December 20, 1965.

Sterns, Matt. Facebook comment, June 13, 2011. William & Mary Facebook Page, www.facebook.com/profile/100064800547992/search/?q=david%20holmes.

Wayne State University Athletics. Thomas B. Adams, Wayne State Sports Hall of Fame. Wayne State University, 1979, https://wsuathletics.com/honors/hall-of -fame/thomas-b-adams-/19.

Wayne University. "Tartar Stars." Wayne University Griffin Yearbook, 1941, 26, 27.

Discussion

- While this chapter is an interview with Tom Adams, it also serves as an introduction to Professor Holmes. When I spoke with my uncle about old track stories, I almost always sensed a melancholy tone that he didn't measure up to his father's athletic expectations. He saw Coach Holmes' love for his athletes and, seemingly, always wished he was one of them. It was something that I felt bothered him right up to his death. Yet, I hope this chapter illustrates how the two men were uncannily similar. They both dedicated decades of their lives to students at their respective universities and were beloved. I know Coach Holmes would have been very proud of Professor Holmes.

- The snowy football game story was not in the interview. The information is true and was added from a couple of newspaper articles. *Sports Illustrated* did a short explanation of why Adams was selected for the 1965 All-American Awards and in that paragraph was the story about the attempted touchdowns in the snow. Adams' account of the game, via *Sports Illustrated*, was quite different than newspaper accounts of the game. The articles told about several plays that didn't work followed by a score by Adams. I liked Adams' version. His telling of that story was created.

- Adams is listed by many sources as the quarterback. However, when he scored the touchdown in the Buffalo game he was given the ball by Frank Cudillo, who was a tailback. In 1940, the quarterback was defined as the play caller. He didn't necessarily always handle the ball first and throw it or hand it off to others.

- The interview did not discuss any of Adams' accomplishments in the Navy during World War II. They are all true, but were added.

- My uncle left no notes about the demeanor of the track athletes he interviewed or about himself during an interview. All of that has been added.

Chapter 2

References

Central Association, Amateur Athletic Union. Running Broad Jump. Program. Track and Field Championship Meet given by the Rogers Park Athletic Association. June 29, 1912, 19.

Daily Northwestern (Evanston, IL.). "Olympic Tryouts Here." March 13, 1912.

Davis, D. J., and E. C. Rosenow. "An Epidemic of Sore Throat Due to Peculiar Streptococcus." *Journal of the American Medical Association* 58, no. 11 (1912): 773.

Detroit Collegian. "Coach Holmes Was No Slouch on Gridiron, Cinders and in the Gym." April 1, 1926.

Dispatch (Moline, IL). "Star Athletes Enter, List for Olympic Trials at Evanston Saturday Is Announced." June 6, 1912.

Holmes, David L. Curriculum Vitae. Personal records of Coach David L. Holmes, 1919.

Holmes, David L. "What of the Future." *Brown and Blue*, June 1, 1908, 8–11.

Hymans, Richard. "Olympic Trials History." Track and Field News website. 2024. https://trackandfieldnews.com/usa-olympic-trials-history/.

Mathys, Jack. "The Men behind Wayne Athletics . . . Holmes." *Detroit Collegian*, January 13, 1936, 4.

Milonas, Lambros. "Profiles of Olympians and All-Americans at Wayne State University." Master's thesis, Wayne State University, 1974.

Oklahoma Agriculture and Mechanical College. "Editorials." *Orange and Black*, February 1909, 29.

Oklahoma Agriculture and Mechanical College. "Graduating Class of '08 Positions." *Orange and Black*, September 1908, 26.

Oklahoma Agricultural and Mechanical College. "Class Notes." *Orange and Black*, May 1908.

Discussion

- There are several articles about D.L. that say he was sick at the Olympic Trials and not at his prime physically.
- A medical journal noted a sore throat epidemic in the Chicago area in 1912 that was so severe some people died from it. He may have had that, but his specific illness is unknown.
- The availability of separate housing at the Olympic Trials for sick athletes is conjecture.
- There is written evidence that at some point during his career he achieved a 25'1" in the long jump when it didn't count. That may or may not have happened at the Olympic Trials practice, but it did happen.
- I'm not sure if it was O.W. who came to support D.L. at the trials, although they had a great relationship and were quite close. There is one

reference to being visited by a brother at the trials, but the brother is not named.

- Olympic Trial records indicate only each athlete's best jump. Any distances stated below the best jump are conjecture. The best jumps of D.L.'s three main competitors are accurate. Because D.L. did not place in the top three in the trials, his jumps were not written in the historical record. A couple sources have said he missed a spot on the team by only inches.
- Due to the rules of amateurism at the time, D.L. would have had an almost impossible challenge trying to be eligible for the 1916 Olympic Trials, even without World War I. His hope of competing in them is conjecture.

Chapter 3

References

Hill, Gordon T. "Chasing the Flying Finn." *Wayne State*, Spring 1988.

Holmes, David L. "A Brief History of Athletics in Junior College." *The Green and Gold*, College of the City of Detroit Yearbook, 1923, 56.

Holmes, David L., Jr. Interview transcript of Gordon Hill, July 24, 1998. From the written records of David L. Holmes Jr.

Discussion

- My uncle did not ask Hill about the race with Nurmi. However, it seemed like a very important part of his running career, so I added it. That part of the transcript is heavily quoted from Hill's own article in a 1988 Wayne State alumni publication.
- The rest of the interview is almost exactly as the transcript was written.

Chapter 4

References

Associated Press. "12 Track Athletes Selected at 'Philly' for Olympic Team." *Binghamton (NY) Press*, July 5, 1928.

Barcus, H. H. "Not So Good on Grid but on Track—Watch Their Dust." *Detroit News*, December 2, 1929.

Bartlett, Lee. Olympic Diary (1928). From the personal papers of David L. Holmes Jr.

Brink, Stanley L. "Colts Better Mark and Win." *Detroit Free Press*, May 31, 1925.

Detroit Free Press. "American Athletes Take Five Firsts in Track Meet—Detroit Negro Takes 400-Meter." August 12, 1928.

Detroit Free Press. "Colts Almost Double Score on Cass Tech." May 18, 1924.

Detroit Free Press. "Four Records Fall in Prep Track Finals." March 5, 1925.

Detroit Free Press. "Four Records Fall in Track Prep Finals, Jimmy Tait Betters Mark of Four Years Standing in 220-Yard Dash." March 5, 1925.

Detroit Free Press. "John Lewis of Detroit Beats Bracey in 200-Meters." August 13, 1928.

Detroit Free Press. "John Lewis on All-Star Track Team." February 1, 1931.

Detroit Free Press. "Lewis Is Big Point Winner for Tartars." April 19, 1931.

Detroit Free Press. "Lewis Stars as Frosh Win." March 29, 1929.

Detroit Free Press. "Records May Fall in Prep Track Meet." May 17, 1924.

Detroit Public Schools. *Metropolitan Detroit High Schools Athletic Year Book 1926–1927.* Detroit: Detroit Public Schools Athletic League, 59–61.

Detroit Times. "City College Sets Track Record." April 27, 1930.

Detroit Tribune. "Lewis and Dues Receive Honors." May 6, 1933.

Gergen, Joe. *The First Lady of Olympic Track: The Life and Times of Betty Robinson.* Evanston, IL: Northwestern University Press, 2014.

Greene, Sam. "New Coach [Doherty] Trained by Masters." *Detroit News*, March 10, 1938.

Holmes, David L. "On Your Marks! Set! Go!" *Athletic Journal*, March 1936.

Holmes, David L. *Track—1929.* Summary of the 1929 track season. Wayne State University Athletic Department records, 1929.

Holmes, David L. *Track—1930.* Summary of the 1930 track season. Wayne State University Athletic Department records, 1930.

Holmes, David L. *Track—1931.* Summary of the 1931 track season. Wayne State University Athletic Department records, 1931.

Holmes, David L. *Track—1932.* Summary of the 1932 track season. Wayne State University Athletic Department records, 1932.

Holmes, David L. "Training for Track and Field." *Coach*, March 1936, 2–3.

Hutsell, Wilbur H. *Report of Assistant Track and Field Coach.* American Olympic Committee Report, Ninth Olympic Games, Amsterdam, Holland, 1928, 99.

Lewis, John W. "My Greatest Sports Thrill." *Detroit Tribune*, March 6, 1954.

McClellan, Keith. *The Hero within Us: A History of Track and Field in the Twentieth Century from a Michigan Perspective.* Oak Park: Eastern Michigan Press, 2001, 105.

Milonas, Lambros. "Profiles of Olympians and All-Americans at Wayne State University." Master's thesis, Wayne State University, 1974.

Nixdorff, Louis S. Olympic Diary (1928). 1928 Olympic Games Collection, Archives Center, National Museum of American History, Smithsonian Institution, Washington, D.C.

United States Lines. *Passenger Accommodation Plan.* Diagram of each deck of SS *President Roosevelt.* New York: United States Lines, 1928.

United States Olympic Team. *Passenger List, American Olympic Team, Amsterdam 1928, S.S. President Roosevelt.* New York: United States Lines, 1928.

Wayne State University Athletics. John W. Lewis, Wayne State Sports Hall of Fame. Wayne State University. https://wsuathletics.com/honors/hall-of-fame/john-w -lewis-/21.

Discussion

- The block party and the anticipation leading up to the Olympics are conjecture. However, going to the Olympics as a Black athlete in the 1920s was a big deal, and there must have been some sort of send-off party. If there was one, D.L. would have been there.

- The background information for the trip to Amsterdam was learned from the diary of Lee Bartlett, javelin thrower from Albion College. Bartlett wrote in his diary daily regarding everything that happened on the ship and in Amsterdam. One of his entries mentions John Lewis as being part of his group that hung out together in Amsterdam. So, John Lewis' noncompetition experiences would be almost identical to those of Lee Bartlett.

- The diary of Louis Nixdorff was also helpful. But because he was a lacrosse player and not a track athlete, his experiences at the Olympics were quite different from Bartlett's. However, he still had great stories from the boat and from Amsterdam.

- The passenger list of the SS *Roosevelt* does not show Ken Doherty as a passenger. It does list a John K. Daugherty. A misspelling perhaps? We know his middle name was Kenneth. Lee Bartlett's diary places Ken Doherty on the ship. There are no records that I could find of the actual room arrangements. It is very possible Black athletes were segregated. It would also have been very normal for Holmes' athletes to room together no matter what their race. The rooming arrangements were conjecture.

- Lewis wrote an article for the *Detroit Tribune* in 1954 where he talks about the thrill of going to Europe to compete. He mentions General MacArthur, but without adding any negative, or positive, opinion. He does not mention being removed from the 1,600-meter relay team. He said his teammates were DeHart Hubbard and Edward Gordon, both broad jumpers. Hubbard was the first American Black athlete to win an individual gold medal in the Olympics. That was in 1924. He placed eleventh in the 1928 Olympics. Gordon placed seventh. It is very possible these were his roommates aboard the SS *Roosevelt*, however the article does not state that. The article says teammates, not roommates. The *Detroit Tribune* was a Black newspaper, so it's also possible he was simply highlighting other great Black athletes on the 1928 Olympic track team.

- In that same *Detroit Tribune* article, Lewis says the trip to the Olympics was his first vacation. We can assume seeing the New York skyline and the Statue of Liberty was a thrill, but his arrival at the SS *Roosevelt* is conjecture based on Bartlett's diary entries.
- In a conversation with Keith McClellan, author of *The Hero within Us*, he said Lewis was distraught after the Olympics, and Coach Holmes helped him to cope with the emotional distress.
- Lewis worked for the Detroit Parks and Recreation Department and was one of the people who Coach Holmes went to for jobs when needed for track men trying to pay their way through college. John Telford (Chapter 15) was employed by Lewis.
- My uncle did not do an interview with John Lewis, who passed away in 1970. Any of the thoughts and feelings associated with him have been created for this chapter. The only feelings we know without doubt are those chronicled in newspaper articles and Keith McClellan's book.

Chapter 5

References

Holmes, David L., Jr. Interview transcript of Richard Brown, June 9, 1997. From the written records of David L. Holmes Jr.

Wayne State University Athletics. Richard Brown, Wayne State Sports Hall of Fame. Wayne State University, 1991. https://wsuathletics.com/honors/hall-of-fame?hof =89.

Discussion

- Almost no changes were made to this interview transcript.
- I looked through all of the faculty directories from Richard Brown's era at Wayne and could not find an Aubrey McCutcheon. He may have been an adjunct staff member and not included in the directory, or the name may have been incorrectly written into the interview transcript.

Chapter 6

References

Detroit Collegian. "Holmes Invents Pacer; Coaches Seek Its Use." March 20, 1942, 4.

Detroit News. "City College Coach Devises 'Movies on Paper' to Teach Track Athletes." March 4, 1932.

Detroit News. "Country's Track Coaches Praise Work of Holmes." May 15, 1932.

Detroit News. "Pace-Setter Machine Invented by Wayne Coach; Tells Boys How Fast They're Running." April 5, 1942.

Detroit Sunday Times. "Drawing by David L. Holmes Shows Proper Form for High Jumping." February 19, 1933.

Giampetroni, Lou. "Holmes All Steel Hurdle Will Alleviate Old Hurdle Ills." *Detroit Collegian*, February 23, 1953.

Holmes, David L. Holmes Folding Hurdle Sales Brochure. From the records of David L. Holmes Jr., 1958.

Holmes, David L. Hurdle. Patent number 175,468. United States Patent Office, 1955.

Holmes, David L. Hurdle. Patent number 2,706,631. United States Patent Office, 1955.

Holmes, David L. Hurdle. Patent number 2,805,062. United States Patent Office, 1957.

Holmes, David L. "Movies on Paper" Sales Brochure. From the records of David L. Holmes Jr., 1934.

Holmes, David L. Starting Device for Track Runners. Patent number 2,890.048. United States Patent Office, 1959.

Jackson (MI) Citizen Patriot. "Coach Draws His Own Athletic Charts." March 20, 1932.

Koscielny, A. S., ed. *Handbook of Detroit City College*. Detroit: Student Club at Detroit City College, 1929–30.

McManis, John E. "Starting Block, Invented Here, Promises New Records." *Detroit News*, January 5, 1936.

Parrott, Harold F. "Would You Believe It? Paper 'Movies' Aid Track Students." *San Antonio (TX) Evening News*, March 18, 1932.

Puscas, George. "Holmes Invents 'Pace-Setter.'" *Detroit Free Press*, January 30, 1949.

Puscas, George. "Mile Is a Mile, but Not at Redford." *Detroit Free Press*, June 4, 1950.

Shaver, Bud. "Holmes' Method." *Detroit Sunday Times*, Detroit, MI, July 23, 1933.

Discussion

- This chapter puts together many different pieces of Coach Holmes' legacy. Holmes invented the folding hurdle, and it was used widely in high schools and colleges. He also held an annual Wayne Relay for high school track athletes. It's also true that he discovered the Redford track was the wrong length.

- The circumstances behind Holmes noticing the error aren't known, but the newspaper article says it was before the sixteenth running of the Wayne Annual Relays. It is unknown if he brought his folding hurdles to that track meet, but it seems unlikely he would have used someone else's hurdles.

- There was a newspaper article written after Holmes' "too short" discovery saying it was too long, not too short. Wherever the truth landed on that topic, both articles agreed it wasn't 440 yards.
- Coach Holmes' reaction to the newspaper article with his incorrect age and years of coaching is unknown.

Chapter 7
References
Detroit Collegian "Little, Hmpf!!" May 3, 1949, 4.

Holmes, David L., Jr. Interview transcript of Paul Pentecost, May 23, 2001. From the written records of David L. Holmes Jr.

Wayne State University Athletics. Paul J. Pentecost, Wayne State Sports Hall of Fame. Wayne State University, 1989. https://wsuathletics.com/honors/hall-of-fame/paul -j-pentecost-/79.

Discussion
- The "shit hole" story was not part of the Pentecost interview. My uncle told me about that terminology and similar stories he heard during many of his interviews. However, I never found that exact wording in any of the transcripts. But I am guessing it was a prominent thought frequently on track travels.
- My uncle told me a story about accompanying his father to a track meet and staying with his dad in a hotel room. The furniture was old and worn, and the armrests on the desk chair were ripped. Coach Holmes thought it was a "fine" hotel.
- Other than the "shit hole" story addition, the chapter runs very close to the interview transcript. The transcript was much longer and was trimmed for the chapter.

Chapter 8
References
Anderson, J. H. "Records Smashed in Annual Meet Run off in Rain." *Wichita Eagle*, April 20, 1929.

Chicago Sunday Tribune. "Name Athletes to Receive Aid on Olympic Trip." July 3, 1932.

College of the City of Detroit. "1931 Football Review." College of the City of Detroit Griffin Yearbook, 1932, 70–73.

Detroit Free Press. "Adams Keeps Track Honors." February 8, 1930.

Detroit Free Press. "Dues Will Compete in Milwaukee Meet." June 1, 1932.

Detroit Free Press. "Kazoo Teachers Outrun Tartars." February 14, 1932.

Detroit Free Press. "Six Records Shattered in State Track Carnival." July 5, 1930.

Detroit Free Press. "Track Results at Evanston." July 3, 1032.

Detroit Tribune. "Capt. Leroy Dues Enters Penn Relays." April 29, 1933.

Fresno (CA) Republican. "Four Records Are Broken in Amateur Meet at Detroit." February 23, 1930.

Holmes, David L. "Movies on Paper." N.p., 1932.

Holmes, David L. "Putting the Shot." *Scholastic Coach*, March 1934, 7–9.

Holmes, David L. *Track—1930.* Summary of the 1930 track season. Wayne State University Athletic Department records, 1930.

Holmes, David L. *Track—1931.* Summary of the 1931 track season. Wayne State University Athletic Department records, 1931.

Holmes, David L. *Track—1932.* Summary of the 1932 track season. Wayne State University Athletic Department records, 1932.

Hymans, Richard. "Olympic Trials History." *Track and Field News*, 2019.

Iola (KS) Register. "Four Records Broken at S.E.K. Track Meet." April 29, 1929.

"Labor Force, Employment and Unemployment, 1929–1939; Estimating Methods." *Monthly Labor Review*, July 1948.

McClellan, Keith. *The Hero within Us: A History of Track and Field in the Twentieth Century from a Michigan Perspective.* Oak Park: Eastern Michigan Press, 2001, 112–13.

Milonas, Lambros. "Profiles of Olympians and All-Americans at Wayne State University." Master's thesis, Wayne State University, 1974.

Nees, Louis A. *McGregor Bay: The Quiet Paradise.* N.p., 1976.

Nicholson, John P. "The Shot Put and Discus Throw." *Athletic Journal*, March 1936.

Oakland (CA) Post Enquirer. "Time and Entries for American Olympic Trials at Stanford Friday and Saturday." July 14, 1932.

Parsons (KS) Sun. "Great Carnival Has New Stars." April 30, 1929.

Parsons (KS) Sun. "Records Fall in High School Track Meet." April 29, 1929.

Peninsula Times Tribune (Palo Alto, CA). "Records Tumble at Olympic Game Finals." July 16, 1932.

Saginaw (MI) News. "Detroit City College Cuts Out Athletics." March 2, 1933.

Smith, Wilfred. "Johnson Beats Simpson, Tolan in Olympic Test." *Chicago Tribune*, July 3, 1932.

Smith, Wilfred. "Southern California Takes National Track Title." *Chicago Tribune*, June 7, 1931.

St. Louis Argus. "More Race Athletes Qualify for Olympics Games Trials Finals." July 8, 1932.

Wayne State University Athletics. Leroy W. Dues, Wayne State Sports Hall of Fame. Wayne State University, 1977. https://wsuathletics.com/honors/hall-of-fame?hof =8.

Welky, David B. "Viking Girls, Mermaids, and Little Brown Men: U.S. Journalism and the 1932 Olympics." *Journal of Sport History* 24, no. 1 (Spring 1997).

Discussion

- It is unknown how Dues and Holmes met. Dues was not from Detroit, so was not recruited. It seems likely Dues walked into the athletic office as portrayed in this chapter. D.L. would have been very excited when he heard Dues' shot put distances.

- All of his shot put distances and performances in various meets are true and were taken from newspaper articles.

- His football injuries were chronicled in The Griffin yearbook. The College of the City of Detroit football team, unfortunately, was as unsuccessful as portrayed.

- My grandfather used Leroy Dues as an example of great shot put form in his 1932 "Movies on Paper" book. My grandfather explained his form perfectly through illustrations.

- I use the term "toeboard" in this chapter as the more accepted term for the block that lets shot-putters know they're at the edge of the circle. In his book "Movies on Paper," my grandfather uses both "toeboard" and "stop-board."

- No one I talked to remembered how Dues got hurt on his way to the Olympic Trials. All I have is a note on a track summary sheet my grandfather did every year that Dues was hurt on his way there.

- There are no records indicating D.L. and Dues stopped in Pittsburg, Kansas, on their way to Palo Alto, California. But, given the routes available to drive from Detroit out to California at the time, it seems likely they would have passed close to Dues' hometown and stopped. The scene involving the shot put demonstration is conjecture.

- In 1933, due to lack of funding caused by the Great Depression, Holmes and the College of the City of Detroit had to cancel all sports for one semester. This important fact was not included because the chapter ends on the car ride home from the 1932 Olympic Trials.

- Dues is remembered by everyone who knew him as a kind and gentle person. He didn't talk much about his accomplishments. His story is almost exactly the same story as Coach Holmes'. Both came from the farmlands, were good at sports, just missed making the Olympics, and went on to become successful track coaches and beloved by their athletes.

- Dues died in 1987, about ten years before my uncle began his interviews. I was able to speak with Dues' daughter and granddaughter for this chapter, but they did not know any of the specifics of his shot put career. His daughter knew he was injured going to the Olympic Trials but did not know the circumstances.

Chapter 9
References

Holmes, David L., Jr. Interview transcript of Jim Coulter and Ray Morgan, May 24, 2001. From the written records of David L. Holmes Jr.

Discussion
- This transcript is almost exactly as it occurred, with just a few off-topic tangents eliminated.

Chapter 10
References

Alderton, George S. "Coach Dave Holmes." The Sport Grist, *Lansing State Journal*, May 19, 1939.

Batchelor, E. A., Jr. "Drill in Halls, but Are Good." *The Detroit Times Extra*, March 20, 1947.

Courier-Journal (Louisville, KY). "Kentucky Notes." March 28, 1912, 4.

Daily Oklahoman (Oklahoma City, OK). "Athletic Director Secured for Tonkawa School—Schedule Arranged." September 16, 1912, 5.

Dann, Marshall. "David L. Holmes Lured to Detroit by Fishing." *Detroit Free Press*, May 11, 1941.

Democrat (Russellville, KY). "Bethel Wins." January 27, 1911, 10.

Democrat (Russellville, KY). "Prof. D.L. Holmes Again Captures the All-a-Round Medal in Athletic Meet." August 16, 1911, 1.

DePauw University. "Coach Dave Holmes, Track." *Mirage*, issued by the junior class of DePauw University, 1915, 28–29.

Detroit Collegian. "Coach Holmes Was No Slouch on the Gridiron, Cinders and in Gym." April 1, 1926.

Detroit Evening Times. "Detroit Junior College, Forerunner of University, Will Be Ready for Fall Term." July 26, 1917, 2.

Detroit Evening Times. "Marriage Licenses." June 18, 1917, 9.

Detroit Free Press. "Coach Holmes, Basketball Mentor at Cass Tech, Is the Very Essence of Pep." December 24, 1914, 9.

Detroit Free Press. "Plans Adopted for the New Central High School." April 28, 1893, 8.

Detroit News Tribune. "Many Changes in Teaching Force." February 28, 1915.

Glover, Lynn, ed. "The 1913 Football Team of the O.I.T.—D.L. Holmes, Coach." *Technical Educator*, Oklahoma State Institute of Technology, November 1913.

Hanawalt, Leslie L. *A Place of Light: The History of Wayne State University*. Detroit: Wayne State University Press, 1968, 162.

Holmes, Carl L. Holmes Family History. In the genealogical records of Jean Holmes Wunderlich, n.d.

Holmes, D.A. "Culture." Speech written by D.L.'s father (D.A.) and read in Philephroncan Hall (possibly at Otterbein College) the evening of January 28, 1882. In the genealogical records of Jean Holmes Wunderlich.

Holmes, David L. "Best Bass Fishing in Canada—Maybe." *Outers' Book—Recreation*, July 1918.

Holmes, David L. Jr. *A Coach's Son: Growing Up in the Ethos of Muscular Christianity and Amateur Athletics in Detroit*. Paper delivered at the meeting of the North American Association of Sports Historians, Windsor, Ontario, Canada, May 1998.

Indianapolis News. "DePauw Wins Track Meet." May 6, 1914, 10.

McClellan, Keith. *The Hero within Us: A History of Track and Field in the Twentieth Century from a Michigan Perspective*. Oak Park: Eastern Michigan Press, 2001, 279–84.

Messer, Warren. "Stardust: Wayne Athletes Expose Tartar Origin." *Detroit Collegian*, February 25, 1938.

Milonas, Lambros. "Profiles of Olympians and All-Americans at Wayne State University." Master's thesis, Wayne State University, 1974.

Nourse, E. M. *Athletics*. Class Book, 1910, Bethel College, Russellville, KY.

Ogle, Claude M., ed. "Holmes. New Coach Here; Plans to Give Track Men Individual Instruction." *DePauw Daily* (Greencastle, IN), DePauw University student newspaper, April 7, 1914, 1.

Ogle, Claude M., ed. "Holmes Starts Track Work with a Bang; Work Outs Every Day Now." *DePauw Daily* (Greencastle, IN), DePauw University student newspaper, April 9, 1914, 4.

Oklahoma News (Oklahoma City, OK). "Tonkawa to Be Hot Contender." September 23, 1912, 8.

President's Athletic Conference. "Dedicated to David L. Holmes." Spring Sports Festival Program, President's Athletic Conference, Detroit, MI, May 17–18, 1957.

Stillwater (OK) Advance. "In Oratories and Athletics." May 18, 1905, 1.

Wallace, Allen. "The Legacy of David Mackenzie: Wayne State and How It Grew." *Michigan History*, March/April 1979.

Warren, J. L., editor in chief. "The Senior Record, Class of June 1916." Cass Technical High School, Detroit, Michigan, 1916.

Wunderlich, Jean Holmes. Personal notes on her father, David L. Holmes. In the genealogical records of Jean Holmes Wunderlich, n.d. Included the information about Laddie and the sugar cubes, as well as the horse on its own schedule.

Discussion

- The Holmes family were pioneers in Oklahoma, arriving there before it became a state. The majority of this chapter is based on written stories that my mother kept in her genealogical records. She researched the family history for decades, much of it before there was an internet. How she found handwritten speeches from 1882, I don't know. But I am so glad she organized all of this information in notebooks that centered around each individual in the family.

- My mother's uncle and D.L.'s brother, Carl Holmes, also kept genealogical information, and notes from his research was included in this chapter also.
- It is true that D.L.'s grandfather was "bound over" (sold) to a family to work by his great grandmother due to family financial hardships. His grandfather never saw his siblings or mother again.
- It is unknown how D.L. became such a good long jumper. There are some photos in my mother's genealogical records that show him practicing long jump in fields in Oklahoma as a young boy. With his love of fishing and the way streams were laid out in Stillwater at that time, it seems plausible he needed the skill for getting to the right fishing location.
- Several newspaper articles say D.L. had to play football under an alias because his parents were against the sport.
- There are conflicting stories about who recruited Coach Holmes to Detroit. Detroit Junior College was absolutely Mackenzie's project. Mackenzie is always given credit for assembling a fine staff to get it started. But Darrel Davis, physical education director for the Detroit Public Schools, has been mentioned as being the person who introduced Holmes to Mackenzie.
- My mother would always tell a story about her mother, Hazel Holmes, and how she met D.L. The way her story went was they were ice-skating—possibly at a Cass Tech High School staff event at Palmer Park in Detroit—and Hazel (an excellent ice-skater) "accidentally" fell right in front of D.L. Being the gentleman he was, he helped her up. And the rest is history.
- When D.L. and Hazel were first married, they lived in a house on Burlingame. According to College of the City of Detroit faculty directories they moved to Faust around 1931. This may seem like odd timing due to the Depression. However, D.L. never lost his job and never stopped getting paid. His income was stable through the entire Depression. It's possible housing prices went down and he was able to snag a nice house at a good price, but that is conjecture.
- The track parties at the Faust home were absolutely true. They were something that the athletes looked forward to every year.
- The reference to "Go Tartars" being said was created; however, it may interest readers to know that it was Coach Holmes who came up with the "Tartar" name for the mascot in 1924 or 1925. He also suggested

the green and yellow school colors. Wayne State University's teams are now known as the Warriors, but the colors remain.

Chapter 11

References

Batchelor, E. A., Jr. "Concealed His Skill in High School." *Detroit News*, March 25, 1937.

Detroit Free Press. "Former Tennis Star Finds Track More to His Liking." April 5, 1936.

Detroit Free Press. "Wayne Track Ace Looms as a Leading Star in Midwest." February 23, 1936.

Harrison, Donald H. "Jewish Athlete Still Bitter about Ruined Shot at Gold Medal." *San Diego Jewish Press-Heritage,* July 2, 1999.

Holmes, David L. "Allan Tolmich." *Athletic Journal*, March 1938.

Holmes, David L., Jr. Interview transcript summary of Allan Tolmich, April 18, 2003. From the written records of David L. Holmes Jr.

McClellan, Keith. *The Hero within Us: A History of Track and Field in the Twentieth Century from a Michigan Perspective.* Oak Park: Eastern Michigan Press, 2001, 188–93.

Rosenberg, Bill. "Skinny Racqueteer Now Husky Sprinter; Holmes Persuades Tolmich to Desert Tennis for Track." *Detroit Collegian*, October 27, 1937.

Wayne State University Athletics. Allan Tolmich, Wayne State Sports Hall of Fame. Wayne State University, 1976. https://wsuathletics.com/honors/hall-of-fame?hof=5.

Winston-Salem Journal. "1940 Olympics Cancelled Definitely." *Winston-Salem Journal,* April 24, 1940.

Discussion

- I was never able to find a tape or the written transcript for the Tolmich interview. All I found was a several-page summary of important points that were covered in the interview. This interview transcript covers all of the important points my uncle and Tolmich talked about, but it is not the actual dialogue. I also added in some important items such as the story about the only two Jewish track athletes being dropped from their race the night before their Olympic competition in 1936.

- Allan Tolmich was one of the most written-about athletes that Coach Holmes ever coached. There are hundreds of articles written about him and his accomplishments. All of the information in the chapter is well founded in fact.

- There are several documented stories with different takes on how Tolmich ended up on the track team. Several articles said my grandfather saw him playing tennis and recruited him. McClellan's book says

Tolmich was a "walk on" for the track team. The Griffin Yearbook has him on both the tennis and track teams, but liking track more. With so many contradictions, the chapter has him coming out for track and Coach Holmes discovering his talent there. However, because I don't have an actual interview transcript, there is no clear answer on how he arrived on the track team.

Chapter 12

References

Cunningham, Glenn. *Never Quit.* Lincoln, VA: Chosen Books Publishing Company, Ltd., 1981.

Detroit Collegian. "Men's Gym Condemned as Fire Trap." November 20, 1936.

Detroit Free Press. "Tolmich Beats Towns in A.A.U. High Hurdles—Wayne Star Also Sets Record Winning Lows." July 4, 1937.

Detroit Free Press. "Tolmich Paces Wayne to 78–53 Track Victory over Butler." May 2, 1937.

Detroit Free Press. "Tolmich Shatters Hurdle Mark at Milwaukee." June 5, 1937.

Detroit Free Press. "Tolmich Speeds to World Record." March 13, 1938.

Detroit News. "Muscles Tense . . . the Final Lunge . . . and Tolmich Is the Winner." July 6, 1937.

Detroit News. "Sophomore Relay Team Will Represent Wayne at Penn Saturday." April 25, 1935.

Detroit News. "Tolmich Leads Wayne to Victory." March 31, 1935.

Detroit News. "Wayne Has Won 6 Out of 7 Races in Philadelphia." April 25, 1935.

Detroit Times. "Detroit's Al Tolmich: Hurdling Champion of the World at 21." March 30, 1938.

Detroit Times Extra. "Coaches Acclaim Tolmich: Defeat of Towns Brings Tribute." July 11, 1937.

Detroit Times Extra. "Rated Unbeatable, 'Spec' Bowed to Tolmich." July 4, 1937.

Detroit Times Extra. "Tolmich Eludes Doc, Wins." March 15, 1937.

Holmes, David L. "Starting and Sprinting." *Scholastic Coach*, February 1934, 6–7.

Holmes, David L., Jr. "A New Race Called Sprinting—With Obstacles." Unpublished paper written by David L. Holmes Jr. while at the College of William and Mary, 2004.

McClellan, Keith. *The Hero within Us: A History of Track and Field in the Twentieth Century from a Michigan Perspective.* Oak Park: Eastern Michigan Press, 2001, 188–93.

McManis, John E. "These Three, and the Greatest of These Is Cunningham." *Detroit News*, June 22, 1934.

Messer, Warren. "Spring? That's for Track." Wayne University Griffin Yearbook, 1936, 8.

Messer, Warren. "Tolmich Ties World Record; Beats 'Spec' Towns by Inches in Hurdle." *Detroit Collegian*, February 14, 1938.

Milonas, Lambros. "Profiles of Olympians and All-Americans at Wayne State University." Master's thesis, Wayne State University, 1974.

Murphy, Bob. "Alan [*sic*] Tolmich Worked Way to Top of Track World the Hard Way." *Detroit Evening Times*, February 28, 1939.

Murphy, Bob. "Wayne's Timber Topper." *Detroit Times Extra*, February 10, 1938.

New York Journal and American Sports. "Tolmich Sets World's Hurdles Mark in National AAU Meet at Garden." February 26, 1939.

Patton, Harvey, Jr. "Once Pampered by a Coach, Now He Doesn't Spare Self." *Detroit News*, March 13, 1938.

Puscas, George. "And Wayne Has It; Track Obstacle Course Unique." *Detroit Free Press*, March 16, 1952.

Rice, Grantland. "Cunningham Loses 1,500 to Lovelock in Olympic Climax." *Lincoln Nebraska State Journal*, August 8, 1936.

Slowick, Anthony. "Tolmich Promises to Rival Former Wayne Stars." *Detroit Collegian*, February 20, 1936.

St. Louis Post-Dispatch. "Tolmich Beats Towns in A.A.U. Track Meet; Cunningham Triumphs." July 4, 1937.

Van, George E. "Wayne Thinclads Drill in Ancient Gym," 1934. [Publication unknown, although Van was a reporter for the *Detroit Times*.]

Wayne University. "Track." Wayne University Griffin Yearbook, 1935, 118–19.

Weekes, William. "'Spec' Towns Loses First in Two Years." *Atlanta Constitution*, July 4, 1937.

Discussion

- Tolmich is the subject of hundreds of newspaper articles, and many of them talk about the small gym and his practicing on just one hurdle.
- Indoor track meets at Wayne were run on tile hallways (some articles say terrazzo hallways) in tennis shoes. Field events were held in the small gymnasium facilities. Running races longer than the main hallway were run on the elevated circular track in the gym.
- The story about the blood infection, including the roadside surgery and Tolmich hiding, is 100 percent true and documented.
- Tolmich and Coach Holmes had a great personal relationship. My uncle wrote down a Tolmich quote that said they enjoyed each other and had fun at practice.
- The Cunningham/San Romani race was included in this chapter because it was such a huge race. Both runners were very well known, especially Cunningham. There was no connection with Wayne University, but it certainly should have been the premier race of that meet.

Fortunately for Wayne, Tolmich made his race the premier race of the meet.

- There are several newspaper articles that speak to the anticipation of the Tolmich/Towns meetup. Towns was unbeaten for two years at the time.
- One *Detroit Free Press* article points out the difficulty of winning the high hurdles and then winning the low hurdles less than one hour apart. Tolmich did that almost every meet.
- I never found any articles that dealt with how Tolmich felt about the 1940 Olympics being canceled. It seems like it would have been devastating to be the potential gold medal winner and not get an opportunity to compete. But it was never discussed in any great depth.

Chapter 13

References

Duggan, Dennis. "Four Athletes Place Wayne in Headlines." *Detroit Collegian*, May 3, 1949, 6.

Filsinger, Bob. "Wayne Thinclads Sweep Penn Relays." *Detroit Collegian*, May 2, 1949, 1.

Holmes, David L., Jr. Interview transcript of Pete Petross and Robert Wingo, June 7, 1997. From the written records of David L. Holmes Jr.

Wayne State University Athletics. Irving (Pete) Petross, Wayne State Sports Hall of Fame. Wayne State University, 1982. https://wsuathletics.com/honors/hall-of-fame?hof=40.

Wayne State University Athletics. Robert Wingo, Wayne State Sports Hall of Fame. Wayne State University, 1982. https://wsuathletics.com/honors/hall-of-fame?hof=41.

Discussion

- Very few changes were made to this interview transcript.

Chapter 14

References

Batchelor, E. A., Jr. "Wright May Realize Tutor's Olympic Hope." *Detroit Times Extra*, March 5, 1948, 25.

Bresnahan, George. "Broad-Jump Olympic Champions." *Athletic Journal*, December 1947, 6.

Chicago Daily Sun Times. "It Was a Legal Pass after All." August 11, 1948, 75.

Daily Telegraph (London, UK). "U.S. Accepts Relay Medal." August 12, 1948.

Detroit Evening Times. "Wayne Thinclads Whip Chicago." February 11, 1945.

Detroit Free Press. "16 Michigan Athletes Hope to Win Olympic Gold." July 25, 1948.

Detroit Free Press. "Tartar Takes Four Firsts, but Spartans Win Meet." February 18, 1945.

Detroit Free Press. "U.S. Awarded Disputed Olympic Relay: Films Show Baton Was Passed OK." August 11, 1948.

Detroit Free Press. "Wayne Set to Celebrate 'Wright Day.'" November 12, 1948, 29.

Detroit Free Press. "Wright First in Five Events as Wayne Wins." May 20, 1945.

Detroit Free Press. "Wright Stars Again." May 2, 1948.

Detroit Free Press. "Wright Tops Own Marks in Illinois Tech Relay." March 14, 1948.

Detroit Free Press. "Wright Wins Junior AAU Broad Jump." July 5, 1947.

Detroit Free Press. "Wright Wins U.S. Crown." February 22, 1948.

Detroit Tribune. "Wayne's Lorenzo Wright Qualifies for Three Olympic Events." July 10, 1948.

Detroit Tribune. "Wright Hailed as Great Athlete by Wayne President." November 20, 1948, 2.

Holmes, David L. "Broad Jumping the 'Wright Way.'" *Scholastic Coach*, April 1951.

International Olympics Committee. "Team USA Sprints to 4x100m Relay Olympic Gold—1948 Olympics" [film]. Olympics You Tube Channel, www.youtube.com/watch?v=3geJSt3geSw.

McClellan, Keith. *The Hero within Us: A History of Track and Field in the Twentieth Century from a Michigan Perspective.* Oak Park: Eastern Michigan Press, 2001, 266–81.

Milonas, Lambros. "Profiles of Olympians and All-Americans at Wayne State University." Master's thesis, Wayne State University, 1974.

Smits, Ted. "Americans Disqualified for Illegal Passing of Baton." *St. Louis Star and Times*, August 7, 1948.

Smits, Ted. "Wayne Star Tells of Olympic Baton Mixup." *Detroit Free Press*, August 9, 1948.

St. Louis Post-Dispatch. "U.S. Wins 1600 Meter Relay; '400' Team Disqualified." August 7, 1948.

Webb, Clifford. Olympics Should Lead to British Athletics Revival. *Daily Herald* (London, UK), August 9, 1948.

Wilmington Press-Journal. "Disqualification in Relay Protested by Americans." August 7, 1948.

Wayne State University Athletics. Lorenzo C. Wright, Wayne State Sports Hall of Fame. Wayne State University, 1976. https://wsuathletics.com/honors/hall-of-fame?hof=6.

Discussion

- Leroy Dues was sent to London through the funding of some Detroit businessmen. Wright was a former track athlete for Dues in high school, and it was Dues that helped get Wright recruited to Wayne. There is no doubt the two of them had numerous conversations at the Olympics. Unfortunately, we don't have any record of what was said in any of them. Any conversation between them in this chapter is conjecture.

- There are hundreds of newspaper articles that include Lorenzo Wright in high school, college, and the Olympics. The baton pass is very well documented and the chapter follows the facts exactly.

- There was Lorenzo Wright Day on November 13, 1948, declared and celebrated in Detroit. There are newspaper articles to substantiate there was a halftime ceremony to honor him. But the scene at the Wayne football game, while possible, is not documented. The articles written about it say there was a huge trophy and a photo album of Olympic pictures given to Wright. Apparently they were able to calm the crowd, and Mayor Van Antwerp gave a speech filled with accolades about Wright.

- Due to Wayne's lack of facilities, they used the University of Detroit football stadium for that November 13 game and other games. The game was against Omaha, but it seemed more impactful, and less confusing, to portray it as against U of D and to have a rival Detroit team salute a Detroit hero.

- There is one English newspaper report that alludes to the British team giving up their gold medals before the Americans left the Olympics for home. It's possible that Wright had his gold medal before Lorenzo Wright Day. London's *Daily Telegraph*, however, reported that Dan Ferris, secretary of the American Athletic Union (AAU) accepted all of the medals for the 400-meter relay athletes because the athletes were already on the boat home. It is uncertain when Wright received his medal.

Chapter 15

References

McClellan, Keith. *The Hero within Us: A History of Track and Field in the Twentieth Century from a Michigan Perspective*. Oak Park: Eastern Michigan Press, 2001, 317–24.

Milonas, Lambros. "Profiles of Olympians and All-Americans at Wayne State University." Master's thesis, Wayne State University, 1974.

Telford, John. "The Longest Dash: A Running Commentary on the Quarter Mile." *Track and Field News*, 1965.

Wayne State University Athletics. John Telford, Wayne State Sports Hall of Fame. Wayne State University, 1978. https://wsuathletics.com/honors/hall-of-fame?hof =17.

Wunderlich, Keith. Interview transcript of John Telford, January 10, 2023. From the
written records of Keith Wunderlich.

Zak, Bob. "Mile Relay Team Victorious." *Wayne Collegian*, May 1, 1956, 3.

Discussion

- Almost no changes were made to this interview transcript. Telford's memory is sharp. I checked many of the times and records he mentioned and he was 100 percent correct on all of them.

Chapter 16

References

Adams, Thomas B. "David L. Holmes Hall of Fame Induction Speech." State of Michigan Sports Hall of Fame Annual Induction Dinner, Cobo Hall, Detroit, May 15, 1975.

Barcus, Harvey. "Holmes, Veteran Track Coach and Star Builder, Dies at 72." *Detroit News*, June 20, 1960.

Beltaire, Mark. "The Town Crier: It's Almost Tee-Time in Israel." *Detroit Free Press*, June 21, 1960.

Daily Collegian. "Holmes Nominated for Michigan Hall of Fame." March 15, 1967.

Detroit Free Press. "Coaching Great at WSU Dies." June 20, 1960.

Detroit News. "Honor Dave Holmes." June 23, 1960.

Holmes, David L. "After Bass among the Fishing Island." *Outers' Book—Recreation*, June 1918, 494. [References Hazel Holmes using a rifle to shoot fish.]

Holmes, Hazel. Letter from Hazel Holmes (wife of D.L. Holmes) to Leona (unknown last name) and Norma about the passing of D.L. and her feelings then and now, July 15, 1960. In the genealogical records of Jean Holmes Wunderlich.

Holmes, Hazel. Letter from Hazel Holmes to Leona regarding how she is coping, January 9, 1961. In the genealogical records of Jean Holmes Wunderlich.

Holmes, Jean. Letter from Jean Holmes (sister-in-law of D.L. Holmes) to Leona regarding the death and funeral of D.L. Holmes, June 23, 1960. In the genealogical records of Jean Holmes Wunderlich.

McCabe Funeral Home. Memory card noting clergyman Rev. John B. Forsyth, June 22, 1960.

Rosedale Park News. "Hold Funeral Rites for David L. Holmes." August 1960.

Telford, John. "The Longest Dash: A Running Commentary on the Quarter Mile." *Track and Field News*, 1965.

Wunderlich, Jean Holmes. "Obituary of Hazel Holmes," June 20, 1984. In the genealogical records of Jean Holmes Wunderlich. [The *Detroit Free Press* obituary was much shorter and did not mention the ambulance driving in World War II.]

Discussion

- Two handwritten letters about D.L.'s death and funeral provided much of the information for this chapter. They were very detailed letters and evoked much emotion.

- The eulogy presented by Tom Adams was actually a speech Adams delivered when D.L. was inducted into the Michigan Sports Hall of Fame. It was adapted slightly to make it a more appropriate eulogy. It is unknown who gave the eulogy or its content.

- I found a very small, one-paragraph newspaper article from the *Detroit News* that named the pallbearers. I had been looking for this information for two years and found it after one more check of my mother's genealogy folders. Four of the six names are very familiar, and there are chapters about them in this book. The other two names I did not recognize. Al Langtry, class of 1930, was a 220 and 440 runner. Dick Waskin, class of 1951, ran the mile relay and the 880. Neither received much press while on the track team, yet both were given the honor of being a pallbearer for Coach Holmes. It was one last example of athletes who didn't score often in meets but were still treated like champions by Holmes.

- It is true that Lorenzo Wright was the first to arrive at the funeral home and the last to leave each day. He and D.L. had a close bond. According to my uncle, Wright also stayed at the gravesite after everyone else went home. However, only Wright knows what happened there.

- Coach David L. Holmes is buried at Grand Lawn Cemetery in Detroit, Michigan. Grand Lawn is located at 23501 Grand River Avenue, Detroit, MI 48219. He is buried near the southeast corner of section 22. Look for an upright headstone that says HOLMES WUNDERLICH. In front of that marker you will find the graves of David L. Holmes, Hazel Holmes, Jean Holmes Wunderlich, and Robert Wunderlich.

INDEX OF SUBJECTS

Note: Numbers in *italics* refer to photographs.

INDEX OF NAMES

Note: Numbers in *italics* refer to photographs.

ABOUT THE AUTHORS

Keith D. Wunderlich is the grandson of Coach D.L. Holmes and was himself a sprinter in high school. He is the author of *Vernor's Ginger Ale* and is a retired public-school administrator. He earned his doctorate at Wayne State University.

David L. Holmes Jr. (1932–2023) was the son of Coach D.L. Holmes. He retired as professor emeritus from the College of William and Mary and was the author of *A Brief History of the Episcopal Church*. He earned his doctorate at Princeton University.